SOUND DESIGN
FOR MOVING IMAGE

FROM CONCEPT TO REALIZATION

KAHRA SCOTT-JAMES

BLOOMSBURY ACADEMIC
AN IMPRINT OF BLOOMSBURY PUBLISHING PLC

B L O O M S B U R Y
LONDON · OXFORD · NEW YORK · NEW DELHI · SYDNEY

Contents

vi Introduction

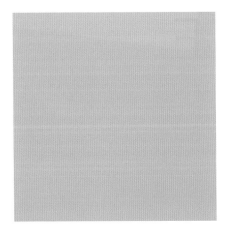

viii Chapter one

Early Practice

1 Noises Off: The Staging of Sound

4 The Picturesque of Sound: Magic Lantern Shows, Installations, and Immersive Entertainment

7 The Fallacy of Silence: Phonography and Mechanical Mimicry

11 Radio with Pictures: Mental Imagery

14 Transitioning to Sound: Amped and In Sync

20 Animation Finds Its Voice: The Thing That Hooked the Crowds

24 Advancing the Craft: Story, Design, Process, People

30 TV Kills the Radio Star: Realism, Limited Animation, and Stylized Animation

36 Chapter two

Sound as Design

37 Experiments in Design: Short Films and Sonic Art

47 The Art of Noise: Sonic Sculpturing

54 Fictions of Science: Synthesis, New Waves, and Ambiguity

64 Chapter three

Contemporary Sound Design

65 The Soundtrack: Dialogue, Music, and Effects

69 The Sound Department

71 Approaches to Sound Design: Modes of Thinking

77 The Sound Designer's Tool Kit: Sound as a Medium

84 Sound as a Place

88 Capturing Sound

91 The Recording Chain

98   Chapter four

Preproduction

99   The Development Stage
103   Sound in Script
109   Audiovisual Development:
      Concept Art
114   Spotlight On: Peter Miller,
      Sound Designer
119   Project Planning

126   Chapter five

Production

127   Production Sound
128   On Location
132   Recording Sound and Foley
      Effects
134   Sound Effect Libraries
135   Studio Recording
138   ADR
141   Foley and Sound Effects
142   Spotlight On: John Simpson,
      Foley Artist
143   Sound Design Effects
145   Spotlight On: Hweiling Ow,
      Filmmaker
147   Development
147   Spotlight On: Adam Elliot,
      Animation Director

154   Chapter six

Postproduction

155   Sound and Picture Editing
165   Audio Post
168   Re-Recording Mixing
170   Mixing Tools and Techniques
176   Spotlight On: Shane Acker,
      Filmmaker
179   Looking Ahead

180   Picture Credits
182   Index

Introduction

Since the advent of moving image, storytellers have used dialogue, sound effects, and music to accompany visuals. Sound design is by no means a new field; the practice has developed over time through various disciplines. The relationship between sound design and visual design is also a long-standing one. Prior to the advent of cinema, there were also many forms of time-based arts that incorporated sound. The first "sound" films and cartoons, however primitive by today's standards, marked the beginning of a field that is continuously evolving. Sound is now a fundamental aspect of nearly every form of art, entertainment, and media, from the inclusion of moving image into contemporary theater, audiovisual installations, broadcasting, film, animation, games, and virtual reality / augmented reality (VR/AR).

Fundamentally, sound design is the capturing, generating, selecting, and shaping of the aural palette that will define the sound of a moving image project. Contemporary sound design can be further defined as the creation of a single sound effect or sound design effect, and the design of an entire soundtrack. Current practice involves the recording, editing, generating, processing, and mixing of sound. Microphones and recorders are used to record sound, while synthesizers, samplers, and virtual instruments are used for generating sound. Processing (manipulation) is the intentional alteration of audio through the use of plug-ins and samplers. Digital audio work stations (DAWs) are used for studio recording, editing, layering, processing, and mixing sound. That's the how to do, but what about the why and when to?

Sound, like image, can contribute to narrative development. Sound is perceived emotionally and aesthetically, as well as intellectually. Both sound and image are equally able to convey information, but it's the combining of sounds and the interplay between sound and image that construct and determine meaning. While audiences don't typically consciously register what they're hearing when watching a film, they feel it, which makes sound design a very powerful emotive device. Sound has the ability to evoke and ***affect.*** The abstraction involved in the creation of sound makes it a difficult subject to articulate and communicate. People have a greater understanding of and are culturally more at ease with visual language, the notion of visual communication, and film as a visual art. However, studies show that if the audio quality and design of a soundtrack are subpar, no matter how great the pictures are, audiences react negatively and are likely to dismiss or disengage from a film. While sound design has traditionally been perceived as a postproduction discipline, the consideration of sound starts in preproduction, with an idea and a script.

This book adopts a specific framework in order to help demystify sound design for moving image. It is not intended to serve as a sound engineering handbook, but as a guide for moving image content creators wanting to explore sound and collaborate with sound designers. The term "film" includes animated film unless stipulating a variation between animation and live action. While there are differences in film and animation production processes, the lines between live action, CGI, and animation are blurring. Regardless of medium, the same or similar concepts can be adopted, adapted, and applied to any project employing sound.

Chapter 1 looks at how the practice has been shaped by invention, innovation, and experimentation across theater, magic lantern shows, the first animated films, radio, and television drama, to the advent of sound on film. Chapter 2 considers the influence of experimental practices, the short film as a vehicle for alternative approaches to audiovisual storytelling, the impact of science fiction on sound design, and the establishment of sound design in the context of contemporary film. Chapter 3 outlines what constitutes the soundtrack, the roles and responsibilities of the sound department, various ways of conceptualizing sound design, sound as a medium, and how practitioners use that knowledge to capture and manipulate sound. Chapter 4 looks at script and sound and early stage development as a vehicle for conceptualizing and planning for sound. Chapter 5 covers the basics of sound production, from recording and the creation of effects to working with story reels. Chapter 6 touches on sound and picture editing, the final mix, and how those stages influence preproduction and story development. Each chapter comes with associated online companion website content to further support key concepts and processes outlined within each chapter: **www.bloomsbury.com/ scott-james-sound-design**.

Sound is the unspoken narrative of our everyday lives. It is the words that feed our unconscious and tell it what to think and do. In real life, we're surrounded by this unwritten narrative, it's the story of real life going on around us constantly. How we interpret or adapt to that narrative is what propels our individual stories. Movies give sound designers the opportunity to control the narrative, real life doesn't. But that doesn't make the power of sound any less potent. Why does sudden silence trigger the fear response? Why do rhythms at 60bpm make us comfortable and double that anxious? Why does the sound of a lawnmower in a neighborhood make it sound friendly and suburban? Why do we distrust someone who jiggles coins in their pocket? We interpret sound constantly in real-life to inform the ceaseless creation of our life narrative. Movies need to do it in two hours. The intelligent sound designer has mastered the ability to create a sonic narrative that supports the spoken one in ways that can be far more potent than the screenplay imagined.

Mark Mangini
Sound Designer/Re-recording Mixer, 2016

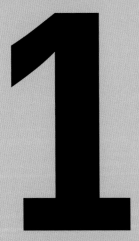

Early Practice

It is difficult to pinpoint the exact birthplace of sound design for moving image, but the practice developed much earlier than is assumed. The history of early sound design is nonlinear, but nevertheless there are many parallels, lines, and interrelationships between audiovisual art forms that have informed sound design as a practice. Although the lineage is complex, it is clear inventors and practitioners adopted and adapted ideas from one discipline into another. The first sound designers were primarily performance artists and concealed offstage, behind the screen, and later behind a microphone. While associated technologies have changed, many of the fundamental concepts and techniques developed are still relevant today.

NOISES OFF

The Staging of Sound

In theater, sound design works in the same way as set, lighting, and performance design; decisions are based on aesthetics, mood, and meaning. The first person to be credited as a "theater sound designer" was Dan Dugan, who began his career as a lighting designer before migrating to sound design. He introduced more complex and atmospheric soundscapes to theater, which led to the introduction of the new title. Another key figure in theater sound is Abe Jacob, who also advanced the concept of sound as a creative and designed element, particularly the use of sound to create mood and atmosphere. Today there is a growing interest in cinematic theater, which involves the integration of preproduced moving image elements. Live streaming of theater and on-demand theater content is also becoming popular.

Despite the differences between theater and film, theater existed long before moving image, and many of the techniques used in early theater were adopted for moving image production. Elizabethan theater (1562–1642) used sound effects (or "noises off"), which were performed backstage (or offstage) while musicians were housed in one of the balconies above the stage. Thunder runs (rolling cannon balls) were built into the ceiling and cannons were housed inside the roof to emulate the sounds of battle and thunder. Actors or voice artists mimicked everything from birds to the wailing of ghosts. The most frequently used sound effects were alarms, clocks, whistles, chimes, bells, thunder, storms, gunshots, cannons, wolves, crickets, owls, roosters, croaking toads, hounds, horses, armor, and swords. Most early theater productions involved the imitation of "natural" sounds by artificial or mechanical means; however, Kabuki, a form of traditional seventeenth-century Japanese theater, called for both literal and stylized sound effects. Drums, flutes, bells, and gongs were used to create textural sound effects and sound props for the more literal effects.

Stealing One's Thunder

One of the most common early theatrical sound effects was thunder, and it served three purposes, the *real* (thunder in the physical world), the *subconscious* (thunder as the sense of impending doom or danger), and the supernatural or the *unreal*. Nicola Sabbatini, an Italian architect of the Baroque and a pioneering inventor of set, lighting, and stage machinery, was among the first designers to create sophisticated machines for audiovisual effects such as sea, storms, lightning, fire, hell, flying gods, clouds, and thunder. In 1683, Sabbatini published *Pratica di Fabricar Scene e Machine ne' Teatri* (*Manual for Constructing Scenes and Machines in the Theater*), which depicts an illustration for the thunder box. The design calls for thirty-pound (approximately 13.6-kilogram) iron or stone balls and a case of stairs. The balls rolling down the stairs simulated the "roll" of thunder and thunder "claps" as the balls fell onto the next step below. The individual design of thunder sound props was of some importance in early theater. In 1708, British theater critic and writer John Dennis designed the more controllable and realistic sounding thunder sheet for one of his new plays at Drury Lane Theatre in London. However, his play was not a success and management withdrew it. A later production of *Macbeth* at the Drury used the thunder sheet, which angered Dennis, and he accused the theater of stealing his thunder.

Various designs for thunder sound effect props

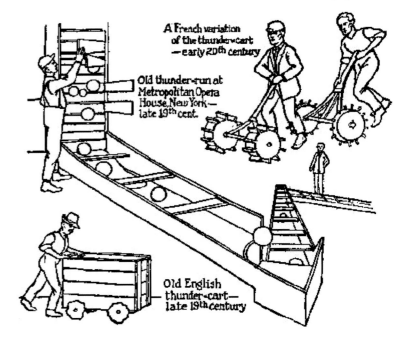

Behind the Scenes

Van Dyke Browne's *Secrets of Scene Painting and Stage Effects* (1900) includes a section on sound effects offering an insight into early practices. Browne was a scene painter, but one of his "bug-bears" (things that annoyed him) was the lack of attention to sound in amateur theater productions. He illustrated his discontent by discussing specific scenarios such as the opening of a house window in a busy London street:

Thanks to motorcars the sound of traffic is easily produced on the stage. Two or three motor horns will produce some of the sounds with which people are familiar, but to get the right effect the men using the horns must retire from the window; indeed, one of the horns should be some distance from it in the first place. The only way to get this effect of distance is to stand in the auditorium and have the horns sounded from different places behind the scenes. (Browne, 1900 p. 65)

Browne was not just identifying the type of sound effects used to create a distant city atmosphere but also isolating a sound effect that is quick and easy for audiences to recognize and understand. Browne also pinpointed the need for considering perspective and the combining of sounds. It's unlikely and therefore unrealistic for a car to be too close to a window, and for a number of cars to be the exact same distance from a window. His suggestion of standing in the auditorium and listening (to the mix) was a way of checking that the balance of sounds was creating the intended outcome, a city atmosphere, from the perspective of the audience. Browne also discussed "horses off," or what would now be described as the creation of Foley effects, in similar detail:

The sound of horses trotting up the imaginary road outside the imaginary house of stage-land is easily produced. The man whose business it is to produce this sound has a couple of wooden blocks, each fitted with a short band of webbing, into which he slips his hands. The blocks are knocked on a board placed on the floor of the stage, and when the horses are supposed to be very near the scene the board is discarded and the wooden blocks are knocked on a slab of slate or marble. Some men prefer to use cocoanut shells instead of the blocks of wood; the shells, which must be cut or ground flat, give a better ring to the sound. (Browne, 1900, p. 65)

Browne was again identifying perspective, and in combination with the choice of contact materials, to create the right sound, within the context of perspective. Materials like slate and marble will generally produce a higher pitched and therefore closer perspective sounding sound than a material like wood. Wood contacting wood does not give a realistic rendering of horses trotting on a road; a road is usually concrete, asphalt, paving, dirt, or gravel. Slate and marble surfaces are closer to concrete and paving. Browne also offered a preferable alternative to using wood blocks as hooves, which—as comical as the use of coconut shells always sounds—does sound more like horses trotting than the sound of wooden blocks.

Puppetry, Slapstick, and Vaudeville

Another common sound effect prop in early theatrical performances was the "slapstick," a paddle-like device introduced by sixteenth-century *Commedia dell'arte* ("comedy of skills") troupes,

Van Dyke Browne's *Secrets of Scene Painting and Stage Effects* (1900)

although it has also been traced right back to the theater performances of Plautus in the third century. Commedia dell'arte was an improvisational style of theater originating in 1545 from Italy. Traveling companies of professional actors performed outdoors in public squares, using simple backdrops and props. The slapstick is two pieces of wood hinged together so when snapped a *slap*, *thwack*, *whack*, *shot*, or *whip crack* sound is created. Slapstick comedy, characterized by absurd situations and vigorous or violent action, became popular in vaudeville theater, and also in silent film with comedians such as Charlie Chaplin and Buster Keaton. The slapstick was also a common sound prop used in puppetry. The Punch and Judy puppet shows also had roots in the sixteenth-century Italian Commedia dell'arte and often included the slapstick. While very little is written about sound for the Punch and Judy shows, various illustrations suggest that dialogue, music, and other sound effect devices were also used in performances. Puppetry and hand shadows are thought to be one of the earliest forms of theatrical storytelling. Shadow puppetry originated during the Han Dynasty (121 BC), and shows were also staged with music and sound effects.

Vaudeville theaters were among the first venues to screen early motion pictures during the late 1800s. Vaudeville shows usually featured eight to ten acts, which included magic lantern shows, puppetry, acrobatics, pantomime, performance, and film. *Gertie the Dinosaur* (1914), American cartoonist and pioneer animator Winsor McCay's third short film, was used as part of a vaudeville act that combined animation with a

Promotional poster for *Gertie the Dinosaur* (1914)

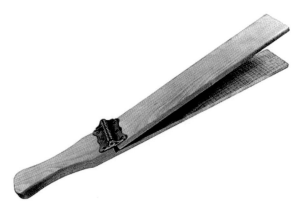

A slapstick

live "interactive" performance. McCay appeared onstage in front of the projection screen, and brandishing a whip ("crack") directed Gertie to perform tricks. In the film's finale, McCay disappeared behind the screen, reappearing in animated form and riding off on Gertie's back. The vaudeville version was later modified so that the film could also be played in regular movie theaters. The film version was prefaced with a live-action sequence and the live dialogue replaced with inter-titles, making it one of the earliest known mixed-media, multi-platform productions.

THE PICTURESQUE OF SOUND

Magic Lantern Shows, Installations, and Immersive Entertainment

The use of sound effects in moving image storytelling originated with magic lantern shows during the 1800s. Magic lantern shows used both painted and then photographic images, which were projected onto a screen or wall. A projectionist could move the slides quickly, and if they contained images of progressive motion, they appeared "animated." Various mechanisms were developed to move glass plates against one another to produce the illusion of movement. Dissolves and other time-based visual effects were also created by using multiple systems. As magic lantern shows were projected, a live showman, sound effect artists, and musicians provided the soundtrack. Magic lantern shows predate film and animation so can be thought of as the birth of animation (painted) and film (photographic). The integration of a live soundtrack also suggests the birth of sound design for moving image.

The most ambitious period in the programming of magic lantern shows began in 1854, when Henry Pepper became the director of the Royal Polytechnic Institution, a London society devoted to the exploration of science and the arts. They employed up to seven magic lanterns simultaneously, with a number of devices installed behind the screen to produce sound effects (Esteban and Segundo, 2010). By the end of the nineteenth century, magic lantern shows were the most popular form of moving image entertainment until the advent of cinema. Most shows were for general audiences, although images of phantoms, devils, and other macabre objects led to phantasmagoria, a precursor to the modern horror film. Etienne-Gaspard Robert, known by his stage name, "Robertson," was a Belgian physicist, stage magician, and developer of phantasmagoria. Robertson's work is documented in an autobiography written in the early 1830s and refers to the use of specific instruments to create sound effects. According to Robertson, terror was best achieved when optical effects coincided with sound effects. In his memoirs he discussed a technique for enlarging and reducing an image of Medusa, combined with the internal movement of her eyes, and the sound of the Chinese tam-tam. Other references include the use of sound effects to emulate wind and thunder, and a glass harmonica to create unsettling and eerie "music." Phantasmagoria marked a shift from the use of "real" sound effects to the use of unreal and surreal sound design effects for moving images.

Early Animated Films

The first documented "animated films" were screened in Paris by Frenchman Charles Émile Reynaud, a painter of magic lantern slides who had refined the Zoetrope, creating the Praxinoscope. In 1892, he gave the first

Making sound effects at the Polytechnic in the mid-nineteenth century

public performance of Théâtre Optique (Optical Theater) at the Musée Grévin in Paris. The show included three animated films, *Pauvre Pierrot* (*Poor Pete*), *Un Bon Bock* (*A Good Beer*), and *Le Clown et ses Chiens* (*The Clown and His Dogs*). The films were back-projected onto a screen while Reynaud manipulated the images. He created composite imagery by using static background images from one magic lantern projected with animated characters and objects from another. Reynaud designed some of the drawings to be played backward and forward, creating sequential moves. These early screenings were also accompanied by a live soundtrack. As a painter of magic lantern slides, Reynaud would have been privy to the sound techniques already employed or being explored by magic lantern and theater producers. There is little documentation about the use of sound in these screenings, but songs were sung in time with characters' gestures and sound effects were triggered. It is unclear if Reynaud was using a phonograph, sound effect artists, or sound effect devices, but it is possible he had developed a basic system for either triggering sound effects or cueing sound artists to perform live sound effects.

Audiovisual Events and Installations

Scientists, psychologists, and epistemologists often assisted in the design of early audiovisual events. Investigations into the fields of optics and acoustics were quite extensive in the eighteenth and nineteenth centuries. German physicist and musician Ernst Chladni (1756–1827) experimented with sound-image visualizations by drawing a bow across the edge of metal plates covered with sand to show how different pitches produced different geometrical figures. Visual artists were also experimenting with the creation of audiovisual experiences during the late 1700s. English artist Robert Barker's 1781 patent for a 360-degree painting set up the groundwork for the panorama, which developed into a form of large-scale audiovisual entertainment. Artists employed techniques such as placing foreground props at the edge of the painting to create the illusion of looking into a 3D (three-dimensional) space. With the aid of

Reynaud's Théâtre Optique, Musée Grévin in Paris 1892

lighting and the integration of viewing platforms, spectators were placed "in" the picture. Panoramas were also accompanied by sound effects, which involved teams of concealed sound effect artists manipulating a variety of sound props to create soundtracks. The *Mareorama* created by Hugo d'Alesi combined a large replica of a passenger ship deck, which rested on a universal joint and simulated the effect of a ship pitching and rolling, with moving panoramic paintings of landscapes. Props were used to hide the cylinders that supported two large canvases unrolled from port to starboard. The illusion was enhanced with the use of lighting, sound effects, costumed actors, and olfactory elements such as seaweed and tar to create an immersive experience.

The diorama, which originated in Paris in 1822, was another form of popular entertainment. Scenes were hand-painted on linen and selected areas were made transparent. A series of these multilayered panels were arranged in a deep, truncated tunnel and illuminated by sunlight redirected via skylights, screens, shutters, and colored blinds. Dioramas were also accompanied by music and sound effects, which helped to create immersive experiences. British artists Clarkson Stanfield and David Roberts produced elaborate dioramas with sound effects, music, and live performers throughout the 1830s. Typical diorama illusions included sound and image effects such as moonlit nights, winter snow turning into a summer meadow, rainbows after a storm, fountains, waterfalls, thunder, lightning, and ringing bells.

A New Art

Prior to the panorama and diorama, multimedia styled presentations also integrated sound with visual effects. Eidophusikon (taken from Greek words meaning "image of nature") was a mechanical, theater-inspired, moving image exhibition invented by artist Philip James de Loutherbourg during the late eighteenth century. Loutherbourg's most commented upon works were the exhibitions held in a small theater he built in his home. He used lights, mirrors, colored glass, paintings, and sound effects to depict various scenes. To create the sound of thunder and lightning, Loutherbourg employed a sheet of thin copper suspended by a chain, which later became known as the "thunder sheet." When the thunder sheet was shaken by one of the lower corners, it produced the rumbling of thunder and could also

"mimic" the crash of lightning. Loutherbourg also integrated sound props for the creation of waves, wind, rain, and hail sound effects. An octagonal box with internal shelves containing small shells, peas, and light balls was wheeled upon its axis to create the sound of waves. Rain sound effects were created through a long four-sided tube with small seeds, which, depending on the degree of motion, forced the seeds to create a "pattering" stream to the bottom. Two circular machines were covered with tightly strained silk, which when pressed against each other through a swift motion, created a hollow "whistling" sound and gusts of wind. Accounts of these exhibitions from an artist called William Henry Pyne (1823) describe the events as genius, and "as prolific in imitations of nature to astonish the ear, as to charm the sight" (Pyne in Longman, Hurst, Rees, Orme and Brown, 1823, p. 296). He credited Loutherbourg with introducing a new art, which he called the "picturesque of sound." Pyne's descriptions of each of the sound props match descriptions and images of theater sound devices published in the early 1900s. The same devices were later used in the creation of radio drama, film, and animation soundtracks.

The Eidophusikon showing Satan arraying his troop on the Banks of a Fiery Lake (ca. 1782), painted by Edward Francis Burney

THE FALLACY OF SILENCE

Phonography and Mechanical Mimicry

The idea of combining recorded sound with moving images is older than film itself. The first movie ever made was Eadweard Muybridge's *The Horse in Motion* (1878), whereas the first sound recording device was invented twenty years earlier. Édouard-Léon Scott de Martinville, a French printer, built a sound recorder in the late 1850s. His "phonautograph" used a mouthpiece horn and membrane fixed to a stylus, which recorded sound waves on a rotating cylinder wrapped with smoke-blackened paper. He discovered sound waves could be traced as a visual image through the vibrations of a bristle. There was no means to reproduce the sound, but it was an important forerunner to Thomas Edison's phonograph.

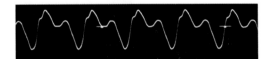

Facsimile of an early Phonautograph tracing

A number of inventors around the world were working on various systems, but credit for inventing the phonograph is usually attributed to Thomas Edison. In 1877, Edison designed the "tinfoil phonograph," which consisted of a cylindrical drum wrapped in tinfoil and mounted on a threaded axle. A mouthpiece attached to a diaphragm was connected to a stylus that etched vibrational patterns from a sound source on the rotating foil. For playback, the mouthpiece was replaced with a "reproducer" that used a more sensitive diaphragm. The first recordings were faint and "tinny" sounding, but they marked the start of what became known as sound recording and reproduction.

After inventing the phonograph, Edison started exploring the idea of coupling phonograph records with "instantaneous photography." In 1887, he wrote a paper expressing the possibility of creating a device that would do for the eye what the phonograph had already done for the ear. However, while the sound recording industry was advancing, the film industry was still in its infancy. Synchronized film sound was only made practical in the late 1920s with the introduction of sound-on-disc and sound-on film systems. Despite this, the silent film era (1894–1928) was not actually silent. The soundtrack was created live and in much the same way as it had been performed for magic lantern and theater shows.

Live Film Soundtracks

It was quickly recognized that music contributed atmosphere to the film experience and provided additional advantages such as masking the sound of the projector, preventing audiences from talking during screenings, and creating a sense of continuity between shots. Small town and neighborhood movie theaters usually had a pianist, while large city theaters employed organists or ensembles of musicians. Lesser documented is the use of sound effects, which also became a common practice. Massive theater organs were designed to create sound effects, plus fill the gap between the simple piano soloist and a larger orchestra. The organ provided a cost-effective alternative and could simulate orchestral sounds, percussion, and sound effects such as train and boat whistles, car horns, bird whistles, pistol shots, ringing phones, the sound of surf, horses' hooves, smashing pottery, thunder, and rain.

American entertainer and filmmaker Lyman Howe is believed to be the first person to use a phonograph and live sound effects in the presentation of movies. Howe started his career by touring with a phonograph presenting recorded "concerts" of music, speech, and sound effects, which were a hit with audiences. Howe presented his first movie in Pennsylvania, USA, in December 1896, making him the first person to use sound and film in tandem for commercial purposes. After acquiring Edison's *Black Diamond Express* (1896), he recorded an approaching train. According to various accounts the rushing of steam, ringing of the bells, and the roar of the wheels made the scene feel so realistic it startled audiences into physically getting out of the way. Audiences flocked to Howe's shows, and by 1899 he had added a backstage crew to provide sound effects. On some films the sound team comprised up to thirty people who, after having rehearsed with the pictures, performed the soundtrack concealed behind the screen. These early films were not perceived as films in the modern sense of the term, but as "animated photographs," "living" or "magic pictures." Voice actors and sound effects performers were employed in an effort to make the pictures feel more "real."

Performing behind the screen, 1908

By 1908 a number of entertainers were presenting "talking" films, using actors behind the screen, some twenty years before "the talkies." The use of voice actors was not a new practice; a narrator or lecturer was often hired by a film exhibitor to introduce and interpret a film for the audience. This also involved reading the inter-titles, which were the short written lines of text descriptions and dialogue inserted into films. In Japan a person, or a group of people, always supplied a live verbal component to films. Benshi, as they were called, were influential and considered an integral part of early cinema. They appeared before a screening to give introductory remarks about the content of the film about to be presented, sometimes voiced the on-screen characters, and provided translation for foreign films.

Sound Effect Machines

Standalone sound effect machines were later developed specifically for the creation of cinema sound effects. These units had various handles, which when turned created sound effects. The first machine was patented in France (1907), followed by the "Allefex" in 1909, which was invented by A. H. Moorhouse and described as "the most comprehensive and ingenious machine ever made for the mimicry of sound" (Talbot, 1912, p. 140). Striking a drum at the top of the machine where a chain mat had been placed created a gunshot. A machine gun was created by turning a shaft with tappets that struck and lifted up wooden laths, which subsequently released them to strike against the framework of the machine. The interior of the drum was fitted with three drumsticks, which could be manipulated by turning a handle to vary the number and speed of shots according to the picture being screened. At the bottom of the machine was a large bellow controlled by the foot, which in conjunction with two handles produced the sound of exhaust steam from a locomotive and the rumbling of a train rushing through a tunnel. Running water, rain, hail, and the sound of rolling waves were created by turning a handle to rotate a ribbed wooden cylinder against a board set at an angle, from the top of which was a hanging chain. The crash of pots and pans was produced by the revolution of a shaft with mounted tappets striking against hammers, which in turn came into contact with a number of steel plates. Pendant tubes produced church bells, a fire alarm, and a ship bell. A revolving shaft carrying three tappets that lifted up inverted cups created the sound of trotting horses. The shaft was movable so that a trot could be converted into gallop, and a muffling attachment created the illusion of distance. Thunder was made by shaking a thunder sheet of steel hanging on one side of the machine. Revolving a cylinder against a steel brush made the puffing of an engine. The press of a bulb produced the bark of a dog, bellows and another attachment produced a warbling bird, and the cry of the baby was created through the manipulation of a plughole and bellows.

Trap Drummers

During early 1900s, the "trap drummer" (or pit-drummer) migrated from theater and vaudeville into performing sound effects for silent films. The first drum sets emerged in the second half of the 1800s when it was realized there were advantages to having one person play a bass drum, snare drum, and cymbal at the same time. Later drummers began adding other "noise-making" devices like woodblocks, temple blocks, gongs, chimes, glockenspiel, timpani, and various sound effects. A newspaper article from 1914 indicates there was probably a range of skill levels and variations in sound effect props. In the article, the author marvels at the drummer's ability to drum and perform sound effects to moving images at the same time. The "traps" mentioned include sleigh bells, sandpaper, an eggbeater, and a nutmeg grater (*The Tropical Sun*, 1914). Given the need for synchronization of sound effects with pictures, highly skilled drummers were perceived as having the sense of rhythm, timing, and hand-eye coordination needed to play sound effects for moving images.

Reviews of films with live sound effect performers were initially mixed, and it is impossible to tell if an organ, live sound effects artists, a machine, a drummer, or a phonograph record produced the sound effects for "silent" films. Some film reviewers noted the ill-considered and overuse of sound effects, while others responded favorably:

> Where a sound will have a direct bearing and effect upon something that is happening in a picture, such as the ringing of a door bell, the shot of a gun, wind in a storm, etc., then by all means come in with it strong, but on the other hand, when you see a calf in the background of a pretty farm scene don't detract from the acting by jangling a cow bell when it has no bearing on the picture. (Hoffman, 1910, p. 185)

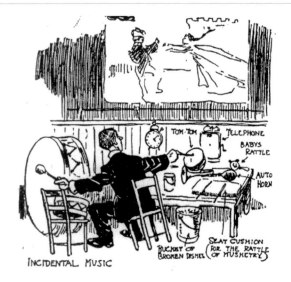

An American effects setup, "The Lure of the Moving Picture Shows," *New York Herald*, 17 April 1910

The sound effects during the presentation of "Trawler Fishing in a Hurricane" fairly captured the audience. The shriek and moan of the wind, the swish of the flying scud, the resounding chug of heavy seas, as they were shipped, were all reproduced with a realism that carried the spectator into the throes of the storm. (McQuade, 1912, p. 1107)

From around 1910, the idea of accompanying pictures with sound effects was fashionable. British writer Frederick A. Talbot wrote, "When a horse gallops, the sound of its feet striking the road are heard; the departure of a train is accompanied by a whistle and a puff as the engine gets under weigh; the breaking of waves upon a pebbly beach is reproduced by a roaring sound" (Talbot, 1912, p. 139). Talbot also wrote about some of the problems that had started to emerge, such as the "unpleasant shock" of hearing the wrong sound effect, "when the realism of a medieval battle is heightened by the vigorous rattling of a machine gun, or when horses galloping over the turf make a clatter that only a city pavement could cause" (p. 139). Problems aside, Talbot argued that since sound effects were indispensable to the "legitimate" stage (meaning theater), it was only logical that the use of sound effects should extend to moving images. He identified and advocated for what he saw as an emerging trend, employing sound effects with as much care as the pictures. It was proposed that high-quality and well-rehearsed sound effects were good for business.

Many early films have been lost due to the fragility of early film (celluloid) and phonograph records. Often when a film is restored, a new soundtrack is added or the film is presented mute. The *Dickson Experimental Sound Film* is one of the few early films to be restored with the original sound. The film was produced by William Dickson in late 1894 or early 1895 and

is considered the first known film with recorded sound. It also appears to be the first motion picture made for the Kinetophone, the proto-sound-film system developed by Dickson and Edison. In 2010, over 100 silent films were discovered in an archive in New Zealand, including a film by Lyman Howe called *Lyman Howe's Ride on a Runaway Train* (1921). The film has been recently restored and is described as a thrill-packed short accompanied by sound discs. It's an experimental live-action animated film with sound, and, given the limited technology at the time, it's not surprising it caused quite a sensation.

Lyman Howe's famous *Ride on a Runaway Train* (1921)

RADIO WITH
PICTURES

Mental Imagery

Often overlooked is the impact early radio production had on the development of sound design practice and techniques. During the 1920s, radio and recorded music were growing in popularity, and new developments paved the way for film sound. In much the same way, radio sound effect artists also paved the way for film sound design. Radio was initially a military communication tool, which evolved into a popular entertainment, culture, and news medium. Research in "wireless telephony" during World War I led to viable microphones and amplifiers that made radio broadcasting possible. Early radio drama was essentially broadcasted theater, and the first shows were broadcast directly from theaters. It took a while for producers to realize radio, as a purely aural medium, needed a different approach to scripting and production. Frequently described as "theater of the mind," the success of a show hinged on involving the listeners' imagination. Unlike theater and film, radio drama didn't need costumes or sets; sound, or more precisely sound effects, created the imagery.

Ora Nichols and her husband, Arthur, are believed to be among the first to bring sound effects to radio. Ora, who led the first in-house sound effect team, is considered one of the most pioneering figures in early sound effects creation. She and Arthur were both musicians who migrated from vaudeville to silent film and then to radio. Arthur was a violinist but had switched to playing drums so he could play sound effects for silent films. When the silent era ended and the sound film was introduced, they both started working in radio. While this might sound like a strange choice in mediums, their decision to work in radio production was most likely due to the nature of early sound films ("the talkies"), which were dialogue-driven so presented limited opportunities for creative sound artists.

Sound Effect Artistry

By the late 1930s, radio drama was hugely popular. Sound effects were initially created manually or vocally, until superseded by sound effects on records followed by tape. Common manual effects included running a fingernail along the edge of pocket comb for the sound of crickets, snapping open an umbrella for the sudden ignition of fire, cellophane or a bundle of bamboo splints twisted together to produce the sound of fire crackling, squeezing seltzer bottles into a pail for milking a cow, shaking cups containing BBs for a rattlesnake, twisting wallets for getting in or out of a saddle, plunging a knife into a cabbage or melon for body stabs, shaking a small chain attached to piece of leather for a horse harness, and scratching rough paper with a paper clip for writing with a pen. Radio sound effect departments grew to house numerous sound props. Some were custom designed and often for the production of multiple sound effects. A slatted metal device was used to create the sound of a guillotine and the sound of footsteps on a fire escape. Props like kitchen sinks were built to cover everything from dishwashing to drink pouring, kettle filling and rainstorms. Foley sound effects such as footsteps, impacts, and falls were especially important in radio drama as they gave stories movement, a sense of perspective, and realism. Plywood and marble slabs were used for different hard surfaces, and boxes were filled with different materials such as gravel. Palm fronds and other plant materials were used for footsteps in the forest, bush, or jungle.

Sound effects chief Ora Nichols assisted by George McDonnell, at work on the CBS radio program *The March of Time* (1935)

On comedy shows, sound effect artists were considered comedians in their own right. Typical comedy effects included hollow wood hits and boings, which were also common in early animation. To "personify" a car in a comedic sense involved combining sounds for the car with additional and typically vocal effects, of the car coughing, wheezing, gasping, and spluttering. Old motors attached to riveted metal buckets for nuts, bolts, and nails to be dropped in created rattles, clanks, and bangs. "Authentic" sounds lack comedic character, whereas combining sound and vocal effects created a "personality" and added comic value. Comedy shows also used studio audiences to provide live laughter, and sometimes "claques," who were people hired to laugh in different styles. Another common strategy for devising effects was based on phonetic imitation, or onomatopoeia, which are words that phonetically resemble or suggest the source of the sound that they describe. This includes animal sounds such as "oink" or "meow" and also applies to the naming conventions of sound props designed to create specific effects. One of the most obvious examples is the "boing" box, which was used for creating comic "boing" sound effects.

Early sound effect artists faced many of the issues still prevalent today. There was a perception that all sound people thought and worked in exactly the same way and that all sound effects

took the same amount of preparation regardless of the actual sound. Playing the sound effect of a thunderclap from a sound effect record was not the same as physically creating the sound of body falling in mud, or performing two live sound effects at the same time, such as typing and a door knock, which required one hand typing and one hand knocking, or two people were needed. Even with the introduction of sound effects on records, certain sounds were difficult to create and involved the use of several turntables or performers. Creating a steam train crash consists of several different sound effects: the sounds leading to the crash, the crash, metal skids, iron wheels locking, brakes on rails, steam, and the collision. The less obvious or complex types of sound effects required deconstructing the intended sound and finding items to create the "right" combination of sounds; for example, the sound of blood boiling was created through blowing bubbles in syrup with a straw. Syrup has a similar consistency to blood, and blowing bubbles through a straw provides the boiling action. Late script changes also posed problems because sound effects always needed to be rehearsed before the live performance. Another common misconception sound effect artists faced stemmed from the lack of understanding concerning weight, scale, and volume. Robert Mott tells the story of Jim Rogan, a sound effect artist working for CBS who needed to create the sound of a turbulent river and a stampede of horses. Rogan stood in a tub of water and thrashed his feet while drumming coconut shells in dirt. The director of the show was underwhelmed with the results, which would have sounded too "small" and not what the director had envisioned.

An additional complication was the "visual director," who based the appropriateness of a sound effect on how the props looked, as opposed to how they actually sounded. Orson Welles was known as a visual director. In a scene that required the sound of a lawn being mowed, he requested the studio be filled with "real" grass and a "real" lawn mower to be pushed by a "real" actor. The usual technique for creating the sound of lawn mowing was using an eggbeater or a stripped-back lawn mower and shredded newspaper. Welles wanted realism but overlooked how sometimes the "real" sound does not actually sound real. The show also required a number of rehearsals, which left no grass to cut, which made the resulting

Sound effect artists in *Back of the Mike* (1938)

sound even more unconvincing. In another show that required footsteps on sand, Welles organized for the studio to be filled with sand. The usual technique for creating footsteps in sand is using a pit or box filled with dirt or cornstarch. Footsteps in sand are a difficult sound effect to create because the "real" sound is very subtle and low in level (volume/amplitude). If the level is raised, so are the actors' voices and any other sounds such as script rustles. Sand is very fine, while dirt is grittier and gravel even grittier. Certain sounds ("grit") contain more mid-high frequency content, which are perceived as being louder. In both situations, the original technique was reemployed.

Radio shows took anywhere between a day and a week to prepare for, and busy shows needed at least two sound effect artists. Everyone involved in a show attended a read-through while the director worked out rough timings. Corrections were made and then the show was rehearsed with sound effects. Rehearsals were necessary because if mistakes were made, the whole show had to be re-performed. The studio engineer was responsible for making sure the various sound components were mixed appropriately.

As the popularity of radio drama increased, producers and directors sought greater realism, or at least the idea of realism. Some producers considered sound effects as artificial and deceptive, although this was more of an issue on news and current affairs shows. Various sound effects were used in news shows, although they were generally restricted to simple signature sounds. Current affairs shows such as *The March of Time* (1931–35) made no attempt to hide the use of sound effects because the show was considered news "dramatizing." A similar debate arises in documentary filmmaking; some documentary filmmakers avoid using sound design and music because of the emotive and subjective impact, while others take a more cinematic approach to the use of sound. One of the most famous radio dramas was Orson Welles's adaptation of H. G. Wells's novel *The War of the Worlds*, broadcast in the 1930s. Welles's version of the story was sound designed and suggested aliens from Mars were invading New Jersey, leaving a trail of death and destruction in their wake. According to various sources, people thought it was real and believed that the end of the world had arrived, which later caused widespread outrage in the media. Despite complaints or

Performing sound effects for *The March of Time* (1935)

possibly because of them, Welles's career took off. The use of sound in his films, most notably *Citizen Kane* (1941), was informed by his prior experiences in radio drama production.

As radio fidelity and recording technologies improved, manual sound effects were considered inadequate and the use of sound effect records started to replace the performing of effects. A record library of hundreds of sound effects took up less space than sound props. Sound effects records were more economical; a single person with three turntables could create an effect that would require three manual sound artists. Record companies started releasing more sound effect records and improved on the quality. As recording technology evolved, audiotape and cartridge machines replaced records, followed by CD libraries. Today radio drama's popularity waxes and wanes. Advances in digital recording and the Internet have revived it to an extent, and some countries still produce radio drama, radio art (or sound art), and radio documentaries. Audio books employ the same techniques and sometimes to a scale that rivals the film soundtrack. Despite changes in technology, the practice is still employed in moving image disciplines by sound designers and Foley artists. While there are numerous sound effects libraries, many sound and Foley effects are unique to a project, so are still recorded "live" while performing to pictures.

TRANSITIONING TO SOUND

Amped and In Sync

The silent film era ended in 1927 with the arrival of the "sound film," a motion picture with synchronized sound or sound coupled with image, as opposed to a film accompanied with a live soundtrack. While the union of sound and image was a long-standing ambition, the two mediums were not so easily combined. Image was recorded in a linear and discontinuous fashion and sound in a circular and continuous fashion, which posed a problem. In addition, early recording mechanisms were not sensitive enough to capture quality dialogue, and the lack of amplification made it impossible to reproduce sound for large audiences. Films with sound were screened during the early 1900s through the use of a phonograph running in mechanical synchronism with pictures; however, reliable synchronization was difficult to achieve due to mechanical failures. A number of inventors throughout the world had been trying to create the technology to combine sound and image, and effectively the "silent" film era was a period of development. While inventors were intent on the unification of sound and image, the film industry was initially resistant to the idea. Poor sound quality, synchronization problems, and inadequate amplification were all significant hurdles.

Sound-on-Disc
The very first sound films were limited to short loops viewed and heard by a single person through the combination of a Kinetoscope and Kinetophone. The Kinetoscope created the illusion of movement through a strip of perforated film bearing sequential images over a light source with a high-speed shutter. Edison introduced the Kinetophone in 1895, which incorporated a cylinder phonograph, effectively creating one of the first audiovisual entertainment devices. Sound was heard through tubes similar to a stethoscope, connected to a diaphragm and stylus assembly.

Kinetophone/Kinetoscope

In addition to the work undertaken by Edison, a number of other inventors were experimenting with sound and image synchronization. In 1902, Léon Gaumont developed the Chronophone to synchronize pictures with a phonograph using a switchboard. Chronophone films were created using a similar technique to modern music videos, with the artist miming to a preexisting audio recording. French civil engineer, musician, and painter Auguste Baron was also one of the first to experiment with sound films. In 1896, Baron and Fréderic Bureau patented a system of shooting and projecting sound films recorded on disc. An electrical device on the motor-driven camera regulated the wax cylinder recorder to maintain synchronization. Between 1896 and the early 1900s, a number of other inventors were working on linking phonograph records and films with various degrees of success and failure.

By 1925, Western Electric's Bell Telephone Laboratories believed they had perfected the

Vitaphone, which was based on the synchronization of film with a phonograph record. A
recording lathe cut an audio signal–modulated
spiral groove into the polished surface of a slab
of wax-like material rotating on a turntable. The
wax was too soft to be played in the usual way,
but a specially supported and guided pickup
was used to play it back immediately to detect
any sound problems that might have gone
unnoticed. If there were problems, scenes could
be re-shot while everything was still in place.
Edward Craft, the executive vice president at
Bell, described the Vitaphone as "a development
which is destined to create an entirely new art
where the medium of expression is the synchronized reproduction of sound and scene" (Craft,
1926). A turntable was geared to a projector and
driven by a constant-speed electric motor. The
needle generated an electrical current with the
same characteristics as the sound that produced
the original record and was amplified providing
enough energy to power loudspeakers behind the
screen. The first Warner Bros. Vitaphone features
were *Don Juan* (1926) and *The Better 'Ole* (1926);
however, they had only synchronized music and
sound effects. *The Jazz Singer* (Crosland, 1927) is
considered the first feature-length motion picture
with synchronized dialogue sequences and is
hailed as the birth of the "talkies." The film contains synchronized singing sequences and about
two minutes of synchronized dialogue. The rest of
the dialogue was presented through inter-titles,
the common standard in silent movies. Early feature films with recorded sound typically included
music and sound effects only. Major Hollywood
studios made a "silent" version (with music and
effects) and a "sound" version (with dialogue),
which may be why many still consider non-
dialogue-driven films as "silent" today.

   The Vitaphone was still susceptible to synchronization problems. If records weren't cued
correctly, the sound would start out of synchronization with the image. Projectors had special
levers to advance and delay synchronization,
but only to a certain extent. The other limitation
was the inability to physically edit material. The
process entailed a microphone recording the
sound performed on set directly to a phonograph
master, which made it impossible to edit recordings. There was some experimentation with

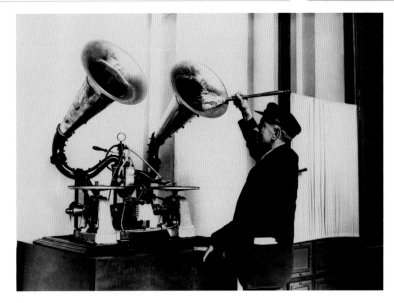

Chronophone

mixing, and dubbing systems were developed so
that source discs could be cued and dubbed to a
new master disc, but the wax master could not be
paused, so each playback turntable had to start
at just the right moment. The Vitaphone system
was the leading brand of sound-on-disc technology at that time, but as sound-on-film systems
were improved on, they became the dominant
industry standard for talking pictures.

First-nighters
outside the
Warners' Theater
before the
premiere of *Don
Juan* (1926)

Sound-on-disc, Warners Vitaphone

Sound-on-Film

The problems associated with sound-on-disc systems led to the exploration of other concepts, most importantly the printing of picture and sound on the same piece of film. Sound was converted into electrical signals, translated into light signals and printed. Eugene Lauste, a French inventor, developed an optical system called "Phonocinematophone" in 1910, but the system lacked the amplification needed for playback in theaters. Another system, developed by Polish-American inventor Joseph Tykocinski-Tykociner, was successfully demonstrated to a large audience in 1922. Tykociner is believed to be the first, or one of the first, to consider the idea of photographing sound. He was an assistant research professor at the University of Illinois and given permission to experiment with sound pictures. Jacob Kunz, a colleague and theoretical physicist, had developed a photoelectric cell, which Tykociner used to convert sound impulses to light.

Three competing technologies surfaced during the 1920s: RCA's Photophone, an optical sound, "variable-area" film exposure system, and two "variable-density" sound-on-film systems, Fox-Case's Movietone and Lee de Forest's Phonofilm. Variable density meant that the density of the soundtrack varied in accordance with the amplitude of the audio signal. Variable area meant that the width of the soundtrack varied in accordance with the amplitude of the audio signal. The soundtrack was photographically recorded on the film by a beam of light modulated by the sound waves. Sound was reproduced during projection by directing a beam of light through the soundtrack onto a photocell. The photographically recorded electrical waveforms were then translated back into sound waves and amplified as a film was projected.

Varying accounts suggest de Forest improved on the work of Finnish inventor Eric Tigerstedt and German inventors Josef Engl, Hans Vogt, and Joseph Massole, who were developing the Tri-Ergon process. Tigerstedt had a big interest in sound recording technology and made significant improvements to the amplification capacity of the vacuum valve. He developed a prototype for recording sound on a metal wire as early as 1912 and was confident sound could be recorded directly on motion picture film. While his sound-on-film technology wasn't commercialized, he also developed directional loudspeakers and predicted future inventions such as the mobile phone. The first sound short to use the system, *Das Mädchen mit den Schwefelhölzern* (*The Little Match Girl*), premiered in 1925 but ended in catastrophe. The sound cut out and the audience responded negatively. Years later, a sound-on-film technique based on the Tri-Ergon system gained wider acceptance in Europe.

The quality of de Forest's Phonofilm was initially poor, but with help from American inventor Theodore Case, de Forest made some enhancements, which led to the first commercial screening of a short sound film in 1923. From 1922 to 1925, Case and de Forest collaborated in the development of the Phonofilm system; however, Case ended the relationship due to de Forest's tendency to claim sole credit. Case had developed an interest in using modulated light to carry speech as a student at Yale University. In 1914, he established a laboratory to study the photoelectric properties of materials, which led to the development of the Thallofide tube, a light-sensitive vacuum tube. He also contributed to the development of the Aeo-light, a light source that could be modulated by audio signals and used to expose sound in sound cameras. In 1922, Case and his assistant Earl I. Sponable developed the Movietone, a modification of the earlier Phonofilm system.

Charles Hoxie created the Pallophotophone, which became the RCA Photophone. Hoxie worked for General Electric (GE) following World War I and developed a photographic recorder to record transoceanic wireless telegraphy signals. The recorder was later adapted to record voice and used to record speeches for broadcast. The Pallophotophone could record and replay multiple audio tracks and is considered the world's first effective multitrack recording system, predating magnetic tape–based systems. In 1925, GE launched a program to commercialize sound-on-film equipment based on Hoxie's work. A number of demonstrations were given in 1926 and 1927 under the new name of Photophone, and the first public screening was a sound version (music plus sound effects only) of the "silent" film *Wings* (Wellman, 1927).

End of an Era

The invention of the Audion tube in 1906 by Lee de Forest was integral to the sound film. Western Electric acquired the rights to it in 1913 and developed it into a more reliable device. It was the first widely used electrical device that could provide enough amplification for a large theater. In 1929, Max Fleischer codirected a short animated film called *Finding His Voice* (Goldman and Fleischer, 1929). Western Electric sponsored the film as a way of educating moviegoers about their sound-on-film process. The film is an "animated cartoon synchronized to voice and sound" that outlines how the Western Electric sound-on-film recording system worked. The film opens with a hand drawing a strip of film that comes to life as a talking filmstrip ("Talkie"), joined by an "out of work" silent filmstrip ("Mutie") wanting to make the transition to sound. Talkie takes Mutie to see "Dr. Western," who guides him through the film sound process. The film effectively marks the end of the silent era, which created an upheaval in the industry. Silent film studios became obsolete and movie theaters began installing sound systems. Films that began production as silent films were transformed into sound films.

However, not all filmmakers embraced the sound film. It was argued that the "talkie" was nothing more than a filmed play, which subverted the aesthetic virtues of cinema. Cameras were noisy, so needed to be housed in large sound-insulated booths. Acting suffered due to the use stationary or hidden microphones, which constricted the movement of actors. Directors became frustrated by the reliance on dialogue and the immobilized camera. In 1928, Russian

Finding His Voice (1929, dir. Max Fleischer and F. Lyle Goldman)

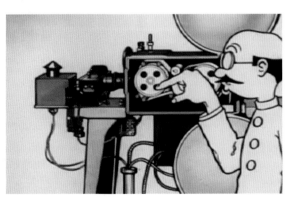

filmmakers Eisenstein, Pudovkin, and Alexandrov issued a joint statement to voice their concerns. They saw sound recording and the sound film as something of a double-edged sword. While it was a significant development, they feared sound would be commercially exploited by Hollywood in the form of "talking" films, which would destroy the visual montage they were responsible for developing. Another concern was international sales. A film produced in London would be in English and therefore only understood by people who also spoke English. Foreign language dubs were considered complex and expensive, and subtitles were not given much thought at that time. While the negativity toward the sound film appears "anti-sound," Eisenstein, Pudovkin, and Alexandrov were concerned with what they perceived as sound being employed "incorrectly," primarily the preoccupation with dialogue to the detriment of other elements. The problems caused by the transition to sound were soon solved with "blimps," designed to suppress camera noise, dollies, and boom microphones that could be held out of frame and move with the actors. Initial misgivings eventually gave way to creative exploration of sound and sound-image arrangements.

A New Form of Composition

Eisenstein, Pudomn, and Alexandrov were principally concerned with the contrapuntal use of sound, which they believed would elevate the visual montage and perfect the cinematic art form.

Hitchcock and Anny Ondra on the set of *Blackmail*

The term "contrapuntal" is commonly associated with music and counterpoint, the technique of combining melodies. In the broader context, counterpoint describes any element that is juxtaposed with another. Filmmakers started to recognize the opportunities for aural and visual counterpoint, and creative manipulation of sound and image was seen as a means for revealing meaning, adding depth, and heightening perceptions.

Sound, treated as a new montage element (as a factor divorced from the visual image), will inevitably introduce new means of enormous power to the expression and solution of the most complicated tasks that now oppress us with the impossibility of overcoming them by means of an imperfect film method, working only with visual images. (Eisenstein, Pudovkin, and Alexandrov, in Weis and Belton 1985, p. 85)

In the United Kingdom, Alfred Hitchcock directed the first all-talking film, *Blackmail* (1929). The film is based on a play about a woman who is blackmailed after killing a man. After starting production as a silent film, British International Pictures decided to convert *Blackmail* into a sound film. Hitchcock initially ridiculed talking films, but he later deemed the arrival of sound as bringing a new dimension to cinematic expression. While music had previously dominated the film soundtrack, Hitchcock pared back music to experiment with the expressionistic use of dialogue and sound effects. He was later known for preparing detailed lists of sounds for his films. For the knife sound in *Psycho*'s shower scene, he conducted blind sound tests using different types of melons. Although uncredited until 1939, British sound editor Harry Miller worked on *Blackmail* and became one of the first known "dubbing editors."

M (1931) was Austrian-German filmmaker Fritz Lang's first sound film. The film, credited with establishing the serial killer and police procedural genres, depicts a manhunt for a serial killer of children. The soundtrack includes a narrator, dialogue, Foley, sound effects, and silence to inform the narrative. Like Hitchcock's work, *M* experiments with the expressionistic use of sound. Dialogue is fairly minimal, especially for a "talkie," and there's an absence of music. The film was one of the first to use a leitmotif, associated with the central character, Franz Becker, who whistles "In the Hall of the Mountain King" from Edvard Grieg's Peer Gynt Suite No. 1. Later in the film, whistling lets the audience know that he is nearby. His presence is heard rather than seen; the whistling is a stand-in for the murders.

From 1928 to 1931, the major emphasis in film sound was on production (location) sound, and film studios, labs, and equipment suppliers were largely focused on sound capture. Soundtracks were mono and had a limited bandwidth (40Hz to 10kHz) and dynamic range (around 40dB). Systems were also noisy. It was not until 1966 that Dolby created the first product to reduce noise in music recordings. *A Clockwork Orange* (Kubrick, 1971) was the first film to use Dolby noise reduction. As the quality of recording and reproduction technology increased, it become apparent that other enhancements could be made, after production. Innovations in technology presented an opportunity to revisit the soundtrack in postproduction. The sound film initiated "multitracking," which meant that separately recorded audio sources could be replayed and mixed together. Re-recording, which had previously only involved the parts of a film requiring music and effects, started to become a production standard for the entire soundtrack. In 1931, engineer Kenneth Morgan anticipated the importance of this change and predicted postproduction sound would become an art in itself, "a new form of composition in sound where the artist's keyboard commands the sounds of the universe" (Morgan, 1931, p. 154). While the term "sound design" was introduced decades later, the concepts that underpin contemporary sound design and re-recording were being established shortly after the transition to sound.

Today film critics and reviewers often consider non-dialogue or non-musically-driven films as silent or visual, when in reality they are reliant on sound effects, the treatment of sound, and the overall soundtrack mix. Sylvain Chomet's first feature-length animated film, *The Triplets of Belleville* (*Les Triplettes de Belleville*, 2003), is a good example of a film that reviewers described as silent. The film centers around Madame Souza and her orphaned grandson, Champion. Madame Souza encourages and trains Champion for the Tour de France. While competing in the race he is kidnapped by the French mafia. Madame Souza and Champion's dog, Bruno, set out to find him. They make their way to the city of Belleville and encounter a former jazz-singing trio called the Triplets of Belleville. The women band together to rescue

M (1931, dir. Fritz Lang)

Champion. The story is narrated through the use of atmosphere, sound effects, and broadcast segments. Sound becomes character, punctuates individual narratives, and adds a sense of realism to environments. The lack of dialogue allows sound design and music to actively partake in the storytelling, which in turn focuses the audience on the visual storytelling. As a consequence, there is an illusion of silence and a perception that the film is visual, despite the storytelling being very audiovisual. The other interesting aspect of the film is that the Triplets are sound effect artists, and props become "instruments" when they perform live with a newspaper, a fridge, and a vacuum cleaner. Sound is *in* the narrative and becomes an active part of the film's overall aesthetic.

The Triplets of Belleville (2003, dir. Sylvain Chomet)

ANIMATION FINDS ITS VOICE

The Thing That Hooked the Crowds

During the silent film era, animated films (or "cartoons") had minimal status, and many of the studios specializing in "silent cartoons" went bankrupt before the coming of sound. The studios that survived did in part by embracing sound. Like live-action films, the first sound cartoons had very few sound effects and everything was recorded in one take, usually after the film was produced. Instruments and sound props created most of the sound effects, often percussive in nature, or created by instruments such as slide whistles and xylophone bells. Early cartoons were often "musical" and frequently depicted characters dancing, singing, and playing instruments or props.

Max Fleischer was the first to experiment with the synchronization of sound and animation. He saw the potential in integrating sound and began working with Lee de Forest to create recorded soundtracks. The short animated film series *Song Car-Tunes* (1924–27) were the first sound cartoons. Fleischer also invented the "follow the bouncing ball" technique used in the *Song Car-Tunes*, which visually indicated the rhythm of a song to help audiences sing along to the lyrics. A similar technique was later used by Walt Disney to synchronize sound and image. There were thirty-six titles in the *Song Car-Tune* series; seventeen were silent films accompanied by live music and nineteen were sound films, which used the Phonofilm sound-on-film process developed by de Forest. The first sound film from the series was *Oh, Mabel*, released in 1924, produced some years before Paul Terry's *Dinner Time* (1928) and Walt Disney's *Steamboat Willie* (1928).

Fleischer brought *Koko the Clown*, *Betty Boop*, *Popeye*, and *Superman* to the screen and was also responsible for a number of technological innovations, such as the Rotoscope. Animated films were primitive and jerky to begin with, which was something that bothered Fleischer.

Max got his brother Dave Fleischer to perform choreographed movements dressed in a clown costume. The live-action images were then projected onto a frosted glass panel and redrawn. World War I interrupted Fleischer's work due to a stint producing training films for the U.S. Army. After the war ended, he returned to his *Out of the Inkwell* series with Dave, who had been working as a film editor at an army medical museum. The series proved popular with audiences and transformed animated films from being considered a "curiosity" into an industry (Fleischer, 2005). In 1921, Fleischer launched his own studio, Out of the Inkwell Inc. He improved on the Rotoscope with the Rotograph, which allowed an animated figure to be superimposed over a moving background. The Rotograph also made combining animation with live-action easier, which became a popular technique in early films, in the same way the combining of live-action and CGI is today.

Incorporating Sound

The incorporating of sound integrated Max and Dave Fleischer's brother, musician Lou Fleischer, into the production team; he became the head of the Fleischer Studios Music Department. Cartoons during this era usually had wall-to-wall music and minimal dialogue, which was typically vocal sound effects such as grunts and groans. *My Old Kentucky Home* (Fleischer, 1926) was their first attempt at using synchronized dialogue, with a doglike character saying, "Follow the ball, and join in, everybody." The film was not very successful, but Max continued producing cartoons with dialogue, devising a new series called *Talkartoons*. The popularity of Walt Disney's Mickey Mouse also inspired the creation of a new character, Bimbo, who first appeared in the *Out of the Inkwell* series as a character called Fitz. The studio's sixth Talkartoon, *Dizzy Dishes* (1930), required a female character, and as Bimbo was a dog, Max developed a half-dog half-female character that after refinements became Betty Boop. In *Dizzy Dishes*, Bimbo plays a chef who gets distracted by Betty Boop (before her doglike ears were revised) performing a "Boop Boop a Doop" on stage. While the story is simplistic, the animation and soundtrack were an improvement on *My Old Kentucky Home*, featuring more dialogue, sound, and Foley effects.

Due to a lack of screen crediting and documentation, it's unclear who was responsible

Dizzy Dishes (1930, dir. Dave Fleischer)

for the sound effects in Fleischer's early films, although there are two distinct possibilities, Max and Maurice (or Morris) Manne. The Manne brothers most likely worked as freelance sound artists for various directors and studios. Morris Manne appears with an effects credit in an Aesop's fable called *House Cleaning Time* (1929) and was rumored to be the sound effects editor at Famous/Paramount. Max Manne is credited as "effects artist" on *Dinner Time* (1928), an animated short film produced and directed by Paul Terry and codirected by John Foster. *Dinner Time* was one of the first publicly shown "all talking" sound-on-film cartoons. Max Manne also features in a *Popular Mechanics* magazine article entitled "Expert in Noise Making Adds Joy to Theatregoing" (1927). The article suggests Manne was the resident sound artist at the Roxy Theatre in New York. Scattered references imply he held a number of positions: production manager, drummer, sound effect device creator, and artist for theater, film, and animation productions.

To make as much noise as he can and in as many different ways as possible is the task of Max H. Manne, who produces sound effects to accompany the films and feature numbers at Roxy's theater. Wire brushes rubbed over the kettledrum, give the effect of a locomotive's noise; a reed whistle has been made to imitate an infant's cry; catgut, variously used, mimics the calls of a number of animals and to reproduce a dog's bark, a string drawn through a tin can and caressed by rosined fingers is effective. Mr. Manne has been granted a number of patents on noisemakers, and the

percussion room of the theater, where articles are stored, is an interesting museum of musical novelties. (*Popular Mechanics*, 1927, p. 818)

Full Steam Ahead

The soundtracks for *Dinner Time* and *House Cleaning Time* were quite rudimentary, bordering incoherent. Walt Disney criticized *Dinner Time* for being "a lot of racket and nothing else" (Disney in Barrier, 1999, p. 55). According to some sources, it was *Dinner Time* that actually inspired Disney to produce a better sound cartoon. His brother Roy O. Disney also cites the success of *The Jazz Singer* (1927) as a motivating factor in Disney's interest in sound. In 1927, Carl Laemmle from Universal Studios approached Disney requesting a new all-animated series featuring a rabbit. Disney and animator Ub Iwerks created Oswald the Lucky Rabbit. *Poor Papa* (1927) was the first

Oswald cartoon; it was criticized by producer and distributor Charles Mintz because Oswald looked too old. The second film, *Trolley Troubles* (1927), featuring a younger version of Oswald, received positive reviews and launched the series. The first Oswald films were produced as silent films, sound effects were added later, and they were then re-advertised as sound films. Sound had quickly become an attraction and featured heavily in film and animation marketing materials. Facing ownership issues, and in collaboration with Ub Iwerks and Les Clark, Disney created Mickey Mouse to replace Oswald, who faded into obscurity. It wasn't until 2006 that the Walt Disney Company actually got the rights to Oswald back, and he returned in Disney's 2010 video game, *Epic Mickey*, with a plot that parallels Oswald's real-world history. The first two Mickey Mouse cartoons, *Plane Crazy* (1928) and *The Gallopin' Gaucho* (1929), were produced as silent films and failed to gain a distributor. *Gallopin' Gaucho* was the second short and although completed in August 1928, Disney decided not to release it in favor of working on *Steamboat Willie*.

To help make Mickey stand out from other cartoons, *Steamboat Willie* was released with a postproduced synchronized soundtrack. Disney realized that sound effects and music could function narratively, so while the soundtrack was postproduced, it was actually conceived in preproduction. Preliminary ideas were discussed at a "gag meeting" and later Ub Iwerks created polished sketches with a synopsis of each scene beside the sketch. According to Wilfred Jackson, Disney either wrote the synopsis or proofed and finalized Iwerks's initial descriptions. During the preproduction phase, a "bar sheet" was devised with each sound effect and musical measure linked to the screen action. Using a metronome and mouth organ, Jackson, who had some music knowledge, helped Disney time the action. Jackson prepared the rudimentary bar sheet and Disney devised exposure sheets indicating which frames the musical beats would fall on. The two documents were prepared before the animators started so that sound and image would work in synchronization. Disney wanted the film to feel real, and as if the sound was coming from what the characters were doing. While work was being undertaken on the rest of the film, a sequence was inked, painted, photographed, and put together for a test screening. Jackson

played the mouth organ, Ub Iwerks banged on pots and pans, Johnny Cannon provided sound effects using various props, and Disney provided dialogue effects, namely grunts, laughs, and squawks. The screening proved successful, and once the film was completed, Disney hired a seventeen-piece orchestra and three sound effect artists for the soundtrack recording session.

Despite money being an issue at the time, Disney's insistence on marrying sound and image as tightly as possible paid off. *Steamboat Willie* was recognized as "a real sound cartoon" instead of "a silent cartoon with an added soundtrack" (Barrier, 1999, p. 55). The film is considered Mickey Mouse's screen debut, although it was not until *The Karnival Kid* (1929) that Walt Disney first voiced Mickey. *Steamboat Willie* premiered in November 1928 and "the thing that hooked the crowds—was its sound" (Leslie, 2002, p. 21). Rave reviews for cartoons were unusual, but *Variety* magazine (1928) acknowledged that while it was not the first animated cartoon to be synchronized with sound effects, it represented "a high order of cartoon ingenuity, cleverly combined with sound effects" (p. 13). Disney and his artists had made sound a part of the art of animation. Disney initially adopted the Cinephone system, which was rumored to be a pirated version of the RCA Phonofilm system. Patrick Powers, an American businessperson involved in the film industry, had hired a former de Forest technician to produce a cloned or similar version of the Phonofilm system, which became known as the Powers Cinephone. The former technician was Bill Garity, who ended up working for Disney as his special effects and sound technician. Garity later headed the department that helped extend the capabilities of the animated films. One of their key developments was the multi-plane camera, which gave depth to animated films and made it possible to create camera movements, which simulated live-action films. Another major development was "Fantasound," an innovative stereo system installed in theaters for Disney's classic, *Fantasia* (1940), which was the first commercial film to be released in stereo. Fantasound was also a precursor to what is now known as surround sound. Fantasound created the illusion of movement across speakers by introducing the pan pot (panoramic potentiometer), which allowed sound to be panned with a left, center, and right speaker configuration. Increasing the volume during loud passages and reducing it during quiet ones also addressed the lack of dynamic range, which is the difference in volume between the loudest and quietest sounds in a soundtrack.

Synchronized Dialogue, Silence, and SFX

A year after the release of *Steamboat Willie*, animators Hugh Harman and Rudolf Ising created *Bosko The TalkInk Kid* (1929), a live-action/animated short film produced as a demo to pitch a series of Bosko cartoons. Harman and Ising worked at Walt Disney's studio in Kansas City and later founded the Warner Bros. and Metro-Goldwyn-Mayer animation studios. Harman had considered producing a sound cartoon in 1927, with the intention of capitalizing on the coming of sound. He filmed *Bosko The TalkInk Kid* with a sound camera in a Hollywood recording studio. The film features live-action footage of Rudolph Ising drawing Bosko, who comes to life. The short is a landmark film in animation sound history because it was the first sound cartoon to use prerecorded dialogue as opposed to vocal effects, and it emphasized dialogue over music, which was unusual at the time. It wasn't released in theaters and was only seen

by a wide audience when it was screened on Cartoon Network's television special Toonheads: The Lost Cartoons in 2000. *Sinkin' in the Bathtub* (1930) was the first Warner Bros. theatrical short, the first of the Looney Tunes series, and Bosko's theatrical debut. It was also the first publicly released non-Disney cartoon to have a prerecorded soundtrack produced with the Vitaphone system. The film is presented as a musical cartoon and resembles *Steamboat Willie* in both story design and production process. The dialogue is minimal, although it does contain more dialogue than *Steamboat Willie*. Most notable is a deviation from wall-to-wall music and the accenting of certain gags with silence and sound effects.

By the early 1930s, the talkies were a global phenomenon, and even critically acclaimed silent films were playing to near-empty theaters. The silent film had become unviable. Theaters rushed to install sound equipment and studios built soundproof facilities. The soundtrack started to evolve quickly and became more clearly defined in terms of dialogue, music, and effects. The success of *Steamboat Willie* and the first live-action "talkies" motivated directors to start developing projects with sound in mind.

Sinkin' in the Bathtub (1930, dir. Hugh Harman and Rudolf Ising)

ADVANCING THE CRAFT

Story, Design, Process, People

The second major development after "the coming of sound" was the introduction of color. The world's earliest color film, only discovered recently, was actually shot in 1902 by Edward Turner, a little-known Edwardian photographer. The first sound cartoon photographed in two-strip Technicolor was "Flip the Frog," who debuted in the short film *Fiddlesticks* (1930). As a result, *Fiddlesticks* is considered a landmark in animation history. After a falling out with Disney, Ub Iwerks founded Iwerks Studio and created Flip. In the film, Flip is seen dancing across lily pads and quacking like a duck until a tortoise he mistakes for a lily pad throws him into the pond. He swims ashore and joins a party in full swing. After performing a dance, Flip plays a duet with a mouse on violin (resembling Mortimer Mouse, the original Mickey Mouse). The mouse becomes infuriated by Flip's diminishing playing skills and clouts him with the violin. They resume playing and start dancing. As the music becomes sadder, the mouse starts crying. Flip also starts crying, which makes the piano cry. Flip starts stroking the piano, which kicks him, and Flip retaliates by beating the piano. While color was a novelty

for audiences, *Fiddlestick* offered nothing new and garnered limited success. The film lacked cohesion and a plot, and adhered to what had become something of a cliché in pre-1930s sound cartoons, synchronization and syncopation of movement with music and mainly musical sound effects.

The ongoing success of Mickey Mouse inspired Disney to forge ahead with the sound cartoon. He created the *Silly Symphonies*, which were designed to capitalize on sound's capabilities. The *Silly Symphonies* series comprised seventy-five animated short films produced from 1929 to 1939 and won an Academy Award for Best Animated Short Film seven times. Disney also started to explore the use of color. *Flowers and Trees* (Gillett, 1932) was the first film to be theatrically exhibited in the full-color three-strip Technicolor process and won the first Academy Award ever given to an animated film. It was originally produced as a black-and-white short; however, after seeing some Technicolor tests and factoring in the public's interest in color films, Disney had the short redone in color. The film depicts trees and flowers coexisting in a tranquil environment, disrupted by the advances of an evil tree. A fight unfolds between the two male trees and the evil tree strikes back by lighting a fire. While singing and dancing was a cartoon cliché, the film also had a coherent narrative, which music and sound effects effectively support without overpowering the visuals.

Sound, Story, and Workflow

The Three Little Pigs (1933), *The Tortoise and the Hare* (1934), *Three Orphan Kittens* (1935), *The Country Cousin* (1936), and *The Old Mill* (1937) followed *Flowers and Trees* and were all Academy Award winners. Disney realized that success depended upon telling emotionally engaging stories, and he established a story department, separate from the animators, with storyboard artists dedicated to working on story development. Disney also set up up a sound effects department. Jimmy MacDonald was one of the first sound effects artists employed at Disney. He was a drummer in a band contracted to record music for a Mickey Mouse short in 1934. After the recording was over, Disney asked MacDonald to stay and help develop the sound effects department. Within two years, the sound effects team

Fiddlesticks (1930, Ub Iwerks)

expanded to include five sound artists. The period signified a shift away from the dominant use of musical instruments to create sound effects in cartoons. The role became not just about inventing or finding the right sound effects but also required greater analysis of the film narrative and the editing of sound effects to pictures. The ability to record sound on film meant sounds could be assembled and cut into separate tracks, which made the role more complex and specialized.

As Disney cartoons became more detailed and lifelike, MacDonald designed and built custom sound props to create more detailed and lifelike sound effects. Disney gave the new department ample time to experiment with the creating of sound props and sound effect creation. A number of his devices mirrored and extended upon those used by Loutherbourg in early theater, silent film, and radio drama. MacDonald had a major impact on the development of sound design as a distinct practice and has since been described as "the dean emeritus of sound designers." He created hundreds of sound effect devices throughout the 1930s and an estimated 28,000 individual sound effects, resulting in one of the largest sound effects libraries in motion picture history. MacDonald's techniques included the use of voice as a sound effect, editing and mixing prerecorded sounds, the manipulation of sound props, and performing sound effects live. Despite being responsible for some of the most familiar sounds in cinema between 1934 and 1977, MacDonald is not actually credited on many of the films he worked on. His first major credit was for *Snow White* (1937), which required years of preparation before it was released. In addition to creating sound effects and voicing Mickey Mouse, he also produced numerous other vocal effects.

During the mid-1930s, Walt Disney, composer Carl Stalling, and Jimmy MacDonald also streamlined their sound production processes (Strauss, 2002). Stalling devised a tick system, which was a precursor to the click track, a series of cues used to indicate exact timings for musicians to accompany films. The Disney team used a reel of unexposed film punched with holes, which created audible clicks and pops when the film ran over a projector sound head. The emergence of the storyboard and specialization of roles also influenced soundtrack production. Storyboard

artists were assisting writers by giving visual shape to story ideas, and the use of dialogue in cartoons became more prevalent. While it had been possible to record dialogue on film in advance and then animate mouth movements to match, it was not until around 1934 that dialogue was "narrative" based. Previously dialogue was often tied to the music, and usually rhymed, which made it nearly indistinguishable from lyrics and song. Animators worked with exposure sheets that broke the dialogue down into frames so they could animate mouth movements without even needing to hear the voices. However, postrecording dialogue could (and can) result in voice, body, personality, and performance mismatches, if casting and directing are not thoroughly considered. On the other hand, recording dialogue in advance was (and can be) problematic if script and animation changes occur. Disney wanted more personality in his characters and had a tendency to favor the recording of dialogue early. According to his daughter, during the casting of *Snow White* he organized for a microphone to be installed on a sound stage connected to a speaker in his office so that he could only hear the auditions (Miller, 1956). His casting selections were not influenced by visual appearances, but by critical listening.

The first *Silly Symphony* to employ a significant amount of dialogue was *The Flying Mouse* (1934). The film tells the story of a young mouse who fantasizes about flying. He attempts to fly using leaves as wings and is ridiculed by his family. He keeps trying, but his efforts are in vain. After a scolding from his mother, he hears pleas for help from a butterfly caught in a spider's web. The mouse fends off the spider and saves the butterfly, which turns out to be a fairy, and she grants him his wish to fly. The shadow cast by his wings when in flight gives him the appearance of a bat and he frightens his family into hiding. An outcast, he finds himself in a forest and is taunted by bats. Crying, one of his tears causes the fairy to return, and she removes his wings. The dialogue is not timed to the rhythm of music and therefore is more natural sounding. The sound effects are still quite sparse and fairly typical of early cartoons but also include organic and realistic sounds such as a bottom spanking and water. The score is narratively driven and overall there is a smoother and more dynamic balance between dialogue, effects, and music/song compared to earlier sound cartoons.

The next major development for Disney films was the multi-plane camera. The earlier success of *The Three Little Pigs* and *The Tortoise and the Hare* influenced Disney's decision to progress with development of the multi-plane camera and *Snow White* (1937), the first feature-length animated movie. Disney wanted to make cartoons more realistic, like live-action films, with greater depth and dimension (Disney, 1957). There was no way of creating successful tracking shots using traditional animation methods, and animating forward motion was time-consuming, therefore costly. *The Old Mill* (1937) was specifically designed to test the multi-plane camera, and it solved tracking issues by splitting a field of view into different planes. Separate levels were used for the foreground, middle ground, and background. For a forward-motion tracking shot, a more realistic effect was accomplished by moving foreground and middle-ground planes toward the camera, while the background plane remained stationary. The multi-plane camera could take up to seven layers of artwork (painted in oils on glass) mounted a foot or more apart and shot under a vertical and moveable camera. While a development like this might not seem significant for sound design, it parallels the depth and perspective potentials in both sound design and sound mixing. Sound designers and mixers consider depth and dimension in much the same way as visuals. *The Old Mill* was also developed as an experiment in the visualization of musical moods. According to the principal writer, Dick Rickard, the aim was to create the type of imagery that might be visualized while listening to a symphony or a concert (Barrier, 1999). Also significant for sound is the incorporating of lighting and color effects, representations of rain, wind, lightning, ripples, splashes, reflections, and 3D rotations of objects. VFX (visual effects) often go hand in hand with SFX (sound effects), and the greater the visual detail, the greater the aural detail. When considering the attention to both visual and sound design, *The Old Mill* is understandably considered the first Disney cartoon to be truly designed (Barrier, 1999). Critics described the film as poetic, which proved to Disney he had achieved the kind of depth he was aiming for.

The Old Mill depicts a community of animals living in an old abandoned windmill, and how they deal with a violent thunderstorm that nearly destroys their home. It opens with music and a shot of the mill. As the film progresses, sound effects and music interweave, creating the soundtrack. A single firefly circles a frog, which he gulps, causing his croaks to tinkle. The wind rises with a chorus of female voices. Reeds sway in the wind, and the frogs spooked by the wind leap into the pond and hide under a lily pad. Shutters bang in the wind as the windmill blades start to move. Inside the windmill a mother bird nesting in a sprocket hole is endangered by a fraying rope. Lightning strikes, thunder rumbles, and the rope snaps. The mother bird covers her nest as she and the nest are thrown under the wheel. Luckily, a missing cog saves them from being crushed. Roof slates are blown off as the rain intensifies. Pond reeds are battered against a broken gate, playing part of the score, and plant stems snap, becoming flutes. The storm and music intensify as the shutter smashes and the pace quickens, culminating in a crash of lightning. The inhabitants are knocked around inside until the savaged windmill slows to a stop. The image fades to black momentarily, transitioning to the next morning and life resuming. Leigh Harline, who composed more than fifty tunes for Disney, created the score, and MacDonald and his team created the sound effects. There is no dialogue; therefore, the story is driven by the visuals, music, and sound effects. For rain sound effects, MacDonald lined the inside of a rotating drum with finishing nails nailed onto strips. Inside the drum were Mexican peas, and when it was rotated, the peas hitting the nails produced the sound of rain. The sound of a frog croak was created by bowing a taut string connected to a coffee can, a thunder sheet created the thunder and lightning, and a wind machine was used for the wind.

In 1937, Disney produced the animated feature film *Snow White* using the experience gained from the production of previous shorts. At the time, he was worried that short films would not keep the studio profitable. The cost of producing shorts was increasing, and double features were taking the place of short films being screened before features in theaters.

The film industry was skeptical of his plans and predicted *Snow White* would ruin Disney financially. The opposite happened. *Snow White* was a worldwide box office success and another landmark in the development of animation as an art form.

Looney Tunes

Rival company Warner Bros. opted for producing *Looney Tunes*, a series of comedy shorts named after Walt Disney's *Silly Symphonies*. After adding animation directors such as Tex Avery and Chuck Jones and voice actor Mel Blanc, Warner Bros. created popular cartoon stars such as Bugs Bunny, Daffy Duck, Porky Pig, Elmer Fudd, Tweety Bird, Sylvester the Cat, Speedy Gonzales, Wile E. Coyote, the Road Runner, and the Tasmanian Devil. *Looney Tunes* and sister series *Merrie Melodies* became the most popular animated shorts at that time. A part of that success is attributed to Mel Blanc's ability to bring personality and life to characters through voice. Blanc began his career performing in radio before voicing Bugs Bunny, Daffy Duck, Porky Pig, Tweety Bird, Sylvester the Cat, Speedy Gonzales, and many other characters. He's had a vast repertoire of dialects, voice characterizations, and vocal sound effects and is regarded as one of the most influential people in the voice acting industry.

Tregoweth (Treg) Brown was another influential sound effect artist and was responsible for the sound effects in *Looney Tunes* and *Merrie Melodies* cartoons from 1936. He was not credited for his work until 1956, and was initially credited as "Film Editor." According to director Chuck Jones, the film editor credit also referred to the sound effects editor, but it's unclear as to whether this was common considering sound effects artists had been credited for sound effects decades earlier. Nonetheless, Jones described Brown as "one of the most brilliant sound effect editors that ever lived" (Jones in Furniss, 2005, p. 96). Prior to working in animation, Brown was a sound editor on Warner Bros. live-action feature films and one of the first people to enter the field of film sound editing. He worked with Cecil B. DeMille and won the 1965 Academy Award for Sound Editing for the classic comedy *The Great Race* (Edwards, 1965).

Porky's Hare Hunt (Hardaway, 1938) marked the first appearance of the rabbit that would later become known as Bugs Bunny. Mel Blanc voiced all the characters, Treg Brown created the sound effects, and Carl Stalling was the musical director. Combined, the trio had a substantial amount of experience in dialogue, sound effects, and music and came to dominate Warner cartoon soundtracks. The soundtrack, which had previously been fairly inconsequential, became one of the studio's greatest assets. *Porky's Hare Hunt* partly conforms to the binding of music to action and the use of instruments such as slide whistles and percussion as effects, but it also incorporates the mixing of real and realistic-sounding sounds, such as gunshots, Foley, and a mechanical toy rabbit. The combining of real and comedic sounds adds a sense of realism to the gags, while punctuating

Porky's Hare Hunt (1938, dir. Ben Hardaway & Cal Dalton)

comedic moments. At times the music drives the action and at other times music and effects interplay to support the action.

Treg Brown's approach to sound effects and comedy is most noted within discussions of Roadrunner cartoons. *Fast and Furry-ous* (Jones, 1949) was Wile E. Coyote and the Road Runner's debut and set the template for what later became a series. It was originally intended to be a one-off short film, but after favorable feedback from exhibitors a second film was produced. The premise of the series is a parody of chase scenes involving two characters alone in the desert, one the pursuer (Wile E. Coyote) and the other the pursued (Road Runner). The hungry Wile E. Coyote tries to catch the speedy Road Runner through various schemes and traps. Neither character speaks, except for the "beep beep" (or "meep meep," as some argue) of the Road Runner. Artist Paul Julian imitated a car horn sound he made when he was in a hurry, which was recorded and became the Road Runner's calling card.

In *Fast and Furry-ous*, the characters are introduced and freeze-framed with text as a way of identification; Road Runner's text description reads "Accelleratii Incredibus" and is marked

Fast and Furry-ous (1949, Chuck Jones)

with a beat of silence and a bell sound effect, before breaking into a dramatic slow-motion run with short skid sound effects coinciding with his feet contacting the road. Music also punctuates the motion; the skid sound effect is edited a fraction before the beat, allowing both music and sound effects to play at perceivably the same time even though they are marginally apart. There is a variation in pitch/frequency and level (volume) between sound effects and music so that one does not mask the other. The result is exaggeration; the event seems bigger and more dramatic than it is. As the Road Runner takes off we hear zips, ricochets, and an aircraft sound effect, which are all sounds that indicate speed. The Road Runner is very fast. Wile E. Coyote is seen watching the Road Runner with binoculars. He half licks his chops and is freeze-framed as his text description reads "Carnivorous Vulgaris," which is punctuated with a beat before the full chop lick is completed. This tells us Wile E. Coyote is very hungry and sets up what unfolds. Classic gags follow as he attempts to capture and eat the Road Runner. In a similar style to *Porky's Hare Hunt*, sound effects and music score the action, which is essentially Wile E. Coyote's painful inability to catch the Road Runner.

Stop-Motion Film

During the early 1930s, sound design experimentation also took place through the stop-motion feature *King Kong* (Cooper and Schoedsack, 1933). Murray Spivack at RKO created the sound effects for the film and is recognized as one of the first sound editors to use sound in a creative way. Spivack was also a professional theater and movie drummer and drum teacher. He started playing drums professionally at the age of twelve and in the decade that followed became house drummer at the Strand Theater, an early movie palace in New York. Spivack was also a percussionist in the New York symphonic orchestra and specialized in recording music for silent films. He worked in radio and later opened his own drum teaching and recording studio. Spivak was one of the first drummers to play for conductor Josiah Zuro, who worked on scores for film and animation. In 1929, Spivack moved to Los Angeles and managed the sound effects and music department at the RKO Studios, which is where he devised the sound effects for *King Kong*. He was a founding member of the Cinema Audio Society, and his contributions to the field of recording percussion led to his induction into the Percussive Arts Society Hall of Fame in 1991.

In 1975, *King Kong* (Goldner and Turner, 1975) was named one of the fifty best American films by the American Film Institute. The film is often hailed as the greatest classic adventure-fantasy film of all time and was a significant development in special effects and stop-motion animation. It also launched the "giant beast" or "giant monster" subgenre of science fiction. Audio technology was still quite limited around the time of production, and Spivack had only a vague idea as to how to create the necessary sound effects for Kong. He studied the script and itemized the sounds that needed to be created. Over a period of nine months, Spivack recorded and designed all the sound effects he had identified from the script.

Spivack recorded zoo lion and tiger roars, which he edited together, played backwards, and slowed down. He rerecorded the effect, edited together the peaks of the sound, and added a tail so the roar would end naturally. This was due to the long duration of King Kong's visual roar and because the original roars would be too familiar-sounding and lack the weight and depth of King Kong. For the scenes where Kong expressed affection, Spivak recorded himself grunting through a megaphone, pitched them down, and rerecorded them. He used a similar technique for animal cries and the Tyrannosaurus screeches. A bellows or pair of bellows, which is a device used for blowing on a fire to supply it with air, were used for monster breaths. The death rattle of the dying Tyrannosaurus was a mouthful of water gurgled through a megaphone. The sound of King Kong beating his chest was created through hitting Spivack's assistant on the chest with a tymp stick while another assistant held a microphone to his back. Kong's footsteps were a plumber's friend (a plunger) on gravel. Spivack recorded a slapstick for the gunshots but later discovered that by removing half of the powder from a .22 bullet he could get a more realistic and controlled sound. Once the music had been completed, he then altered the pitch of the sound effects to compliment Max Steiner's score.

The 1930s marked the beginning of a shift in approaches to soundtrack design. The expression "mickey mousing," coined by producer David O. Selznick, is often used to describe the close synchronization of music to action and animated motions of the characters. Max Steiner is frequently credited with inventing the technique, but Disney had been employing it since *Steamboat Willie*. Selznick felt that it was obtrusive and distracting and believed music should help the mood of the scene without audiences being aware that they are listening to music. He advocated for composers working with the script, rather than a finished film. Today the technique is considered a cliché and overused, although arguably it can still serve comedy well. The decrease in "mickey mousing" coincided with a general move from musically driven films to narratives with greater psychological depth. Consequently, dialogue, sound effects, and music became less constrained by synchronization with visuals, and vice versa.

King Kong (1933, dir. Merian C. Cooper and Ernest B. Schoedsack)

TV KILLS THE RADIO STAR

Realism, Limited Animation, and Stylized Animation

Television became commercially available in the late 1920s; however, television sets were not commonplace until after World War II. As a new medium, television introduced new problems. Sound effects were not high on the list of priorities; picture and dialogue quality took precedence. Theaters were converted into TV studios with little attention to audio requirements, and some producers even considered sound effects the territory of radio, not television. However, as television become more popular, the demand for better-quality content increased. It was quite common for early radio dramas to be reworked as television dramas, but not all shows transferred across equally as well; sometimes the listener's imagination surpassed the quality of production and visuals. Shows were shot live, which meant major set changes had to occur during commercials. There was no such thing as a "second take." Transitions like time or scene changes were also problematic. In radio drama, sound and music could act as a bridge; film could be edited; and in theater, scene changes were customary and accepted by audiences. As competition between mediums increased, comparisons were also made between the higher production values in film, which led to some television directors complaining about the lower quality of television sound. Like today, television productions had smaller budgets and faster turnaround times compared to film. Despite a slow start, television production advanced quickly; it had the benefit of stage, radio, and motion picture production experience to draw from.

Bang Bang

Guns and gun sound effects were especially problematic in early television shows. Audiences had been hearing Western and gangster films since the 1930s so had developed certain expectations. Film sound editors had the luxury of combining gun sound effects in postproduction to create bigger and more dramatic-sounding guns. Prior to the development of audiotape, record companies tried to solve the problem with realistic-sounding guns on sound effect records, but this made the cueing up of gunshot sound effects difficult. If a second shot was required, then the sound effect record had to be cued again or a second record was needed. Records were produced with multiple shots, but this meant the timing of shots was predetermined and rarely matched or synchronized with the associated visuals. Guns and gunshots needed to look and sound realistic. Blanks caused a flame from the barrel, and the paper waddings holding the powder in the casing would shoot out. An alternative or compromise was to shoot pictures with an empty gun. The actor would turn his or her back to the camera and move as if firing while the sound effect artist manually performed the sound effect. A second alternative was to have the camera cut away from the actor. Both options were problematic, especially if the actor wasn't in the right position and the audience saw that the gun wasn't actually doing the firing.

Don Foster, a CBS sound effect artist and inventor, came up with another solution, which was a shot machine aptly named the "Foster Gun" and something of an early electronic "instrument." The Foster Gun could generate various gunshots, ranging from machine gun fire, antiaircraft fire, cannons, explosions, and ricochets. The right audio frequency could be manually selected or the shot could be triggered by the sound of a blank firing. If the shots were offscreen, it was triggered manually, and if they were on-screen, the sound of a blank would trigger the sound effect. It was sensitive enough to pick up a quieter blank sound, while rejecting anything below a threshold, effectively functioning like a "Gate," a common plug-in used in audio production today. The downside was that a louder sound or another sound at the same frequency the machine was tuned to would also trigger the shot, which made tuning critical. The gunshot problem was eventually resolved in 1954 when two sound effect artists, Ray Kemper and Tom Hanley, recorded a series of real gunshots out on location for a television show called *Gunsmoke* (French and Siegel, 2014). Kemper and Hanley's gunshots rivaled those used in films and became an industry standard.

Gunsmoke was a Western that successfully migrated from radio to television and ran for twenty seasons, from 1955 to 1975. The show featured U.S. Marshal Matt Dillon, who was responsible for Dodge City, a town in the Wild West. Norm Macdonnel, the producer, prioritized music and sound effects, or "exaggerated sound patterns," as he called them. The term is misleading because he was using it to describe the use of sound design narratively, as a replacement for dialogue and music. The show received critical acclaim due to its unprecedented realism and attention to detail, which was in part because of the focus on and approach to sound design.

When Dillon and Chester rode the plains, the listener heard the **faraway prairie wind** and the **dry squeak** of Matt's **pants against the saddle leather**. When Dillon **opened the jail door**, the listener heard every **key drop on the ring**. Dillon's **spurs rang out with a dull clink-clink**, missing occasionally, and the **hollow boardwalk echoed dully as the nails creaked** in the worn wood around them. **Buckboards passed** [horse-drawn carriages], and the listener heard **extraneous dialogue in the background**, just above the **muted shouts of kids** playing in the alley. He heard noises from the next block, too, where the inevitable **dog was barking**. (Dunning, 1998, p. 305)

Limited Animation

In 1939, W2XBS "telecasted" Walt Disney's *Donald's Cousin Gus*, directed by Jack King, which was the first prerecorded program and animated film televised as part of a show that also included music, songs, a film, and a play.

James Arness as Matt Dillon in the television version of *Gunsmoke* (1956)

Donald's Cousin Gus was not made for television; animation was considered too expensive for broadcast, so animation studios wanting to enter the television market had to create more economical content. This resulted in the production of "limited animation." Limited animation reduced production costs by minimizing the use of synchronized dialogue, using walk cycles, keeping character bodies static when possible, and animating moving body parts on a separate level. Many felt that this reduced the quality of animation and led to Chuck Jones coining the term "illustrated radio." Jones was referring to the simple visual style, which relied more heavily on sound to tell the story. A cartoon series called *Crusader Rabbit* (1949) was the first animated series produced specifically for television and was broadcast on KNBH in 1950. *Crusader Rabbit* was a cliffhanger-styled adventure series featuring a white rabbit, which

became quite popular and helped establish the made-for-TV mode of production (Butler, 2007). The animation and synchronized dialogue were minimal and the narrative driven largely by voice-over narration, with music and spot sound effects created by Ray Erlenborn and Gene Twambley. Twombly was an actor and created sound effects for several radio shows, including *The Jack Benny Show*. Erlenborn was a vaude-villian, voice actor, and sound effects artist. Prior to his involvement in sound, he played one of the newspaper boys in Charlie Chaplin's *City Lights* (1931) and appeared in the TV series *The

Buster Keaton Show (1950). He also created the animal sound effects for the original live-action musical film *Dr. Dolittle* (Fleischer, 1967) and voiced the rabbit from Walt Disney's *Winnie the Pooh Discovers the Seasons* (1981).

In 1942, Disney animators Dick Moores and Jack Boyd formed Telecomics, Inc. and in 1945 created a pilot for a low-cost series, which led to the production of a television program consisting of four three-minute stories. NBC optioned the material in 1950 and renamed the series *NBC Comics*. *Space Barton* (1950) was one of the three-minute stories and stars Horace "Space" Barton Jr., a college football star who, after enlisting in the Army Air Corps, lands on Mars in a rocket ship with his stowaway brother Jackie. Mars is experiencing a civil war and Space Barton is pitted against a group led by a deranged Earth scientist who preceded them to Mars. The production style is similar to that of *Crusader Rabbit* except pared right back to mostly static images, a voice-over, and a few spot sound effects, which gives the film the appearance of a storyboard with a voice-over (or a story reel).

Stylized Animation and Sound Effects

In 1957, former Metro Goldwyn Mayer (MGM) animation directors William Hanna and Joseph Barbera and live-action director George Sidney formed Hanna-Barbera. Their first involvement in television was *Colonel Bleep* (Schleh, 1957),

the first animated series produced specifically for color television. Futuristic, stylized, but still in the domain of limited animation, the series takes place on Zero Zero Island, which is where Earth's equator meets the Greenwich Meridian. Colonel Bleep is an extraterrestrial life form from the planet Futura, with the ability to manipulate "futomic energy" and propel himself through space or use it as a weapon. His "space deputies" are a mute cowboy puppet boy called Squeek, representing the present day, and a Caveman awakened from a sleep of several thousand years, representing the past. The trio's main nemeses are Dr. Destructo, the Black Knight, and Black Patch, a space pirate. Each story is predominantly told through narration and sound effects, and it's possibly the first, or one of the first, animated series to use electronic sound effects, predating television shows like *The Jetsons* and *Futurama*.

Huckleberry Hound was Hanna-Barbera's next television cartoon and premiered in 1959, *The Flintstones* following in 1960. Hanna-Barbera also produced the first television special to combine live-action with animation, *Jack and The Beanstalk* (1967). Alongside their cartoons and characters, they developed a reputation for their sound effects library, which was largely developed by Fred McAlpin through the production of *Tom and Jerry*, short slapstick films that center on the rivalry between the two main characters, Tom the Cat and Jerry the Mouse. The films are known for their non-gory (aural and visual) violence and won seven Academy Awards for Best Short Subject (Cartoons). According to Hanna, their sound effects library preexisted their MGM days. Prior to creating most of the sound effects for MGM, Fred McAlpin worked for Harman and Ising Studios and took the library to MGM, and when Hanna

Colonel Bleep (1956-57, dir. Robert D. Buchanan and Jack Schleh)

and Barbera left MGM, they took the library and expanded on it. Hanna described McAlpin as a "true pioneer" who built and collected sound props, which included everything from dishpans to whistles (Hanna, 1995, para. 4). Some of their most famous sound effects include a rapid bongo drum used for a character's feet scrambling before taking off, tires squealing for a sudden stop, a bass drum and cymbal mix for a fall, and a xylophone being struck rapidly for a tiptoeing effect. Short theatrical film studios, both live-action and animation, were falling into decline by the 1950s. This was partly due to a decrease in film audiences in favor of television. Hanna and Barbera realized early on that sound effects were just as important in television animation as they were in full or theatrical animation, so despite budget restraints, they always factored in sound effects. In the late 1960s, they launched the short-lived Hanna-Barbera Records and released a set of LP (long-playing) records, which contained some of the classic sound effects. In 1993, Fred Seibert, the last president of the studio, commissioned sound effects company Sound Ideas to release a digitally remastered, four-CD set version entitled *The Hanna-Barbera Sound FX Library*, which features many of their original sound effects. Many other studios and production houses have been using these effects for decades.

Gerald McBoing-Boing (1950) also used classic cartoon sound effects, except in *Gerald*

McBoing-Boing, sound effects are his dialogue. The story was written by Dr. Seuss and previously featured as an audio story on a children's record in the late 1940s. The film was adapted by Phil Eastman and Bill Scott, directed by Robert Cannon, and produced by John Hubley from United Productions of America (UPA). In 1943, Hubley formed a studio with former Disney animators Stephen Bosustow, David Hilberman, and Zachary Schwartz. Hubley wanted to experiment with new styles of animation and break away from the overt realism developed by Walt Disney. Realism was aesthetically limiting and UPA wanted to explore the use of caricatures rather than lifelike representations. *Gerald McBoing-Boing* tells the story of Gerald McCloy, who at the age of two begins "talking" in sound effects. As Gerald grows up, his speaking in sound effects intensifies, earning him the nickname of "Gerald McBoing Boing." After angering his father, the distraught Gerald decides to run away but is stopped by a talent scout from the NBC Radio Network, who hires him as a sound effect artist. The film proved to be a major step in the development of limited animation. Some likened the design to art movements such as abstract expressionism and the style, pacing, and editing to the French New Wave films of the late 1950s and early 1960s (Butler, 2007). Similarly, the more prominent use of sound effects furthered the abstract and design quality of the film. *Gerald McBoing-Boing* won an Oscar and later became *The Gerald McBoing Boing Show* (1956–58).

In summary, sound design is an old field; sound has always been used as a storytelling device. As films became more narratively complex, the importance of sound became more apparent, making the selection of the sound palette as important as the selection of images, and the practice of sound design evolved into a specific discipline. Sound became integral, a key selling point, and a way of differentiating work. The development of limited and stylized animation furthered the interest in soundtrack design, not only in terms of economical filmmaking but also as part of a film's narrative and aesthetic. Despite negativity around limited animation, the basic process is very similar to the way story reels or animatics are created for films today.

Gerald McBoing Boing (1950, dir. Robert Cannon)

Sound as Design

Early film and sound technology opened the door to more than just the synchronization of sound with image. Sound-on-film processes encouraged artists to experiment with graphic-sonic art, animated, hand-drawn, and ornamental sound. The short film lent itself to audiovisual experimentation and provided a vehicle for filmmakers to explore the creative use of sound. Experimental compositional techniques such as musique concrète were particularly influential in the evolution of sound design practice. Film movements like the French New Wave, the science fiction genre, and art house films also determined the need for a more stylistic approach to soundtrack design. Methods employed by contemporary sound designers are diverse and multifaceted, but they draw from very similar sound-sculpting techniques pioneered by earlier artists.

EXPERIMENTS IN DESIGN

Short Films and Sonic Art

Arseny Avraamov was a Russian composer, journalist, music theorist, and inventor. He was involved in the production of the first Russian sound films, led a sound laboratory at the Cinematic Institute of Scientific Research, and lectured on the history and theory of sound at the Moscow Conservatory. Among his many achievements was the invention of graphic-sonic art, a technique that created sound by drawing onto the optical soundtrack of film. While working on *The Plan for Great Works* (Room, 1930), Avraamov, inventor Evgeny Sholpo, and animator Mikhail Tsekhanovsky noticed the "ornamental" nature of variable-width film sound. Engineer Eric Humphriss, who had previously worked on RCA's Photophone sound-on-film technology, later demonstrated the reproduction of the first "synthetic" voice. He analyzed the sound wave patterns that corresponded to phonetic components of voice recorded on film. In 1931, Humphriss painted a waveform to create the phrase "all of a tremble" on a strip of cardboard, which he photographed onto film. Around the same

time, a number of other artists were also creating sound by drawing or photographing patterns on film. German animator Oscar Fischinger experimented with "sound ornaments" and Rudolph Pfenninger with hand-drawn "music." Fischinger used graphical icons to create sounds and in 1932 demonstrated how the parameters of pitch, time, and amplitude interact to create a composite optical waveform. Among the first generation of artists to adopt these new ideas were Len Lye, Harry Smith, Jordan Belson, and Norman McLaren.

Sound Cards

Canadian filmmaker Norman McLaren produced the award-winning *Neighbours* in 1952, using live actors as stop-motion objects and a soundtrack created by what he called "animated sound." In documentation of his work, McLaren describes three methods of creating sound using film: painting or inking directly onto blank film, scratching into black film, and photographing film "soundcards," a technique that he adopted and advanced. He created a library of one-inch by twelve-inch strips with one to 120 repetitions of hand-drawn sound wave patterns to reproduce every semitone across a five-octave range. The drawings consisted of a basic figure or shape repeated to form a patterned band, which resulted in a series of sound waves having a definite tone or color. Using simple and easily drawn shapes, he also made new kinds of sound waves. The drawings were photographed in the same way animated films were shot. One drawing was placed in front of the camera and one

Ornament Sound Experiments (1932, dir. Oscar Fischinger)

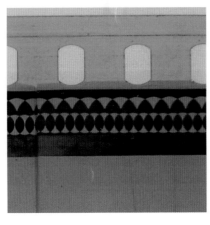
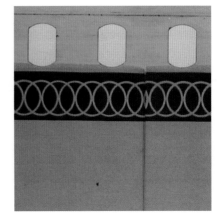

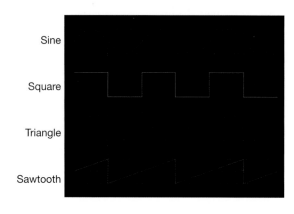

The basic audio waveforms

frame of film was taken. Then the first drawing was removed and replaced with another drawing, and so on. The cards were photographed on the narrow vertical strip normally reserved for the soundtrack. After the film was developed and run on a sound projector, the photographed images of the drawings were reproduced as sound.

On some cards, the basic figure was repeated about four times within the card area to produce a low pitch. Twenty to thirty repetitions created mid-range pitches and high-pitched notes, as many as 120. To produce notes of a very low pitch, the cards were shot twice as fast and in the process of re-recording onto magnetic tape the audio was slowed down by half, which resulted in an octave drop. As a film camera shoots by the frame as opposed to continuously like sound recording equipment, the soundtrack was built

up from small units, each one twenty-fourth of a second in duration. If a longer duration note was desired, several successive frames of the same card were shot, building up a sustained effect by rapid repetition of the same note. For a very short note, one or two frames were used, and for rests or pauses, a black card was photographed. By photographing combinations of sound and black cards for varying lengths of time and at varying speeds, pitch and rhythm could be controlled. McLaren's drawn patterns relate to the four different types of basic waveforms (sine, square, triangle and sawtooth) in audio synthesis, and this is why the term "synthetic" sound is often used to describe the results.

McLaren's experimental film *Synchromy* (1971) was produced through photographing square wave cards. It was created in three parts, shot on separate strips of film, rerecorded, and then mixed on magnetic tape. McLaren controlled the volume by varying the width of the soundtrack through a moveable shutter. Almost closed, the extremely narrow band of striations would give a pianissimo (very soft) note, and when the shutter was wide open, the broad band of stripes would produce a fortissimo (loud) note. After photographing the cards, McLaren used an optical printer to reproduce the sequence of shapes, which were colorized. Since the shape of the soundtrack opposite a single frame of film is a long, narrow column and the visual frame is rectangular, up to eleven columns side by side were used in the picture area. The visual image, whether one or several columns, was the image of the original sound card used to create the corresponding sound. No "color-sound-theory" was applied, although the quieter passages are muted hues and louder passages more highly

Synchromy (1971, dir. Norman McLaren)

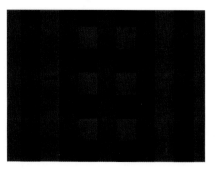

saturated. The production process and resulting effect allows the audience to see the shapes that generated the soundtrack.

Rated X

In 1953, UPA released *The Tell-Tale Heart* (Parmelee, 1953), an adaption of a short story by Edgar Allan Poe (1843) and considered a classic of the Gothic fiction genre. Designed by Paul Julian (the artist who had previously voiced Road Runner's "beep beep" at Warner Bros.), the grim tale fuses elements of surrealism with expressionism. It was a major departure from *Gerald McBoing-Boing* and the first cartoon in film history to be rated "X." While considered a flop when released, it was nominated for an Oscar and is now listed as one of the fifty greatest cartoons of all time.

The story is told "through the eyes of a madman," an unnamed first-person narrator voiced by British actor James Mason. The narrator attempts to convince the audience he is sane while describing a murder he committed. He qualifies his actions by claiming he suffers from a nervous disorder causing an over-acuteness of the senses. His victim is an elderly man. While he professes to care for the old man, he declares a hatred for his milky white, staring eye. The eye is blamed for his murderous intent. The narrator plots to murder the elderly man, insisting that his careful planning proves his sanity. Every night he sneaks into the old man's room to observe him. On the eighth night, while the narrator is watching the old man sleep, the old man is disturbed by a sound and wakes. The narrator remains still as the old man sits in bed, frightened. A dull pounding is heard, which the narrator interprets as the old man's terrified heartbeat, as if the old man suspects something is about to happen. The heartbeat gets louder and faster, which drives the narrator to kill the old man and hide the body beneath the floorboards. A knock at the door reveals the police have arrived, alerted by a neighbor who heard a scream. The narrator explains it was his scream while having a dream. The police enquire as to the whereabouts of the old man and the narrator tells them he is away in the city. As the police are about to leave, he invites them to stay for tea. In the process, a cup is dropped and smashes on the floor, drawing

his attention to the floor, and he starts to hear something. At first he thinks it's a clock ticking, but when the sound gets louder and deeper, he recognizes it's the heart of the old man, pounding away beneath the floorboards. He starts to panic, believing that the police must also hear the sound. As the sound gets louder, he cracks and admits to the murder. The final shot reveals the narrator in a prison cell.

The Tell-Tale Heart (1953, dir. Ted Parmelee)

The soundtrack is as experimental as the pictures, especially for the period, with specific sounds integral to the narrative; the beating heart is a catalyst for murder. The film starts with a bell tolling on an exterior shot of the house, which cross-fades into a sinister musical score composed by Boris Kremenliev. The narrator opens with, "True I'm nervous, very very dreadfully nervous, but why would you say that I'm mad," which is the central theme and repeated in the final scene. The film is set in a house where light, shadows, and shifting geometric planes appear, as if a metaphor for the narrator's conflicted psychological state. The color palette is muted and the narrator depicted in silhouettes, shadows, and a textural image of eyes staring. The offending eye is described as having a milky white film, which is a reoccurring visual motif that links the eye with other imagery; branch-like broken capillaries, a moon, a milk jug that smashes, and cracks in a mirror all reflect the narrator's obsessive hatred of the eye.

The narration leads the sound mix, underscored by music, which combined with tempo, pacing, and level changes creates dramatic tension. Music interplays with the shifting light and what the narrator implies, emphatically and sub-texturally. The soundtrack builds to breaking points using sound effects to heighten the tension and mark changes in the narrator's mood and psychological state. Momentary pauses in narration and the use of silence create dynamics and a sense of recognition; the narrator knows he's giving too much away, exposing his questionable state of mind. Foley effects are used sparingly, as subtle effects: footsteps, the creaking of a door, the movement of floorboards, the rustle of the bed, a clock ticking, fluttering of paper birds. The Foley is "real" and organic, which contrasts with the sound of the pounding heart, despite being organic by association (with a human heart). Black frames focus the audience on the act of listening, mirroring the narrator, who is hiding in the dark listening to the house, waiting for the right time to murder the elderly man. The heartbeat starts on black, intercutting the beat with a textural image suggestive of an internal organ. As the beat grows stronger, the image is intercut with a fast zoom; the editing quickens as the beat gets louder and faster, with the narration matching in pace and energy. The

sequence climaxes with the murder, a combination of Foley effects and abstract imagery, which cuts to black and silence, before fading up on the old man's hand and strewn bedcover. The effect is a "graphic" murder, yet nothing is actually seen; the image and Foley effects imply that the old man is beaten or possibly strangled. The narrator pulls the bedcover over the body and calmly states that it is over: "The heart was still. . .the eye was dead. . .I was free." As he rejoices in his freedom, music punctuates the word "free" as we see the moon whole and the house without walls, implying a freedom that entails giving in to madness. With a creaking of floorboards, the narrator acknowledges there is still work to be done—concealing the body. The creaking preempts his preconceived plan to hide the body under the floor. Again, like the murder scene, the audience does not witness the act but sees the hole in the floor, which dissolves to reveal the hole boarded up. A clock strikes four (a.m.) and there is a knock at the door, heard while the narrator, in a point-of-view (POV) shot, reviews his handiwork. Panning, he turns to the direction of the knocking and the front door. The following sequence splits into his POV, intercut with the reoccurring textural image of eyes staring, as if he is both watching himself and feeling under scrutiny, being watched.

There is an undercurrent of paranoia and suspicion throughout the film. As the police investigate the house, their dialogue is treated with reverb, which alludes to spatial reality, the adding of room reverb, and subtext, in the form of a hollow, soulless emptiness. The narrator, sounding desperate, asks the police to stay for tea, and in such a way that insinuates he wants to get caught. He describes the hour as "wretched" and says, "It would surprise good people how much evil the night conceals from their eyes." A cup spilling water as it smashes on the floor acts as another aural-visual motif, a catalyst for the film's resolve, the narrator admitting to the murder. The cup and saucer are white, like the filmy eye and the moon. The narrator, while attempting to downplay the incident, also draws attention to the floorboards. He starts to hear an imagined heartbeat on an overlaying image depicting a drop of water causing ripples. Believing the police must also hear the heartbeat but are pretending otherwise, the narrator is tortured by the sound.

As the beat grows louder and more insistent, he screams his guilt and reveals the body wrapped in the bedcover under the floor. The final shot fades up from black to a metal jail door with the narrator's line of dialogue from the opening, treated with room reverb, with a metallic edge, as it would sound inside a jail cell. We hear a door slam, cut with his hand on the door, as if while acknowledging he's been locked up, he still considers himself sane. Through bars in the door, we see what looks like a prison as the sound of the door slam echoes through the space.

Now Hear This!

On a much lighter note, Looney Tunes experimental cartoon *Now Hear This* (1962), directed by Chuck Jones and Maurice Noble, was also

nominated for an Oscar. In the style of limited animation, the film experiments with the combination of sound, image, and text. Treg Brown's exaggerated sound effects are coupled with animation and graphics to tell the tale of Satan's misplaced horn. The film opens with the title forming and sound effects playing with the concept of onomatopoeia. The "OW" says "ow" and is hit by the "N" to create "NOW." The "HE" laughs itself on screen, and when joined with a monkey screeching "AR," forms "HEAR." The "THIS" sounds like a train and the quotation marks are deflating balloons. A worried and confused Satan then appears, minus one of his horns. After he wanders off, the title splashes into an ocean, which a boat chugs across, then is sucked down a "plughole." Music and sound

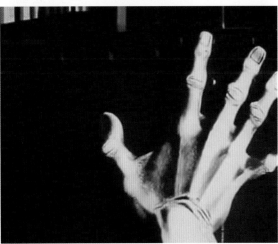

The Tell-Tale Heart (1953, dir. Ted Parmelee)

effects combine to create a cacophonic graphic credit sequence, until an unseen voice yells for quiet. Silence follows, in silence and text, which evolves into a parody of the "follow the ball" animation technique, with music, effects, and the voice of Bugs Bunny. A man appears with a horn-shaped hearing device, footsteps crunching, and discovers Satan's misplaced horn. He inspects it with an eyepiece, which is punctuated with an exaggerated sound effect of scraping glass. He coughs. Perceiving the found horn as superior, he throws his into a trash can, opened by a bodiless leg and accompanied by a number of nonsensical sound effects. At first the man hears music through the horn, but then he experiences a series of aural and visual hallucinations that become increasingly bizarre; a bug sounds like a train; chickens cackle; a butterfly "toots"; a bird sings like a music box and walks into the horn; he hears "patterns"; a phone rings and becomes

a shower; laugher and bubbles erupt; a little man dries himself loudly in a bubble; he gets run down by a train; he hears his own beating heart; he hears traffic; shots are fired; horns sound; a car appears and disappears with a "zip"; the little man reappears, takes the horn, and attaches it to a phonograph; the record is "sprung" and the little man shoots it; it rains; an umbrella becomes a rocket ship; and it all culminates into a gigantic explosion of sound and text. The battered man retrieves his original horn from the trash, and Satan reappears in a blaze of fire and reattaches his missing horn.

Mixing It Up

Award-winning Czech filmmaker and surrealist artist Jan Švankmajer started making films in the 1960s when the "Czech New Wave" was gaining ground in the film industry. Švankmajer's films combine live action, puppets, collage, drawn animation, montage, stop-motion animation, and sound, giving life to everyday and unusual objects. Švankmajer made his first short film, *The Last Trick of Mr. Schwarcewallde and Mr. Edgar*, in 1964. The film depicts two stage performers attempting to outdo each other through various stage tricks for an unseen but audible audience. After each act, the performers congratulate each other with a handshake, but as the competition heats up, the relationship becomes tense. The last trick is a disappearing act; the two performers make themselves disappear by tearing each other to pieces. The film mixes live action with puppetry and stop-motion animation. The soundtrack is a blend of music, song, sound, and Foley effects, percussive in nature, which coincide with montage sequences and fast cutting between images.

Švankmajer's third film, *A Game with Stones* (1965), opens with the sound of a ticking clock on a close-up textural image of an old wooden door. The door creaks open into what appears to be an empty room. The sound of the clock ticking is juxtaposed with pans and tilts of room details: the corners, dirt, and cracks in the wall. The ticking slows prior to a reveal of a clock, the source of the sound. The camera zooms in and cuts to a fast montage of clock mechanisms, with comb and pins from a music box, a tap, and a bucket. The clock strikes twelve and two stones "pop" out of the tap into the bucket. A montage

Now Hear This
(1962, dir. Chuck Jones and Maurice Noble)

The Last Trick of Mr. Schwarcewallde and Mr. Edgar (1964, dir. Jan Švankmajer)

of stone images follows: black stones on white stones, black stones on white backgrounds, and vice versa, stacked in different arrangements, which dance to the sound of the music box. The montage cuts as the bucket tips the original two rocks onto the floor. The sequence repeats, with more stones, which are interspersed with flashes of meat. Again the stones are tipped out of the bucket, and the sequence repeats with even more elaborate stone arrangements, people and hands, skeletons and feet. The sequence repeats, except this time the stones become gravel. The final sequence is another repeat, but without the clock ticking, only a chime. The stones collide and crack apart, causing the bucket to break, and the stones fall to the floor. The last sequence is another repeat except the stones fall through the broken bucket to the floor. The music plays but the stones are inanimate, and the clock ticks but makes no sound.

In *Meat Love* (1989), Švankmajer further humanizes the inanimate. In a kitchen, we hear a café atmosphere and walla (background conversation of the diners). A knife chops two slices of fresh meat. We hear the slices and meat fall organically, yet exaggeratedly. The first slice "walks" over to a glass and picks out a spoon. We hear the clink of metal contacting glass. She admires her reflection as the second slice groans into life. He "walks" over to her and expresses his admiration for her reflection with a slap on her rump. She lets out a little cry and drops the spoon to hide shyly behind a tea towel. We hear the spoon hit the table and the sound of cloth being draped around a body. The second slice switches on a radio and beckons her to dance. The meat slices dance and then jump into a plate

of flour, writhing ecstatically until being skewered and sizzled in a frying pan. The soundtrack is dialogue effects (groan, cry), atmosphere (café), walla (people in a café), Foley (cutlery, impacts, slaps, drops, walks), sound effects (sizzling), and source music (the radio).

A Game with Stones (1967, dir. Jan Švankmajer)

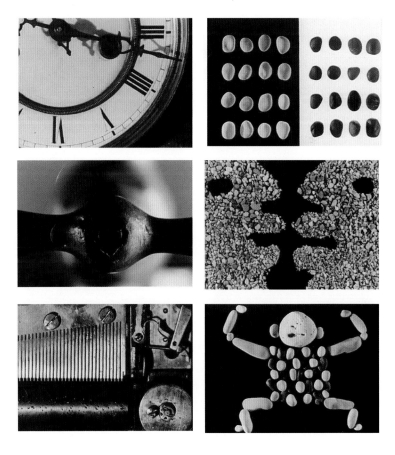

Meat Love
(1989, dir. Jan
Švankmajer)

own sound and sound design effects. The raw audio used in the film included pencil sharpeners, plungers, and various items of "junk" from a machine shop. They also experimented with adding effects such as reverb to a whistle. At the time, they didn't have access to reverb devices, so they used aluminum heat ducting with a speaker on one end and a microphone on the other, blew the whistle, and rerecorded the result a number of times.

The soundtrack for *The Grandmother* was essentially created from "found" sounds either left intact, layered, or processed, creating an audio collage that emotionally charges the visual images. "Audio expressionism" is another term used to describe the same approach to sound for image, recognizing the nonliteral aspects of sound design:

I tend to amplify what you see on the screen. . .to heighten the picture by sort of interpreting what´s there. The sound may or may not correspond with the visible movements of the things on screen. Instead, it kind of adds to it to create a mood, an atmosphere. (Splet in Gentry, 1984, p. 62)

The film resulted in Splet being offered a position running the sound department for the new American Film Institute (AFI) Center in Los Angeles, joined by Lynch, who became a fellow. While at the AFI, Lynch conceived his debut feature film, *Eraserhead* (1977). A surrealist horror film shot in black and white, it tells the story of Henry Spencer, a printer on vacation who suffers strange visions and hallucinations. The opening sequence depicts "The Man in the Planet" moving levers in his home in space, while Spencer's head is seen floating in the sky. A worm-sperm-like creature emerges from Spencer's mouth and floats into the void and he silently screams. The primary setting for the film is a bleak industrial neighborhood with imposing factories and thick pipes blowing steam. It's a wasteland, devoid of life, yet machinery rumbles, clangs, creaks, and groans; a dog barks; a freight train passes; and music drifts in the air. Spencer returns home to a shabby one-room apartment with a single window facing a brick wall. His neighbor tells him that his girlfriend (Mary X) has invited

Aural Junk

David Lynch was also experimenting with abstract short films during the 1960s. His first film, *Six Men Getting Sick* (1966), was a one-minute animation that consisted of six loops depicting six people getting sick. It initially screened as part of a mixed-media installation, accompanied with the sound of a siren. His second film, *The Alphabet* (1968), reflected the fear of learning through the use of animation and live action. After the success of *The Alphabet*, Lynch made *The Grandmother* (1970), which revolves around a boy who grows a grandmother to escape neglect from his parents. *The Grandmother* was also Lynch's first collaboration with Alan Splet, who sound designed all his films through to *Blue Velvet* (1986).

Lynch and Splet planned to use sound effect records to create the soundtrack for *The Grandmother*, but they found them unsuitable. Lynch had also developed an interest in counterpointing picture with atmospheric and exaggerated sound rather than realistic sound effects. So instead of relying on records, Lynch and Splet spent several weeks creating their him to dinner with her family. The dinner is an uncomfortable and awkward event. Henry is confronted with Mary's deranged and dysfunctional parents, a catatonic grandmother, and a small man-made roast chicken that gushes blood. The dialogue exchanges are banal and tense, and the situation takes an even stranger twist when it is revealed that Mary has just given birth to a premature baby. She and Spencer are married and start living together in his apartment. The infant is beyond deformed, a grotesque bundle with an inhuman, alien-like head. It refuses to eat and cries incessantly, driving the sleep-deprived Mary back to her parents' house. Henry is left to care for the sickly creature and begins experiencing visions. He sees "The Lady in the Radiator," who performs to organ music on an old-fashioned stage while squashing worm-sperm-like creatures as they drop onto the stage. Later Mary returns and in a fitful sleep with the bedclothes wrapped around her, like a straightjacket, she clicks her mouth and rubs an eye, which sounds hideous. The scene becomes even more grotesque when Spencer discovers the worm-sperm-like creatures are in the bed. Later a knock at the door leads to an encounter with the neighbor and another vision. The Lady in the Radiator sings and a large chicken is wheeled in. Spencer literally loses his head, revealing a stump that resembles the creature-child. His head sinks into a pool of blood and lands on a street below, where a young boy collects it and takes it to a pencil factory to be made into erasers. Spencer, who has an encounter with the neighbor, sees her with another man and is crushed. For the first time he removes the baby's bandages to find the baby has no skin. Spencer cuts into the creature's organs, which foam with a strange substance. The power in the room overloads and the child grows to huge proportions. As the lights burn out, the planet from the film's opening sequence replaces the child's head, and Spencer is seen in a billowing cloud of eraser shavings. The side of the planet bursts and the Man in the Planet is seen struggling with his now-sparking levers. The final sequence depicts The Lady in the Radiator embracing Spencer.

There have been a number of attempts to explain the film's meaning. The most common view is a take on the perils of domesticity;

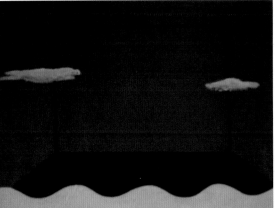

The Grandmother (1970, dir. David Lynch)

however, according to Lynch, no interpretation of the film has matched his personal vision, and as an abstract work, it is open to interpretation. Critics have also deciphered Henry as a stand-in for Lynch, and the film a manifestation of the fear he experienced while living in Philadelphia in his early twenties. While *Eraserhead* was actually filmed in Los Angeles, Lynch has described it as his own *Philadelphia Story*, "a dream of dark and troubling things." The sound design reflects exactly that, and serves as a pull into Spencer's world.

Sound is 50 per cent of a film, at least. In some scenes it's almost 100 per cent. It's the thing that can add so much emotion to a film. It's a thing that can add all the mood and create a larger world. It sets the tone and it moves things. Sound is a great "pull" into a different world. And it has to work (with the picture)—but without it you've lost half the film. (Lynch, 2003, p. 52).

Eraserhead (1977, dir. David Lynch)

TIPS AND TRICKS

Sound is often perceived as merely a technical discipline, which obscures the opportunities to use sound as a creative storytelling device. Film is frequently described as a "visual" medium, which also negates sound and consequentially hinders the potentials for both sound and image.

Reviewing experimental films, specifically short films, is a good way of exploring the many different approaches to audiovisual storytelling. Short films provide a vehicle for creative experimentation and can function as a "stepping stone" to the creation of longer format works.

The key element in filmmaking is the juxtaposition of sound and picture, so when you're planning a film, step back and consider the story idea from a sound perspective and think audiovisually. *How could sound be used to tell your story?*

THE ART OF NOISE

Sonic Sculpturing

Another area that influenced the practice of sound design is experimental music and sound art. Early sound art was largely influenced by developments in magnetic tape and audio recorders. Danish inventor Valdemar Poulsen invented the telegraphone between 1898 and 1900, which recorded sound by electromagnetism. It consisted of a cylinder wrapped with magnetic wire and a recording head that revolved around the cylinder, magnetizing the wire. The telegraphone was later refined by German-Austrian engineer Fritz Pfleumer, who used a magnetic stripe as an alternative to wire. In 1935, he built the world's first practical tape recorder, called the Magnetophon. The use of magnetic tape for sound recording revolutionized the broadcast and recording industries. Tape gave artists the ability to record and rerecord audio with an acceptable loss in quality. In 1955, Louis Mackenzie introduced the cartridge machine and "carts" that were loaded with quarter-inch tape and adopted by broadcasters. Cartridge machines came in banks, which meant sound effects could be played separately and together. Magnetic tape was also a key technology in early computer development, allowing data to be stored and rapidly accessed.

Musique Concrète

"Musique concrète" is a French term for "concrete music," a composition technique that uses recordings of "real" (concrete) sounds as the raw material for the creation of experimental music. Musique concrète challenges traditional music and music theory: It is not governed by customary parameters such as harmony but by recorded sounds that are separated from their origin and manipulated. The fundamental principle of musique concrète is in the selection, recording, assembly, and manipulation of found sounds, or "sound objects," to produce a montage of sound. Sound design and the creation of sound design effects or elements are a form of musique concrète; the concepts, ideas, and processes behind both practices are much the same.

French composer and writer Pierre Schaeffer developed the techniques involved in the production of musique concrète in 1948 while working at the Studio d'Essai (Experimental Studio). The studio was part of Radiodiffusion Française (RF), the French radio system created during World War II as a resistance hub for broadcasters. Despite coming from a musical family, Schaeffer had no formal music training, and his main interests were literature, philosophy, and technology. In 1942, Schaeffer convinced RF to make him the project director of research into the science of musical acoustics. He was among the first to manipulate and combine recorded sounds, as opposed to instruments, to compose music. Instead of notating musical ideas, he collected and manipulated concrete sounds. Schaeffer believed that traditional music starts as an abstraction, or musical notation, which is produced as music. The concept underpinning musique concrète is the reverse or inverse; it starts with "concrete" sounds and then abstracts them into a composition. Schaeffer considered music to be "patterned sound" and believed compositions could be created by juxtaposing and manipulating preexistent sound. Natural sounds, both animate and inanimate, could be altered and combined in a musical fashion. Schaeffer also believed that "playing" was another important part of the creation process, which is reflected in the improvisational nature of his work.

I have coined the term Musique Concrète for this commitment to compose with materials taken from "given" experimental sound in order to emphasize our dependence, no longer on preconceived sound abstractions, but on sound fragments that exist in reality and that are considered as discrete and complete sound objects, even if and above all when they do not fit in with the elementary definitions of music theory. (Schaeffer, 1948, p. 14)

Pierre Schaeffer

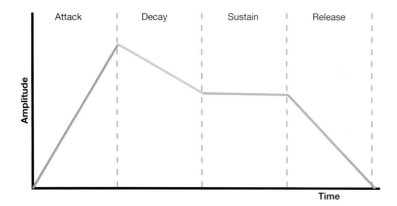

ADSR envelope

Initially Schaeffer concentrated on sounds other than those produced by traditional musical instruments. Schaeffer experimented with alarm clocks, bicycle horns, birdcalls, bits of wood, clappers, coconut shells, klaxons, rattles, vibrating metal strips, whirligigs, bells, and trains to create his compositions. After raw sounds were recorded, they were isolated and then rerecorded with different treatments. Schaeffer later found it was possible to remove the familiarity of musical instruments and abstract them through techniques such as removing the attack of the sound or altering the envelope of a sound. After removing the percussive attack from bells and extending the sound through volume manipulations, he recognized that entirely new sounds could be created. Schaeffer also discovered that sounds could be classified by timbre and volume changes over time (what is now known as the "envelope"). Timbre became as important as pitch had customarily been in music composition.

Schaeffer believed that sounds should be appreciated for their abstract timbral characteristics and not their source, cause, or context. He classified sounds in terms of their psychological effect on the listener. New recording and playback technologies and their ability to present "acousmatic" experiences inspired much of Schaeffer's work. Acousmatic (or *acousmatique*) sound is sound heard without seeing an originating cause and is derived from the Greek word *akousmatikoi* (or "listeners"), which refers to pupils of Greek philosopher Pythagoras. Pythagoras demanded that students listen to his lectures while he was concealed behind a curtain. He believed this would focus the students on the content of his lectures. Schaeffer argued that the "inscrutability of sound—its representational and ontological ambiguity"—could be rectified through recording technology; by separating sound from its origin or source, the listener would focus on the sound in itself. He manipulated sounds in a way that prevented the listener from identifying their original source.

By 1948, Schaeffer had also learned how to lock-groove (or loop) sounds using records. Instead of a disc with a spiral groove that went toward the center of the disc, there was a single or a series of circular grooves that would play as a continuous loop. This involved placing an intentional skip in the record so a sound would repeat, which is similar to a tape loop or a sequencing and looping audio today. Using seven to eight turntables playing individual sounds or loops, Schaeffer created various sound montages. He created *Etude aux Chemins de Fer* (*Study in Locomotives*) from the sounds of locomotive trains recorded at the depot for the Gare des Batignolles in Paris. The composition was derived entirely from sounds of steam whistling, trains accelerating, and compartments moving over rails. Schaeffer based his compositions on natural sounds, although a synthesizer does appear in later works, such as *Etude aux Sons Animes* (*Study on Animated Sounds*) in 1978.

The introduction of audiotape resulted in experimentation with techniques such as tape looping and splicing. Other common practices included playing sounds backwards, editing sounds to become shorter or longer, filtering out or boosting certain frequencies, adding effects such as echo and reverb, and altering the original pitch of a sound. Schaeffer and engineer Jaques Poullin also created the Phonogene, which was able to transpose a tape loop in twelve distinct steps from a keyboard. The keyboard selected one of twelve capstans of different diameters, and a two-speed motor was used for octave transposition. The Morphophone was another invention, a specialized loop deck with an erase head, record head, and ten playback heads with adjustable filters for each to create special timbre effects. Throughout his career Schaeffer also mentored other composers, including French synthesist Jean-Michel Jarre, who regards Schaeffer as an important influence in his work. Today Schaeffer's techniques are recognized as a precursor to contemporary sampling and sound design practices.

A Manifesto

Many of Schaeffer's ideas were drawn from and similar to those of Luigi Russolo, a futurist painter regarded as one of the first experimental "noise-music" composers. Russolo designed and constructed a number of sound-generating devices or experimental musical instruments called Intonarumori ("noise intoners"). In 1913, he authored a manifesto called *The Art of Noises* (*L'arte dei Rumori*), which is considered one of the most influential texts on twentieth-century music aesthetics. Futurism was an international art movement founded in Italy in 1909, and a futurist was someone who studied the future and made predictions based on current trends. It was an offshoot of cubism, initiated by Filippo Marinetti, an Italian writer and author of the *Futurist Manifesto* (1909). At the forefront of futurist painting was a fixation on motion, speed, noise, and machines. Futurist painters introduced time or temporal dimension to their paintings and produced pictures analogous to chronophotography, an early photographic technique that captures movement in several frames of print. In *Dynamism of a Car*, Russolo conveys the idea of motion with the compression of sound waves in front of a car, which resembles the Doppler effect. This is the effect heard when a sound source, such as a car or train, passes by and the pitch changes: It becomes higher as the sound approaches and lower as it passes. It was named after Austrian physicist Christian Doppler (1803–53), who theorized that sound waves from a moving source would be closer together as the sound came closer and farther apart as the sound went farther away. He proved his theory in 1842 by having trumpet players standing on a train pass by at varying speeds.

Luigi Russolo, *Dynamism of a Car* (1912–13)

Russolo's ideas were similar to Marinetti's, whose *Manifesto of Futurism* called for a total revision of aesthetic values. Marinetti favored modernity and technology and developed a poetic technique while working as a war correspondent in the Italo-Turkish War in 1911. He used onomatopoeia in an attempt to liberate the sounds of poetry from the restrictions of grammar and syntax. The sounds of machine guns, bombs, and shrapnel become new words, which he called "noise poetry." *The Art of Noises* was also written as a futurist manifesto. Prior to writing the manifesto, Russolo had worked purely in the graphic arts domain. He later abandoned the graphic arts and turned his studio into a workshop for making the Intonarumori. Like Marinetti's, his manifesto advocated for a new approach to music composition. At the time, he was drawing parallels between the evolution of music and the proliferation of machinery, which he saw as a creative opportunity. For Russolo, orchestral instruments were limited in the range of timbres they produced, and he believed technology would allow musicians to create an infinite variety of timbres. He claimed music had reached a point where it no longer had the power to excite or inspire; it lacked the more complex polyphony, tones, and coloring of organic and industrial sounds:

In the pounding atmosphere of great cities as well as in the formerly silent countryside, machines create today such a large number of varied noises that pure sound, with its littleness and its monotony, now fails to arouse any emotion. (Russolo, 1913, para. 3)

Russolo predicted the future of music was in the way sounds could be combined to create new sounds. He considered the rhythmic movements of a sound as infinite possibilities and divided "noise" into six groups, which would form the fundamental building blocks or sonic palate for a futurist orchestra:

1. Roars, Claps, Falling Water, Driving, Bellows
2. Whistles, Snores, Snorts
3. Whispers, Mutterings, Rustlings, Grumbles, Grunts, Gurgles
4. Shrill Sounds, Cracks, Buzzing's, Jungles, Shuffles
5. Percussive Noises using metal, wood, skin, stone, baked earth etc.
6. Animal and human Voices, Shouts, Moans, Screams, Laughter, Rattling's, Sobs (Russolo, 1913, para. 16)

Russolo claimed his new orchestra would produce "the most complex and newest sonic emotions" through "a fantastic association of these varied sounds." He believed this new orchestra would attract "futurist ears as it already has futurist eyes" (Russolo, 1913, para. 23). Russolo concluded that this new sound would require instruments with "special mechanisms" capable of altering the pitch of a sound through built-in resonators and other types of extensions. He built the Intonarumori to create and perform the music outlined in the *Art of Noises*. It's believed he was greatly influenced by the work of Leonardo da Vinci (1452–1519), who had previously experimented with acoustics and the design of mechanical instruments. Leonardo's instruments share commonalities with Russolo's designs—drums with cranked beaters, drum-box apertures, and integrating cones as tuned resonators. The Intonarumori were acoustic devices with varying types of internal constructions designed to produce different sounds. They had a drum skin attached to a string or coiled wire spring and a wheel acting as a continuous bow. The wheel rattled or bowed the string, while the drum skin functioned as an acoustic resonator. Sound was tuned by the tension of the string and the drum skin. Turning a crank generated sound, and a lever controlled the pitch of the sound. The wheel type, materials, positioning, string or spring, and pressure on the wheel defined the timbre of sound. The skin and the cone, similar to a gramophone, amplified the sound. One of the devices was described as a *burster* (or *scoppiatore*) and produced a sound similar to an early automobile engine. Other designs included a *hummer*, which sounded like an electric motor; a *rubber*, which produced a metallic scraping sound; and a *crackler*, which sounded like a cross between a mandolin and a machine gun. The Intonarumori were first presented at a press concert at Milan's Casa Rossa, the headquarters of the futurist movement in 1913.

Sculptors of Sound

Another pioneering figure in musique concrète and experimental music is Pierre Henry, who worked with Pierre Schaeffer at the Studio d'Essai from 1949 to 1958. During that time, he composed the first musique concrète–styled composition to appear in a commercial short film, *Astrologie ou le miroir de la vie* (*Astrology or the Mirror of Life*, 1952). After completing formal musical studies, Henry began his career as a percussionist, yet he aspired to create something new, strange, and unheard-of. His work includes numerous collaborations with poets, dancers, filmmakers, and bands. Henry defined musique concrète as comprising movement and rhythm and being more connected to photography, cinema, and literature than traditional music. He aspired to conceiving a score like a film, with sound and voice.

Daphne Oram, a pioneering British musique concrète composer, or "the mother of electronic music,'" as she became known, cofounded and directed the BBC's Radiophonic Workshop in the late 1950s. Oram started out as a junior studio engineer and "music balancer" at the BBC in 1942 and began experimenting with tape recorders and "synthetic" sound. She was promoted to music studio manager, and after a trip to the RTF studios in Paris, campaigned for the BBC to provide electronic music facilities for composing sounds and music. Oram and colleague Desmond Briscoe established the BBC Radiophonic Workshop in early 1958, where she was the first studio manager. After leaving the BBC, Oram set up her own studio in Kent and worked on designing soundtracks for radio, television, theater installations, exhibitions, and short films, including electronic sound effects (uncredited) for Jack Clayton's horror film *The Innocents* (1961). She was awarded two grants from the Gulbenkian Foundation to support the research into "Oramics." Her Oramics machine was essentially a prototype synthesizer, and she had a very clear vision of how the computer would revolutionize electronic music. Oramics allowed a composer to draw "an alphabet of symbols" on paper and feed it through a machine that would in turn produce sounds on magnetic tape. The first drawn sound composition using the machine, entitled "Contrasts Essonic," was recorded in 1968, and in the 1980s, Oram worked on the development

Russolo's Intonarumori

Pierre Henry

of a software version of Oramics for the Acorn Archimedes computer. In 1972, she published *An Individual Note*, a book that discusses her work and views on sound, music, electronics, and synthesis.

Another seminal figure associated with musique concrète is experimental composer John Cage, who is probably best known for *4'33"(Four Minutes, Thirty-Three Seconds)*, composed in 1952 for any instrument or combination of instruments, with performer(s) instructed not to play their instrument during the entire duration of the performance. The controversial piece is commonly perceived as four minutes and thirty-three seconds of silence. Cage's intention was to redefine the concept of silence, because of the rarity of silence, or the total absence of sound. Cage believed silence was simply the absence of intended sound, which is how "silence" is used in film soundtracks. He studied music but realized that the kind of music he wanted to create was very different from music at the time. His early works were largely percussive and included elements such as pipes and sheets of metal, apparently inspired by a meeting with German abstract animator Oskar Fischinger. He was also inspired by artist Marcel Duchamp, who presented everyday objects in museums as "found art". Cage also experimented with recording technologies and the alteration of instruments.

Virtually unknown but equally significant is Delia Derbyshire, who started working for the BBC as a trainee assistant studio manager in 1960 and later oversaw their "avant-garde" Radiophonic Workshop. Derbyshire had a degree in mathematics and music and an interest in the theory and perception of sound. She created music and sound design for almost 200 radio and television programs, but her most well-known work is the original *Doctor Who* (1963) theme. Ron Grainer composed the basic melody and Derbyshire provided the iconic sounds and form of the theme. Most of her early work remained anonymous or credited as "special sound" by the BBC. *Four Inventions for Radio* (1964–65) is described as the best illustration of Derbyshire's particular style of "soundscaping." She also worked across film, theater, and electronic music events, creating music for a film by Yoko Ono and sharing a bill with Jimi Hendrix. Among those who credit her as an influence are Orbital, Portishead, Aphex Twin, and the Chemical Brothers.

John Cage

Soviet filmmaker Dziga Vertov also experimented with similar concepts to that of musique concrète, most notably in his first sound film, *Enthusiasm: Symphony of the Donbass* (1931), which was also the first Ukrainian sound film. The film is shot in eastern Ukraine and dedicated to Stalin's first Five-Year Plan (1928–32), as a celebration of industrialization and collectivization. Vertov's films heavily influenced the Cinéma Vérité (truthful cinema) style of documentary filmmaking, and *Enthusiasm* is considered an innovation in film, primarily because of the soundtrack and its use of industrial sounds such as the clash of hammers, train whistles, bells, and the songs of workers. Vertov had welcomed the coming of sound and perceived it as a "radio-ear" to accompany the "cinema-eye" (Croce, 2016, p. 58).

I was returning from the railroad station. In my ears, there remained chugs and bursts of steam from a departing train . . . somebody cries out . . . laughter, a whistle, voices, the station bell, the clanking locomotive . . . whispers, shouts, farewells . . . And walking away I thought there is a need to find a machine not only to describe but to register, to photograph these sounds. Otherwise, one cannot organize or assemble them. They fly like time. (Vertov in Feldman, 2014, p. 23)

The methods employed by contemporary sound designers are subjected to very similar sound-sculpting techniques as those developed by these earlier artists, and many film sound designers attribute hearing earlier works as inspiring their interest in sound design. One of the reasons for the confusion that surrounds sound design is that the term is often used in reference to other art forms.

Sound design is an element, and often the main element, in film sound design, sound art, sound sculptures, and sound installations. A *soundscape* is generally defined as a combination of sounds that either forms or arises from an environment, and the study of soundscapes is called acoustic ecology. Canadian composer and sound ecologist R. Murray Schafer coined the term in reference to environments, abstract constructions, and sound montages. *Sound art* considers sound, listening, and hearing as its predominant focus and engages with the subjects of acoustics, found or environmental sound, psychoacoustics, electronics, music, sculpture, screen media, and technology. *Sound sculpture* generally describes an art object that produces sound, or the reverse; sound is manipulated in such a way as to create a sculptural form or mass. *Sound installations* are usually site-specific installations that include a sound component that makes a dialogue with the surrounding space. All forms of sound art involve sound design, but soundscapes, sound art, and installations are generally less narrative or non-narrative and not as visually oriented as sound design for film and animation, which is primarily concerned with story and image.

Enthusiasm: Symphony of the Donbass (1931, dir. Dziga Vertov)

TIPS AND TRICKS

When Luigi Russolo predicted the future of music was in the way sounds could be combined to create new sounds, he was defining one of the key aspects that underpins contemporary sound design, and identifying the potential of emotional responses to nonmusical sound.

Pierre Schaeffer furthered those ideas through creating "musical compositions" by manipulating preexistent or "found" sound. Schaeffer was effectively experimenting with the shape and form of sound. By extracting, altering, and "abstracting" specific qualities, he was sculpting with sound.

"Found sound" is an expression used to describe sounds from the natural or physical world. When conceptualizing sound, it can be difficult to determine a starting point, but thinking about the story world can lead to sound ideas. How could or should that world sound? Additionally, thinking about the character(s) in your story world also triggers sound ideas. Put yourself in your character's shoes. What does she or he hear?

FICTIONS OF SCIENCE

Synthesis, New Waves, and Ambiguity

Science fiction has had a huge impact on sound design. Georges Méliès's *Le Voyage dans la Lune* (1902) is considered the first science fiction film and pioneered the use of special effects in film. By the 1950s, science fiction had become a popular genre, and sound artists were breaking new ground in sound design through creating soundtracks for films such as Forbidden Planet (Wilcox, 1956). Modeled on The Tempest, reviewers reacted enthusiastically to the film's mix of Shakespeare and science fiction. It was nominated for a Special Effects Oscar, and despite losing out to *The Ten Commandments* (DeMille, 1956), the visual effects work was considered very sophisticated for the time. *Forbidden Planet* was also the first film to be produced with an entirely electronic "score."

The film is set in the late twenty-second century. A United Planet cruiser is sent on a special mission to look for survivors from an expedition on distant planet Altair-IV. On the planet, Professor Morbius builds robots and raises his daughter, Altaira, who was born on Altair-IV. When the cruiser from Earth arrives, Morbius tries to warn them off, but they ignore his warning and land. An invisible force kills some of the crew; Morbius believes it is the same unknown entity that killed nearly everyone from the previous expedition. While living on Altair-IV, Morbius had been studying the Krell, a highly advanced race that mysteriously died out 200,000 years previously. In a Krell laboratory, Morbius shows off a device capable of measuring and enhancing intellectual capacity. It was the device that had given him the ability to build Robby the Robot. Altaira falls in love with the commander from the ship, who demands that the Krells' knowledge be turned over. Morbius refuses and chaos unfolds. It's later revealed that the "monster" is actually the professor's repressed subconscious. Morbius eventually accepts the truth—that the Id monster is an extension of his own mind, unleashed by his experiments with Krell technology, and is the same entity that killed the original expedition.

Film and Electronica

Husband and wife team Louis and Bebe Barron created *Forbidden Planet*'s sound design and electronic score, which was credited on the film as "electronic tonalities." Bebe and Louis Barron were both trained musicians with an interest in electronic music. They knew of Pierre Henry's and Pierre Schaeffer's work as well as that of Karlheinz Stockhausen and the "Elektronische Musik" group in Koln, which produced the first music created solely from electronic generators in the early 1950s. They also worked with John Cage and other experimental composers,

Forbidden Planet (1956, dir. Fred M. Wilcox)

collaborating on a number of sound projects for film, dance, and theater. In 1951, John Cage organized a group of musicians and engineers to produce music directly on magnetic tape with technical assistance from Louis and Bebe Barron. Prior to *Forbidden Planet*, they worked on experimental films and theater but wanted to take on larger and more financially rewarding productions.

In his autobiography, MGM head Dore Schary credits Louis and Bebe's score as a primary factor in *Forbidden Planet*'s cult status. Originally the Barrons' music was to be incidental to a more conventional orchestral score, but they ended up creating the whole film soundtrack, including most of the sound effects. Since the Barrons did not belong to the Musicians Union, they could not be considered for an Academy Award, and there was also some debate as to whether their work should even be called "music," as the soundtrack was produced directly to tape and there was no notated score. The Barrons later released their soundtrack in 1976 as an LP album for the film's twentieth anniversary. While their work on *Forbidden Planet* is usually defined as score, it is actually a combination of sound effects, sound design effects, and score. The soundtrack bore no resemblance to the traditional approach to film music, which was something of a first at the time.

While the theremin, an electronic instrument, had been used earlier on the soundtrack of Alfred Hitchcock's *Spellbound* (1945), the Barrons' electronic sound designs preceded the invention of the Moog synthesizer by eight years. The Barrons got some of their ideas from the book

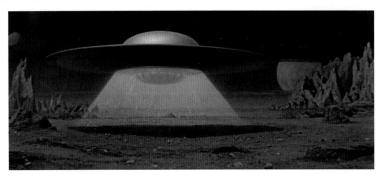

United Planets Cruiser from *Forbidden Planet* (1956, dir. Fred M. Wilcox)

Cybernetics: Or, Control and Communication in the Animal and the Machine (1948), written by the mathematician and electrical engineer Norbert Wiener. Wiener is considered the founding father of cybernetics, which is the science and study of control mechanisms in human and machine systems. Louis followed principles described in the text and designed various oscillator and ring modulator circuits, which were used to generate sound. Striving to create an organic quality despite using electronic circuits, the Barrons likened their work to cybernetic biological processes. They equated their circuit designs with the neural circuitry of an organism, and the resulting sounds were intended to produce an emotional response or effect.

We used many circuits from Norbert Wiener's book *Cybernetics: Or Control and Communication in the Animal and the Machine*. We recorded and amplified the electronic activity and endlessly processed it, since they were all mathematical equations they seemed to have a kind of order and organic rightness. Entropy and information theory contributed ideas on probability and randomness, which we had to use since that was the only thing our circuits were capable of. We thought of our circuits as characters in a script, and used the unfolding of pitches as they came out of the circuits. We didn't control the pitches at all. The emotions which seemed to come out of the circuits such as romance, monsters, space travel were almost always in [sic] upper most in importance. Each circuit we built had life spans of their own . . . [and] once they died we could never revive them. (Bebe Barron in Chasalow, 1997)

Bebe and Louis Barron

The Barrons devised a list of "characters" and approached the soundtrack like a director would direct actors. Circuits were built, activated, and then personified. Bebe undertook most of the selecting and production, while Louis did most of the circuitry design. He constructed various electronic circuits to generate the bleeps, whirs, whines, throbs, and hums for spaceships, robots, and technology in the film. Their process involved isolating suitable fragments or samples they felt had the potential for further work. Together they mixed and manipulated sound by adding effects such as reverberation and delay and reversing or changing the pitch of sounds. Sound design and textural effects were created to express the eeriness of space and the strangeness of Altair-IV; many of these sounds were generated using a ring modulator. A ring modulator multiplies two signals together to create two brand-new frequencies that are the sum and difference of the input frequencies. Ring modulation is often used to simulate the sounds of tuned percussion instruments that produce inharmonic frequency content, such as bells and chimes, which tend to sound metallic or robotic. An oscillator is an electronic circuit that produces a periodic, oscillating electronic signal, often a sine or a square wave. Audio oscillators produce frequencies in the range around 16 Hz to 20 kHz, and a low-frequency oscillator (LFO) generates a frequency below 20 Hz. Oscillators form the basis of sound synthesis.

The roaring Id/beast came out of the circuit sounding not remotely like a beast, it was very high pitched, tinkling, with very complicated harmonic sounds, I would go through all the tapes and select things that had the most

potential for further processing. When I heard all that high-pitched activity, such complicated sounds, I said to Louis, "We've got to slow this way down." We probably lowered the frequencies 60 or 70 times (playing it back at half speed while re-recording at 15 i.p.s.). And each time we slowed it down more of the sound would emerge to the foreground while other parts would disappear. But finally we got to what we thought was the optimum speed—the rhythm was all there. That's the way the monster sound came about.

The preview showing was one of our great experiences because they played the music directly off the magnetic tapes. They had synced up the projector and tape and they gave it so much volume it was embarrassing. It was so effective—they played it stereophonically, which they never did in those days. Then there was the landing of the space ship. That was one of the best cues in the picture—and the audience broke into spontaneous applause. (Bebe in Brockman, 1992, para. 22–33)

New Waves

The 1950s also generated the New Wave (*La Nouvelle Vague*), which refers to a group of French filmmakers who transformed French cinema during the 1950s and 1960s. They also had a pronounced impact on filmmakers throughout the world during and after that period. Through experimental techniques, they fashioned a new cinematic style. Cinema was important in postwar France, and most of the New Wave directors were influenced by everything from realist Italian directors to American noir and B movies. The most common descriptions of early New Wave films was that they were "low budget" and made "outside" the conventional system. New Wave filmmakers rejected the traditional Hollywood tendency to base narrative styles and structures on earlier media, namely books and theater. Previously there were two primary camps of filmmakers: spectacle and special effects, or fact and observation. Many saw popular movies of the era as out of touch with the daily lives of postwar youth, and mainstream audiences were starting to decline due to the impact of television and emergent art cinema. New Wave films often engaged with the social and political upheavals of the time.

Monster of Id from *Forbidden Planet* (1956, dir. Fred M. Wilcox)

The scripts or lack thereof were considered revolutionary, and the modest budgets forced filmmakers to become inventive. Technical developments in cameras, film stock, and sound recording had made it easier for people to experiment with filmmaking. As a result, New Wave films became known for certain stylistic innovations such as unusual camera angles, handheld shots, jump cuts, rapid editing, the use of natural lighting, improvised dialogue, direct sound recording (as opposed to the dubbing), using nonprofessional actors, and long takes. Concurrently, there were echoes of the French New Wave across the globe: the Free Cinema Movement in Britain, *Cinema Novo* in Brazil, and the New German Cinema of the 1960s. They all had their own particular style, but universally they were a reaction against what had come before. While arguably not the only, or even the first, wave, when taking into consideration German expressionism, Italian neorealism, and Soviet formalism, the French New Wave was later acknowledged as a major inspiration for Hollywood's generation of new directors such as George Lucas, Francis Ford Coppola, and Martin Scorsese.

The science fiction genre also became an increasingly popular genre for exploring alternatives in film form, and French New Wave filmmakers recognized the genre as a vehicle for stylistic experimentation. One of the first experimental French short science fiction films was *La Jetée* (*The Jetty*), released in 1962, and the inspiration for the feature film *12 Monkeys* (Gilliam, 1995). Written and directed by Swiss filmmaker Chris Marker, *La Jetée* is set in the aftermath of World War III. Survivors shelter underground while a group of scientists experiment with time travel. The aim is to perfect travel into the future by perfecting travel to the past, and by traveling into the future, the scientists hope to find a way to change the present. A survivor obsessed with memories of a mysterious woman and a man's death on the pier at Orly Airport is chosen to participate in the experiment. The film's title refers to the large "jetty" or pier-like structure at Orly Airport outside Paris, where the time traveler as a boy sees the man killed and the woman who witnesses the event. The story is told through the use of black and white stills, voice-over narration, sound effects, atmos(phere), and music. It contains one brief shot of filmed motion and is described by the credits as a "photo-roman," or photo-graph-fiction. The still images are connected by cuts, fades, and dissolves. The voice-over tells the story, while the airport atmosphere, which includes public address (PA) announcements and sound effects, adds a sense of realness to *La Jetée*. The sound of birds is used in a similar fashion, getting louder as if to provoke a sense of doom and challenge perceptions of reality. The presence of the conspiring scientists is conveyed through whispering, while the psychological effects of the experiments are revealed through the sound and rhythms of a heartbeat.

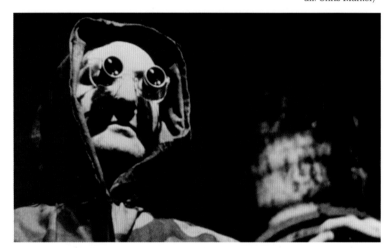

La Jet**é**e (1962, dir. Chris Marker)

Sonic-psychedelia

La Planète Sauvage (*Fantastic Planet*), an abstract science fiction feature film, won the Special Jury Prize at Cannes in 1973 and is considered a landmark in European animation. The film is a cutout stop-motion animated film directed by René Laloux, with production design by Roland Topor, music by composer Alain Goraguer, and sound design by Jean Guérin. It was five years in the making at Prague's Jiri Trnka Studios and is regarded by some as an allegorical statement on the Soviet occupation of Czechoslovakia. Based on Stefan Wul's novel *Oms en série* (*Oms by the Dozen*), the film is set on an alien planet called Ygam, where humans (Oms) are enslaved by a larger and more superior alien race (Draags). The Draags treat humans like animals; some are domesticated and kept as pets, while others live in the wilderness and are periodically slaughtered by the Draags as a form of population control. The

Draags maintain a technologically and spiritually advanced society where education is received through headphones that transmit knowledge straight to the mind.

The film opens with an Om mother being literally teased to death by three Draag children. A Draag leader discovers the woman's orphaned infant and he allows his daughter Tiva to keep him as a pet. Tiva names him Terr and controls him through a collar that can pull him in any direction she wishes. She brings him to her teaching sessions, and a defect in his collar allows him to receive the same knowledge she is receiving. Terr becomes a young man and eventually escapes with Tiva's headphones. He meets a female Om who cuts off his collar and introduces him to her tribe. After a duel, he is permitted to show them how to use the headphones to acquire Draag knowledge. This enables them to read Draag writing, and they discover their area is about to be purged. Some escape and join forces with another tribe. They take over an abandoned Draag rocket depot and with the knowledge acquired from the headphones learn how to adapt Draag technology. When a large-scale Draag purge hits the depot, a group, led by Terr, flees in rockets to the Fantastic Planet. They discover statues that Draags travel to during meditation and through strange rituals with other beings maintain their species. The Oms destroy some of the statues, which threatens the Draags' existence. The purges are halted and, facing a crisis, the Draags opt for peaceful coexistence.

La Planète Sauvage (1973, dir. René Laloux)

The film has an abstract-surrealistic-psychedelic-hallucinatory visual sensibility that mixes seventies avant-garde rock with sound design reminiscent of Bebe and Louis Barron's earlier work on *Forbidden Planet*. The Barrons had to design and build a number of circuits to produce particular sounds, and each could only perform a limited range of functions. Early electronic devices like the theremin were also relatively limited, and the first sound synthesizers were largely impractical. The RCA Mark II sound synthesizer, designed by Herbert Belar and Harry Olson at RCA was the size of a room, and the first programmable electronic synthesizer. By the 1970s, sound designers were using a modular voltage-controlled analog synthesizer pioneered by Dr. Robert Arthur Moog. Moog became interested in the design and construction of complex electronic music systems in the mid-1960s while completing a PhD in engineering physics. The invention of the transistor led to the creation of the Moog synthesizer, which was smaller, cheaper, and more reliable than earlier systems. The introduction of electronic instruments opened the door to creating sounds that sit outside what is typically perceived as a sound effect, further clouding the line between sound effects and music, which is where sound design is often situated.

The Ambiguous Twilight Zone

Walter Murch is a well-known sound designer, re-recording mixer, and picture editor. He studied liberal arts before attending film school at the University of Southern California (USC), and he launched his career through working on the American Zoetrope's first film, *The Rain People* (Coppola, 1969). A core objective for American Zoetrope was to circumvent the departmentalism of the studio system, and as film technology had become more affordable, it made sense for the sound designer to take responsibility for the soundtrack. Murch has since worked on films such as *The Conversation* (1974), *Julia* (1977), *Apocalypse Now* (1979), *The Unbearable Lightness of Being* (1988), *Ghost* (1990), *The Godfather: Part III* (1990), *Romeo Is Bleeding* (1993), *The English Patient* (1996), *The Talented Mr. Ripley* (1999), *Cold Mountain* (2003), *Jarhead* (2005), and *The Wolfman* (2010). He has received numerous awards for both sound and picture work, directed the feature film *Return to Oz* (1985), and in 2001 wrote *In the Blink of an Eye*, a well-regarded book on film editing. Murch is also widely acknowledged for introducing the term "sound design" in the 1970s. On previous films, his work was credited as "sound montage." The term "sound montage" was adopted to avoid altercations with the union—he wasn't a member, so he couldn't be credited as a sound editor—and to more accurately reflect the increasingly conceptual nature of soundtrack design. *THX-1138* (1971), directed by George Lucas, was the first "mainstream" feature film to use the credit of sound designer.

While also attending USC, George Lucas directed the short film *Electronic Labyrinth: THX 1138 4EB* (1967). The screening synopsis described the film as "a nightmare impression of a world in which a man is trying to escape a computerized world which constantly tracks his movements" (USC, 1967). The film is set underground, in a dystopian future, which the lead character attempts to escape. The story is primarily told through POV from video security cameras, which supports the central theme of a totalitarian order reliant on surveillance technology to control the population. The film is abstract and the soundtrack mostly non-sync, consisting of music, phrases, and word fragments treated as radio and intercom communications, electronic hums, beeps, and alarm sound effects. With support from Francis Ford Coppola, the short was reworked as *THX 1138*. Lucas wrote the original story and in collaboration with Walter Murch rewrote the screenplay.

Lucas describes *THX 1138* as a parable or metaphor for how people were living in the 1960s, and Murch describes it as an investigation into the ramifications of a self-contained world, disconnected from the organic world, with an unbridled consumer culture. The film depicts an underground society living in a clinical environment policed by androids. Key themes are conformity, consumerism, and surveillance. The population prays and confesses to their god OMM 0910, who responds through prerecorded messages, but there is no god or leader; the society is controlled by drugs and made bureaucratic by the people who participate in it. Inhabitants are sedated and dressed in white, with shaved heads. Consumerism is encouraged, while any form of emotion is a punishable offence. The story centers on THX 1138 and his female roommate, LUH 3417. THX 1138 handles radioactive materials in a factory, and LUH 3417 is a disenchanted surveillance worker. After she stops taking the emotion-suppressing medication, she gives placebos to THX 1138. He also becomes

The factory in *THX 1138* (1971, dir. George Lucas)

self-aware and they form a relationship. They plan to escape to the "superstructure" but are caught and detained. THX 1138 is imprisoned in a wall-less white void where he is beaten, but later, with the help of a hologram, he escapes. After discovering that the now-pregnant LUH 3417 has been killed, he makes his way to the surface.

Lucas wanted the film to feel like an artifact from the future, as opposed to a film about the future. The aim was to tell the story subliminally, by creating an aural-visual experience that was more atmospheric, more stylized, and grittier than a traditional film narrative. Lucas also drew inspiration from Theatre of the Absurd, a theatrical movement that developed in the late 1950s around the philosophy of existentialism: Humans define their own meaning in life and try to make rational decisions despite existing in an irrational universe. As both Lucas and Murch have pointed out, *THX 1138* is not always coherent. Seeing a lizard doesn't make sense in the setting presented; it's thematic, a living thing trapped in a synthetic environment, an analogy or metaphor for the lead characters. The same concept is applied to the sound design, which functions beyond cause and effect, seeing and hearing, and often counters what's seen. At times, sound is addressing a different element of the story, and sometimes themes are being addressed simultaneously. Images and sound are intentionally disconnected, which creates tension and a feeling of unease.

Murch identifies contemporary films as fitting into two categories, either dialogue-driven films, where the visuals and the sound play a secondary and supporting role, or action-driven films, where the images and accompanying sounds are often powerful and overwhelming, and the dialogue is reduced to a support role. Lucas defines the approach to *THX 1138* as "pure cinema," based on visual and sound design, as opposed to

The prison in *THX 1138* (1971, dir. George Lucas)

overreliance on action, dialogue, or music. While soundtracks are typically broken down and categorized as dialogue, music, and effects, conceptually the lines often overlap—they blur. Between each classification is what Murch describes as an "ambiguous twilight zone."

Sound effects are like people who can travel around the world without any passports. Sound effects have a way of sneaking under the radar so that you can be being affected by them in musical ways, emotional ways but because they seem to be being produced by the visuals, by the world that you're looking at you tend to accept them at face value and not as something the filmmakers are doing to create an emotional effect with you, whereas that's not the case with music. (Murch in Leva, 2004)

Murch also termed his approach to designing the sound for *THX 1138* as "cubistic sound." Cubism is an early twentieth-century avant-garde art movement that inspired related movements in music, literature, and architecture. Cubism is considered the most influential art movement of

Surveillance center in *THX 1138* (1971, dir. George Lucas)

the twentieth century. In artwork, objects are analyzed, broken up, and reassembled in an abstracted form, instead of from a single viewpoint, to represent the subject in a greater context. In *THX 1138*, each scene was treated as a cube of sound, and each cube had a slightly different sound. The prison "room" is a white void with no discernable walls and therefore not actually a room. So the "room tone" needed to be less room and more tone, which was derived from a recording of the Palace of Fine Arts in San Francisco, a curved room that houses science experiments. Like all rooms, it has a tone, but not many rooms are curved and have an unidentifiable "mechanical something" as part of the tone. Most of the material used in the film was from original recordings, except for two stock sound effects, thunder and a punch. It was also decided from the beginning that unlike in many science fiction films at the time, there would be no or minimal electronically generated sounds. While the "cattle prod" the police use to torment THX 1138 is electronic-sounding, or has an electric tinge, it was created from an organic source. Murch recorded different hits on a metal lamp shade, edited out the attack of the hits, and combined one hit played forward and one played backward.

In addition to synchronized dialogue, dialogue effects in the form of radio and intercom communications (or "chatter") are used throughout the film. In the public spaces, like the shopping mall, voice is used to communicate the nature of the society— in the case of the shopping mall, consumerism. The public address broadcasts are also treated to reflect the physical environments. At the time the film was produced, audio processing equipment was limited, so Murch recorded dialogue in real spaces to get authentic-sounding reverbs and echo, a technique he called "worldizing." Murch and Lucas also recorded dialogue material through the use of ham radios, one broadcasting and one receiving, which altered the timbre or tone of the dialogue. The police are all the same, one pervasive voice, which sounds totalitarian and has a logic: The police are robots, and why would you bother to program voice variations? Murch also experimented with temporary music tracks from mainly classical records. He rerecorded tracks backwards, slowed them down, and layered them, effectively treating preexisting music as raw material for the creation of temporary soundscapes. Many of the results were later adapted by composer Lalo Schifrin and rerecorded as a musical score.

Architects of Sound

By the late 1970s, independent filmmakers such as Francis Ford Coppola, Martin Scorsese, and George Lucas had embraced the creative potential of sound. Francis Ford Coppola first credited sound design on *Apocalypse Now* (1979) in recognition of Walter Murch's overall contribution and supervision of sound for the film. *Apocalypse Now* (Coppola, 1979) was central to the progression of film sound design and the development of the surround soundtrack. The film is set during the Vietnam War. Army captain and special operations veteran Benjamin L. Willard (Martin Sheen) is tasked with terminating special forces colonel Walter E. Kurtz (Marlon Brando), who has adopted a demigod-type persona and gone insane. Willard's objective is to travel down the Nyung River by boat and assassinate the defective Kurtz. As Willard and the crew embark on their journey, they confront the same horrors and hypocrisy that pushed Kurtz over the edge. When they arrive at Kurtz's outpost, Willard is brought before Kurtz and lectured on his theories of war, humanity, and civilization. Regardless, Willard attacks and kills Kurtz with a machete. The film depicts the insanity of war, Willard's journey, and his growing understanding of how Kurtz, one of the army's best soldiers, was driven to madness and despair.

In discussions between George Lucas (the original director), Walter Murch, and scriptwriter John Milius, it was identified that one of the elements that made the Vietnam War different and unique was the prevalence of helicopters. In the film, the war is presented from Willard's point of view, which is established in the opening sequence, forming a connection between the sound of helicopters (war) and Willard's state of mind. A synthesized sound design effect is heard "swooping" on a wide shot of the jungle. As it passes across the frame, The Doors' "The End" begins with a fragmentary mix of fog, flames, and helicopters, images of Willard and a ceiling fan. The helicopter sound becomes more realistic as Willard's "reality" comes into focus: He's in a hotel room in Saigon. Realistic sounds were deconstructed on synthesizers to mimic the real sounds; as Murch explained, "The helicopter provides you with the sound equivalent of shining a white light through a prism—you get the hidden colors of the rainbow" (Murch in Isaza, 2009). In the same way sound effects are created, the helicopters were broken down to their individual parts: rotor,

Apocalypse Now (1979, dir. Francis Ford Coppola)

turbine, clanks, thuds, and blades. Combined they sound realistic; individually, and treated, as with the blade, a dreamlike quality surfaces.

At the time, sound libraries had no stereo recordings of weapons, and the location sound material was problematic, so the film had to be thoroughly sound designed. It also needed to be authentic to the location, period, craft, and weapons used during the Vietnam War. The original plan was to make the film soundtrack quadraphonic and release it in 70mm Dolby Stereo. Quadraphonic sound is 4.0 surround sound and uses four channels, in which speakers are positioned at the four corners of the listening space. It was the earliest surround sound consumer product, and thousands of quadraphonic music recordings were made during the 1970s. The format they established while working on *Apocalypse Now* comprised six tracks: three channels in the front, two channels in the rear, and a subwoofer channel. Coppola wanted the explosions to be felt in addition to being heard, and the circular nature and motion of helicopters suited immersive techniques and the surround format; they fly, move around, and hover. Released to wide acclaim, *Apocalypse Now* is frequently held up as one of the most notable examples of creative sound design in filmmaking and integral to the development of 5.1 surround sound. Dolby Atmos takes that another step by supporting up to 128 discrete audio tracks and sixty-four speaker feeds, which allows film-makers to create even more highly immersive and cinematic story experiences.

Star Wars: Episode IV—A New Hope (Lucas, 1977) also marked a definitive turning point in the understanding of and interest in film sound. Lucas founded Industrial Light & Magic (ILM) specifi-cally to create the visual effects for *Star Wars: Episode IV* and Sprocket Systems, which later became Skywalker Sound, for creating the soundtrack. Prior to the production of *Star Wars: Episode IV*, Ben Burtt was a student at USC. Producer Gary Kurtz contacted USC looking for someone to record sounds that might be useful, and Burtt was recom-mended. Burtt's work on *Star Wars* incorporated the roles of sound recordist, sound editor/designer, and sound mixer. He spent a year recording and editing various sounds and created hundreds of different sound effects. Droids, crafts, creatures, and weapons all required sound designing. In discussions with Lucas, it was decided that sound should be organic as opposed to electronic or artificial sounding. Science fiction films still had a tendency to use electronic-sounding effects, and Lucas wanted to create a "used universe," in a similar vein to *THX 1138*.

Star Wars: Episode IV is set in "a galaxy far, far away" (of course), where the Galactic Empire is nearing completion of the Death Star space station and planning to crush the Rebel Alliance. Luke Skywalker, a farm boy, and his step-uncle and aunt purchase astromech droid R2-D2 and protocol droid counterpart C-3PO. While cleaning R2-D2, Luke triggers a message from Princess Leia, a member of the rebellion captured by Darth Vader. In the message, Leia asks for assistance from Jedi knight Obi-Wan Kenobi. Luke and the droids track down Obi-Wan Kenobi and hire smuggler Han Solo and his Wookie copilot Chewbacca to take them to Leia's home world, Alderaan. After discovering the Death Star has destroyed Alderaan, they board the space station to rescue Leia and escape with plans that help them destroy the Death Star.

The aural palette was drawn from the real world, familiar but not necessarily identifiable sounds. The blasters were devised from striking a steel cable on a radio tower and the Tie Fighter was a manipulated elephant bellow. The lightsaber, probably the most, or one of the most, iconic sound effects, was also the first sound design effect Burtt created. While attending USC, he worked as a projectionist and noticed a motor in the booth that hummed when it was idling. Burtt described the hum as having a musical sound and a hypnotic tone. A few weeks later, he had an incident with a broken microphone cable, and the microphone picked up a hum from a nearby television picture tube. Burtt described that sound as having a scin-tillating and angry buzz. The two sounds com-bined became the lightsaber. The Imperial Walkers introduced in *The Empire Strikes Back* (1980) were described in the script as big, heavy, lumbering mechanical beasts. ILM created models rang-ing from six to fifty centimeters in height, which were filmed using stop-motion animation against matte paintings. Burtt needed to design sounds that would give the miniature Walkers mass and weight. Motors and metal clunks were created from recordings Randy Thom made of a metal stamping/shearing machine, and the sound of the Walkers' "joints" were from recordings of a large Dumpster lid. Using purely organic sounds helped create the illusion of reality—the physicality and weight of the lumbering mechanical beasts.

Darth Vader's breathing is also one of the most memorable sounds from the films. In the script, Darth Vader is described as a strange and dark being that breathed abnormally and was sustained by some kind of life-support suit. Burtt went to a local dive shop and recorded different scuba masks and regulators, which he slowed down to become the breathing of Darth Vader. He originally designed a multitude of robotic sounds for the suit but found they overwhelmed the mix. Most sound designers design a number of sounds for any given event, as a way of "seeing" what works, and then pair it back to what's impor-tant. Mix problems aside, not "knowing" can be more engaging than knowing. When Darth Vader first appeared on-screen, he was a very mysterious and imposing figure. Chewbacca's voice was developed when *Star Wars* was still at script stage. Chewbacca (a 200-year-old Wookie) becomes Han Solo's companion after Solo is dismissed from the Imperial Navy for refusing to kill the Wookie. Chewbacca repays the debt by protecting Solo and becomes his copilot on the Millennium Falcon. His character was defined as gentle, hairy, and non-English-speaking. As he was required to act and communicate with other actors, he needed a language that was not recognizable as human or English but was still intelligent and believable. His "dialogue" also needed to look credible and lip-sync with Chewbacca's limited mouth movements. Lucas suggested bear growls as a starting point, and Burtt created his speech principally from recordings of bears, but also dogs, lions, tigers, badgers, and walruses. He edited together fragments of the recordings to create a sense of speech, with emotional associations or expressive tones such as affection, pain, and anger. Designing R2-D2's beeps and whistles proved to be a more difficult task. R2-D2 is a droid, therefore a machine, but he also needed to act, have a personality and be able to communicate. Unlike Chewbacca, he had no human or animal features, no face, eyes, or ears. Burtt's initial designs were deemed too machinelike and lacking in human quality, so he experimented with his own voice by mimicking infant type non-word sounds. What resulted was a combination of his voice and electronic sounds he generated with a synthesizer. By combining synthetic with organic material, he gave R2-D2 emotion, through inflection and intonation of voice.

By the early 1970s, Dolby® noise reduction equipment dominated the music recording industry and Dolby turned its attention to film sound. Senior vice president at Dolby Laboratories Ioan Allen described soundtracks in the 1960s as having poor quality and being little more than "audible subtitles." In 1974, Dolby released the 70mm split stereo format, a precursor to 5.1 surround sound. The technology's commercial breakthrough was *Star Wars*. Lucas wanted something that had never been heard before, and the initial plan was to use "Sensurround," which involved running a soundtrack with low-frequency content through a series of speakers. It was developed to enhance the audio experience during film screenings, specifically for the film *Earthquake* (Robson, 1974). Instead, Stephen Katz from Dolby suggested using the extra speakers in theaters that nobody used, and so *Star Wars* used two of the five speakers behind the screen and made them only low frequency. Dolby called it "baby boom." The film was released as a 70mm film with stereo sound. Projecting 70mm meant the original 65mm film (or 35mm blowup) was printed on 70mm film with the additional 5mm for four magnetic strips holding six tracks of sound. The original six discrete uncompressed channels were reconfigured into a left, center, and right screen channel plus a surround channel. The soundtrack became a big part of the *Star Wars* "spectacle" that continues today.

TIPS AND TRICKS

Film is a form of audiovisual text, and for sound designers, story is paramount. Technology provides the means, but like other film crafts, sound design is an artistic process.

One of the biggest "gray" areas in defining sound design is the blurring of boundaries; voice and music can function as sound effects or become sound design effects, and sound design can function as voice and music. Sound design effects can also be defined as musical sound effects, tonal or textural sound effects. Sound and sound design effects can serve as an alternative to the traditional film score, or the use of preexisting music tracks. Sound effects can be arranged and structured as music, obscuring the line between sound effects, sound design effects, and music.

To articulate sound ideas with sound people requires the ability to communicate. Sound has no codified language, but sound designers understand story, aesthetics, and emotive intent. When engaging with sound and sound designers think about story, key themes, locations/environments, and emotive intent. How do you want a scene to feel? The sound/s of the lightsaber, as Ben Burtt describes it, is scintillating, angry, musical and hypnotic. Despite the lack of a "formal" sound language, ideas can be informed by and exchanged through the consideration of emotion and aesthetics.

Contemporary Sound Design

The role of "sound designer" is now commonplace in contemporary film production, although not always recognized; the Academy presents awards for "Best Sound Editing" and "Best Sound Mixing." This is partly due to the collaborative nature of soundtrack creation and the misconception of sound as a technical discipline. It's still quite rare to see "sound designer" as a film credit, and those responsible for sound design are often listed as "sound editor." When directors use "sound designer" on film credits, it's in acknowledgment of the design and editorial work that goes into creating a soundtrack. Filmmaking is both artistic and technical; the most successful directors know this and employ sound to its full capacity. In the early days of cinema, technology was limited and most live-action films were shot in controlled environments, usually on a sound stage, with everything, including sound effects, recorded. As a result, the postproduction phase was less intensive than it is today. Like in radio and television drama, a desire for realism led to more films being shot on location, which made sound recording more difficult and intensified the need for greater postproduction sound work. The first films relied more heavily on music ("silent film"), and then dialogue ("the talkies"), and there were few sound effects. The art of filmmaking developed as technology and associated skills developed, which resulted in greater experimentation. Consequently, this expanded the possibilities and complexities of both film sound and visual design. Peter Jackson's remake of *King Kong* (2005), for example, looks and sounds nothing like the original film.

THE SOUNDTRACK

Dialogue, Music, and Effects

The soundtrack, often credited with being up to 70 percent of the picture or film experience, suggests a measurable constant. Sound can be 0 percent (complete silence, and just picture) to 100 percent (just sound, with no pictures, just a black screen), and any figure in between. Each element of the soundtrack can function as a storytelling device, which is why understanding the various elements and the potential for interplay between sound and image helps generate ideas for how a film could or should sound.

Typically, the soundtrack is defined as dialogue, music, and sound effects, which is an oversimplification, particularly in the case of sound effects. The soundtrack comprises dialogue, sound effects, sound design effects, Foley effects, walla, atmosphere, room tone, music, and silence. While it was once a singular (or mono) track, contemporary soundtracks can be hundreds of tracks and thousands of individual sounds.

Dialogue

Dialogue is a form of communication from characters or actors. Dialogue can express character and convey thoughts, emotions, and intentions. Dialogue is used to reveal the characters and sets the mood or tone of a story, while also providing direction and advancing the narrative. Synchronized dialogue is on-screen, visible, and typically recorded during production in the case of live action, or before production in animation, which helps to aid in timing and lip-synchronization. Dialogue recordings (or scratch tracks) for animation are often temporary and replaced with higher-quality recordings from voice artists at a later stage. Non-synchronized dialogue can be on-screen and offscreen. This includes additional

vocal material such as grunts, groans, mumbles, breaths, coughs, and laughter. In animation, it's especially important to cast the right voice for the character, character design, and type of film. Animation directors always want authenticity and for the vocal elements to *belong* to the character.

Many animation directors will define animation as being action or movement, and arguably the overuse of dialogue can be seen in a negative light. Both live-action and animation directors often advocate for "pure cinema," which is storytelling through sound and image, not overreliance on dialogue.

Location sound (or production sound) is audio material, such as dialogue, that is recorded on location at the same time as the recording of image (principle photography). Automated dialogue replacement (ADR), or looping, is the process of re-recording dialogue due to problematic recordings, which is very common in the production of live-action films. The priority for production sound is capturing good quality dialogue. Microphones used for location dialogue recording are highly directional, therefore designed to capture dialogue and eliminate background sounds. Location sound recordists record separate recordings of room tone and atmos as a standard practice, and sometimes Foley and sound effects depending on the schedule and feasibility of the location. Sound effects and design

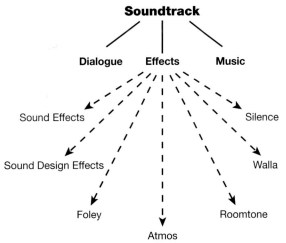

The various elements of a soundtrack

material are usually recorded separately by sound designers and specialist recording teams. Location sound practitioners encounter a wide array of challenges during a production shoot. What is being shot is often the priority, not what is being recorded, which creates issues for postproduction. Ironically, it's more expensive to do ADR, and many argue that no matter how technically correct, ADR rarely measures up to original production dialogue. ADR often fails to match the energy and realism of on-set performances. The process of ADR in live-action film production is much the same as replacing prerecorded dialogue for animated films. In animation, "scratch tracks" are usually recorded prior to storyboarding and rerecorded later.

Dialogue also encompasses voice-over (VO), or narration, and other material such as telephone conversations and radio or television broadcasts. VO and narration typically address the audience directly (non-diegetic sound), as opposed to dialogue from within the film world (diegetic sound). VO usually has a commanding presence in a soundtrack and will always dominate the sound mix. VO and narration are often the voice of the main character, like in *The Tell-Tale Heart* (Parmelee, 1953), and are generally delivered in the first person (in English, "I," "we," "me," and "us"). A narrator can also be a person external to the story, someone who has a more complete knowledge of the events and characters in the film than the characters themselves. In this case, the narrator is invisible and delivers in the third person (in English, "he," "she," "it," and "they").

Dialogue can also be sound design. King Kong, R2-D2, Chewbacca, and WALL-E are good examples of where sound design and dialogue intersect. The voices are designed. Dialogue can also be "gibberish." The Minion voices in *Despicable Me* (Coffin and Renaud, 2010) are codirector Pierre Coffin speaking gibberish pitched up. In the first film, very few words have meaning, but as the Minions became more central, words were added to help carry the story. Their language is a mix of Chinese, Japanese, Korean, Italian, French, and Spanish. Coffin describes it as gibberish, with a magical rhythm and melody, which makes the nonsense make sense. We understand the intent, which is communicated through the use of voice and variations in rhythm, speed, intonation, and pitch.

Sound Effects

Sound effects (spot, sync, or hard effects) tend to be the primary up-front sounds that sync to important events, highlight drama, and help tell the story. Sound effects are also used narratively, to draw the attention of a character to something offscreen to preempt something. A common misconception is that a sound effect is a single sound. Sometimes this is the case, but generally what's perceived as a single sound effect is a number of sounds mixed and/or edited together. Every sound effect in a film is considered, in the same way everything you see in a frame is considered. Sound effects make an event or action feel "real." If we see someone being thrown through a window, we expect to hear it. The glass is fake; it's the sound of real glass that makes the event "real." If we heard the sound of fake glass, or no sound, or the wrong type of glass and impact, the illusion of reality would be broken. Sound effects can also be described as ambient or background sound effects, which are both synchronized and non-synchronized, and used to build atmos tracks.

Sound Design Effects

Sound design effects (and/or elements) tend to be categorized as non-naturalistic and are sometimes called specialty effects; they are designed for imagined objects and places. However, they are frequently combinations of naturalistic, musical, and generated sounds. A sound effect can also become a sound design effect or atmos. A single piano note manipulated beyond recognition and mixed with wind can give wind a "voice" or make a scene "feel" eerie. In the literal (effect) sense, it's wind, whereas the subtext or "feel" (sound design effect) is eerie. The sound of wind can be created through recording the friction of materials (a canvas bag dragged across the floor), the effect of wind (rustling of leaves), custom-built wind machines, and/or the use of synthesizers. Sound design "textures" such as rumbles and drones can also feel like music or score when they have a perceivable musicality and/or rhythm. An example of how and where the terms "sound effect" and "sound design effects" overlap is in the creation of an effect like a laser gun. It's a gun, but it doesn't exist in reality so cannot be recorded. It's designed by combining real gun sounds with other sounds and synthesized and/or processed sounds.

Foley Effects

Foley effects are natural detailed sounds associated with people and movement: sitting on a chair, placing a plate on a table, paper folding, glass breaking, footsteps, rustling of clothing. The technique is named after Jack Foley, who established the process of recording "acted" sounds such as footsteps and clothing rustles. In live-action films, when the dialogue is replaced so is everything else, which includes Foley. Animation, on the other hand, starts as a blank canvas, and Foley helps create a world that's believable and feels authentic. Foley adds a physicality. Foley effects tend to be relatively subtle—a teaspoon clipping the edge of a cup, the jingle of keys, and the unlocking of a door—which helps connect the audience to characters and immerse the audience in the story world. Doors are considered Foley effects and sometimes sound effects. A door opening is not just one click of a latch, so like sound effects, Foley effects will also comprise a number of different sounds. A door can also be a sound design effect, for example the door of a spacecraft, which is a combination of Foley, sound, and sound design effects. Foley can be used narratively, to draw the eye to a specific detail and help define a character. If in a scene a character hears footsteps from behind while walking down a dark, quiet alley, the footsteps suggest he or she is being followed. If the footsteps sound like stilettos, the audience would assume or "know" the character is being followed by a woman.

Atmosphere

Atmosphere (abbreviated as "atmos") and also called ambience, or backgrounds, are the sounds of a location, environment, or space, such as a city or a forest. Atmosphere signifies locations, settings, time of day/night, and historical time periods, and helps convey the story and immerse the audience. Atmosphere establishes a scene and works editorially by staying constant across a picture cut to indicate to the audience that no change of time or location space has occurred. When atmosphere changes abruptly, it indicates a change in location or time to the viewer/listener. Atmospheres are generally exterior environments and consist of added sound effects and often walla, but they can also be interiors, non-naturalistic, and perceived as sound design effects.

Room Tone

Room tone is the sound of a room or interiors, which is the presence of subtle sounds created by the movement of air particles in a particular volume. All rooms are different sizes, shapes, and are constructed from different materials so have different acoustic properties. Interiors are usually reverberant, which indicates the size of the enclosed space. Room tone is generally naturalistic, but like atmos, room tone can be sound designed. For example, combining sound design textures with room tone can make a room feel claustrophobic or add a sense of foreboding. Room tone is recorded on location and used in live-action films to match and intercut with production sound to smooth out any sound edits. For ADR and animation, adding room tone gives realism and authenticity to dialogue recorded or re-recorded "dry" in an acoustically treated studio.

Walla

Walla is human vocal sounds such as the murmur of a crowd or background conversations in a café. Walla is added to a soundtrack and usually to create realism and/or to "cheat" how many people are in a given space. The word "walla" was adopted from the early days of radio for the sound of a crowd in the background. It was discovered that if several people repeated "walla, walla, walla" it sounded like the indistinct chatter of people talking in the background. Today walla is devised using real words and conversations and is sometimes treated as dialogue, depending on the degree of presence in the mix, relative to the visuals.

Silence

Complete silence is very rare in a soundtrack. More often than not, something described or written into a script tends to be expressed as something emotive like "eerie silence" and not actually conceived as pure silence. Silence is the total absence of sound, whereas "eerie" suggests sound design, and something *unsettling*. Silence is typically used to express the absence of dialogue, music, and key or "upfront" effects. When used "silence" can be a very effective, dynamic, and emotive storytelling device or effect. Silence (or near silence as is often the case) can make what happened before or after an event feel bigger and more dramatic, and focus the viewer/listener on the emotional dimensions of a scene.

Music

Music is either source, therefore comes from within the story world and generally from a source visible on the screen (or "diegetic"), or score, which means external to the story world (or "non-diegetic"). A composer creates a score, but a film score can also include preexisting music tracks. Music adds to the emotional quality or effect of a film, and often the most effective scores "work" below the consciousness of the viewer/listener. Most film scores are "underscore" and are used to support atmosphere, plot and narrative and/or reflect the emotional aspects of the narrative and/or characters. On the other hand, music can also drive a scene, sequence, or montage. Music can also help establish historical/period, geographical, social and cultural characteristics of a film. Scoring can involve anything from a 100-piece orchestra to a simple trio or solo instrument. Scores are recorded on scoring stages or in smaller music recording studios, depending on the arrangement and budget.

Music mixers are in charge of recording and mixing music and delivering music stems to the dub stage for final mixing. Common in film scoring is the leitmotif, a term coined to define a theme of easily recognizable melodic, rhythmic, or harmonic identity used in connection with a certain character or incident and used repeatedly, therefore reminiscent of the original association. "The Imperial March (Darth Vader's Theme)" is a classic example of a leitmotif. Thematic music is also frequently used for openings and closings, transitions and credits. Quentin Tarantino uses songs to help him find the personality and spirit of a film, and often during the concept and writing phase. Music tracks and songs are selected for their lyrical content and/or genre because they suit the situation, period, and/or character(s). Sound design can also serve as music, particularly if it involves using elements that are or were musical instruments, in the same way that musique concrète is considered a form of composition.

TIPS AND TRICKS

"Mise-en-scène" is an expression used to describe the design aspects of a film production and is often defined as the "visual theme" or "telling of a story," referring to everything that appears before the "camera" or in the frame. Sound is also part of a film's mise-en-scène because it pertains to anything in a film or story world.

The main difference between sound and image is that audiences rarely notice the soundtrack, especially sound design, unless there is a problem. Images and dialogue sit in the foreground, music primarily in background, and sound design in that "ambiguous twilight zone." People listen to music and have emotional associations with certain instruments, tempos, and rhythms. Sound affects us in the same way, but we are less aware of it when it comes to nonmusical sounds.

Considering what constitutes a soundtrack, there are many options when it comes to design, but it must to suit the story, the film's aesthetic, and engage and immerse the audience. One of the key factors in defining aural direction is questioning the overall approach to narrative design, before a script is locked. Should dialogue drive the scene and to what extent? Will dialogue capture and deliver the emotion of a scene, or should/could sound design and/or music do it better?

The Sound Department

In the media and entertainment industry, the size and scale of the sound department depends on the scale of the project and corresponding budget and schedules. Aside from production sound (location sound), there is minimal difference between live action and animation; both are storytelling mediums, with images that move and have sound. On live-action films, sound recordists record dialogue, wild takes, atmos, and room tone. On animated films, games, and many live-action films, separate recording teams specialize in sound effect recording, or the sound designer(s) working on the film will record sound effects and design material. Key creative staff include the supervising sound editor, sound editors (sound designers), and re-recording mixers. The sound department on a feature film can mass to more than thirty people, sometimes even more, and with overlapping roles. In *WALL-E* (Stanton, 2008), Ben Burtt is credited as character voice designer, sound designer, re-recording mixer, and supervising sound editor.

The Supervising Sound Editor

The first postproduction sound person brought onto a film is the supervising sound editor (or a senior sound designer), during preproduction, for creative planning and the hiring of talent. The supervising sound editor works with the director, producer, and editor and is responsible for managing the sound department. He or she coordinates sound editors, designers, Foley artists, mixers and directs the creative contributions of the postproduction sound team. The supervising sound editor also handles administrative duties like planning and monitoring the postproduction sound budget, securing equipment rental, scheduling staff, and establishing the workflow of the department. On low-budget productions, the supervising sound editor may not be hired until the final picture edit, which

is problematic, and undermines the quality and creative potential of work. In games and virtual reality film (VR), an audio director functions in much the same way as a supervising sound editor, but due to the complexity of working on games and immersive or interactive projects, the audio director is usually involved from the preproduction stage.

The Sound Editor (Dialogue, ADR, Foley, Sound Effects, Music)

A sound editor is responsible for selecting, assembling, spotting, and tracking sound in preparation for the final mix. The need for sound editing developed from the early "talkies" and over the decades has become more closely aligned with sound design, which involves sound editing. The roles of sound editor and sound designer are now interchangeable, as they both involve design. In the case of large-budget films, editors tend to specialize in a specific area: dialogue, effects, or music editing. Dialogue editors work with the dialogue recordings and/or ADR; music editors edit the music tracks; and the role of sound effect editors is usually split between the various categories of sound effects. On small projects, sound editors/designers may handle all three areas, premixing, and sometimes the final mix.

The Sound Designer

A sound designer is defined as someone who practices the art of sound design, which can range from designing individual sound or sound design effects for a film or game to a complete soundtrack. Commercial feature film soundtracks are created by a number of sound personnel, whereas an individual or a small team produces a short film or independent feature soundtrack. A sound designer conceptualizes, designs, and supervises the sound for a film in much the same way that a production designer is responsible for the look of a film. A production designer is concerned with visualizing the script's thematic, emotional, and psychological concerns. Sound designers share the same concerns. The title of sound designer in film is often interchangeable with the designation of supervising sound editor. For interactive projects such as games, the role of the sound designer is similar to the role of a film sound designer. Game sound designers create the sound effects that comprise the game soundtrack. Low-budget projects typically employ a sound designer capable of handling everything from recording to mixing.

The Re-recording Mixer

A re-recording (or dubbing) mixer mixes the dialogue, sound effects, and music premixes to create the final version of a soundtrack. The term "re-recording mixer" refers to the process of taking material that has been recorded once and recording it again. Re-recording mixers are responsible for making sure the soundtrack is both technically and stylistically "correct." During production and postproduction, sound editors, sound designers, sound engineers, and music editors assemble material ready for mixing. The first part of the re-recording process begins with the preparation of "premixes," which involves the premixing of all the separate elements into a more manageable form. Premixes can also be divided further if the mix contains a large number of sound effects; for example, the effects premix can be broken down into separate spot or Foley effects premixes. Dialogue, music, and sound effect premixes are then brought into the final mix stage. During the "final mix," the re-recording mixers combine and balance the various soundtrack elements, which involves volume automation, adding effects, and spatial positioning. In the same way there is an overlap between sound editing and sound design, re-recording mixers work with complex layers of sound, technically, editorially, and aesthetically. Re-recording mixers are usually employed by audio postproduction facilities or work on a freelance basis. On small- to medium-budget films, re-recording mixers may also work as sound editors and designers. A full-size mixing theater or dubbing stage is used for mixing feature films that are going to be released in movie theaters, which is done in consultation with mastering engineers and Dolby consultants.

TIPS AND TRICKS

Due to the confusion surrounding sound design, variations in project requirements, and the blurring of roles, it pays to engage a supervising sound editor or audio director well before a project goes into production. This is important not only in terms of clarifying and furthering creative direction, but also for practical reasons such as budgeting, scheduling, hiring of talent, and general troubleshooting.

Depending on the project, a sound designer/mixer and a composer may be all that is required. An animated film with no dialogue doesn't need voice casting, dialogue recording, or a dialogue premix/mix. A project that relies solely on sound design, or sound design and preexisting music tracks, does not require a composer. VR films are reproduced on headphones so do not need a theatrical mix.

Defining the type of film, mediums/platforms, the approach to narrative design, and the visual aesthetics by talking through the script with a sound designer, supervising sound editor, or audio director early will help ascertain specific project needs.

APPROACHES TO SOUND DESIGN

Modes of Thinking

Sound design can suggest a mood; add or withhold information; evoke a feeling; convey meaning; set a pace; indicate a geographical location; stimulate our visual imagination (or mental imagery); specify a historical period; clarify the plot; define a character; connect otherwise unconnected ideas, characters, places, images, or moments; heighten realism or diminish it; heighten ambiguity or diminish it; draw attention to a detail or away from it; signify changes in time; smooth otherwise abrupt changes between shots or scenes; emphasize transitions; describe an acoustic space; startle or soothe; and exaggerate action or mediate it. Sound can accomplish many of these functions independently (radio drama, for example), but the combining of sound and image is the power in storytelling.

While sound design relates to story and design, in the case of experimental works, a purely conceptual or thematic approach is often a more appropriate methodology. Sound can be literal and mimic what is seen on the screen. Sound can also be "internal" and mirror the subconscious or psychological dimensions of a narrative, character, or story world. Although individual sounds may not be identified as such, the mix of seemingly disparate sounds can "work" visually, conceptually, and aesthetically. The "effect" of many sounds combined can also trigger conceptual resonance. "Resonance" is a term frequently used in audio-related fields and explains the tendency of a system to oscillate with greater or enhanced amplitude at the natural frequency of the system. A more general use of the term is to describe the emotive significance of an association. While the obvious see it/hear it approach to sound design will add realism, a completely "literal" approach is not necessarily the most emotive, effective, or creative use of sound.

As soon as the sounds of the visible word, reflected by the screen, are removed from it, or that world is filled, for the sake of the image, with extraneous sounds that don't exist literally, or if the real sounds are distorted so that they no longer correspond with the image—then the film acquires a resonance. (Tarkovsky, 1989, p. 162)

A basic principle of design is materials and composition, and typically a sound designer will start with a raw sound, usually sounds, that form the "building blocks" or aural palette for the creation of sound and sound design effects. A raw sound could be the right sound or starting point, but rarely on its own or in its original state. The process of creating sound and sound design effects is similar to painting and sculpture. It involves selecting, creating, and shaping the aural palette to define the aural aesthetic of a film. Understanding the "ingredients" of a sound is akin to defining what pigments, and amounts of them, are combined to create a new paint color. Image elements have similar sound equivalents; color and hue are akin to frequency, pitch, or timbre. Sound designers are storytellers, and many have a background in visual arts so naturally draw parallels between sound and image, and communicate in narrative, visual, or emotive terms. Sound has its own distinct terminology but often parallels or has close associations with image terminology. The process of identifying, and rationale behind audio selection, can be complex. There is no right, wrong, or singular path; it is dependent on story, visual aesthetics, and emotional context. We relate to sound emotionally and subconsciously, which is why articulating how a sound effect should sound is difficult. Often it is easier to define something relative to how it should "feel." "Dark," "cold," "frightening," "light," and "warm" are words that evoke certain sound associations. Words can help trigger ideas. Most sound designers describe the process as involving imagination, experimentation, and trial and error. The audio palette is extensive and sound can be very deceiving. Sometimes a sound will not feel, sound, or look right when it could in fact be the right sound(s), but too loud, in need of equalization or pitching up or down. The envelope of the sound itself may need reshaping. When it feels right, it is right, but if it feels wrong, then it's back to the "drawing" board.

A well-known thought experiment asks this hypothetical question: If a tree falls in a forest and there is no one to hear it, does it make a sound? Objectively, the answer is yes, because a falling tree would make a sound. On the other hand, the answer could also be no. How can something exist without being perceived? Sound is only sound if someone actually hears it. The answer depends on the way the word "sound" is interpreted. Sound is used to describe a physical phenomenon and a human experience, because hearing is a mechanical phenomenon of wave propagation and a sensory-perceptual event. Most aspects of sound engineering are concerned with sound from an objective perspective, but soundtracks are created for audiences, audiences are people, and people respond to sound emotionally. If a tree is seen falling soundlessly, an audience may react negatively because they see and expect to hear something: branches cracking and splintering, and the impact of the tree hitting the ground. If there is a reason for

silence—for example, if it is being used as an *effect*, which is understood by an audience— then the reaction is likely to be positive. People are different, but there are commonalities in the way people respond to sound. So, when designing a soundtrack, if something "feels" wrong, then it probably is wrong, and will be perceived as wrong by an audience.

In film, objective sound is understood as sound that the physical world generates and is considered literal. Objective information is fact-based, observable, and measurable. Subjective sound mirrors the world inside our minds, affected by the processes of hearing and perception, and considered psychological. Subjective information is based on opinions, interpretations, and emotions. Sound designers oscillate between these two states of consciousness, which often overlap. How should something sound from a "real-world" physical, literal, and external perspective, and how could something sound from a psychological, emotional, intellectual, and internal perspective?

Real and Literal Sound

Realistic sound is sound that would logically and authentically exist in the world depicted on the screen. There are times when the real and literal sound is appropriate, for example the sound of a car arriving. But real sound is also used narratively and expressively. For example, a knock on the door is a real sound, but is it delivered with a clenched fist or a polite tap? If we're on the other side of the door, we don't see the knock, but the sound of the knock could tell us something about the person doing the knocking. Real sound can also be fabricated. In *Saving Private Ryan* (Spielberg, 1998), Gary Rydstrom scraped concrete to create squealing tank treads, with rhythms from motors for the German tanks. While not authentic, audiences and war veterans perceived the sound design as authentic. So while real and literal sound are preoccupied with authenticity and physicality, how something is designed, why, and from what is often a fabrication. In defining how something should sound from a literal perspective sound, designers think about it from a physical and objective point of view.

Perspectives on sound

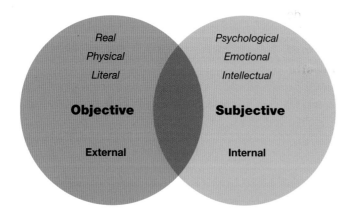

- What's it made of?
- How does it work?
- How fast/slow, big/small is it?
- What environment is it in?
- Will the audience accept/believe it?

Hyperreal and Surreal Sound

Hyperreality is described as the inability of consciousness to distinguish reality from a simulation of reality. In sound design, that takes the form of heightening or exaggerating "reality." The effect can be unsettling, can add an emotive and psychological depth, and can be used to draw the eye/ear/mind to a specific detail. When pushed to the extreme, the hyperreal can become surreal, which is often associated with nightmares, dreams, flashbacks, memories, altered states, and hallucinations. In defining how something should sound from a hyperreal perspective, sound designers think about it from a physical and beyond physical, into a more subjective and emotive, point of view.

- What should, and then what could it sound like?
- What's it made of, and do I want to exaggerate that?
- How does it work, and do I want to exaggerate that?
- How fast/slow, big/small is it, and do I want to exaggerate that?
- What environment is it in, and do I want to exaggerate that?
- What do I want the audience to accept/believe/feel/think/see?

Psychological and Emotive Sound

Psychological and emotive states can be difficult to convey and communicate in pictures alone. The combining of real, generated, and manipulated sound, from a psychological and "internal" position, can be dramatic and emotive; can set up a mood, tone, or idea; and can place the audience inside a character's head. Certain types of sounds and different frequencies evoke certain emotional responses; low frequencies suggest *danger*, *foreboding*, *doom*, *dread*, and *panic*, while higher frequencies can

suggest *pain*, *isolation*, and *anxiety*. In defining how something should sound from a psychological and emotive perspective, sound designers think about it from a narrative-emotive point of view.

- What is the character's emotional state? Why?
- What do I want the audience to think, know, or suspect?
- How do I want the audience to feel and react?

Metaphorical/Figurative Sound

The word "figurative" comes from the French word *figuratif* and is frequently associated with the "metaphorical" and relates to something that isn't intended to be understood literally. Dialogue is usually the literal and informative part of a soundtrack and music typically perceived as the emotive. Metaphors in film are usually thematic and a combination of sound and image, often reliant on the approach to picture editing techniques, primarily the juxtaposition of images and sound. Conceptual metaphors are often used to communicate emotions, abstract ideas, and "invisible states." In defining how something should sound from a metaphorical perspective, sound designers think about it from a more abstract and representational point of view.

- What are we seeing and not seeing, and what could we hear?
- What do I want the audience to think, know, or suspect?
- How do I want the audience to feel and react?

Symbolic and Subliminal Sound

Symbolic sound is generally abstract and not usually associated to a given visual; for example, the sound of thunder could suggest something bad is about to happen, even though we don't see thunder, so there's no visual reference. The sound can be low in a mix and barely discernable, to the point of subliminal. Viewers can see and separate elements in a picture, but they hear the soundtrack as a whole, despite its being constructed from many elements. Sound affects audiences subconsciously, and symbolic or subliminal sound creates an emotional involvement and/or suggests an underlying subtext.

- What is the character's emotional state? Why?
- What are we seeing and not seeing, and what could we hear?
- What do I want the audience to think, know, or suspect?
- How do I want the audience to feel and react?

There is no singular or definitive path to designing a soundtrack; real can become hyperreal and function symbolically. All "categories" are narrative, aesthetic, and emotive choices. It depends on the type and style of film. The goal is to design the film with sound and image in mind, and the question is always, what "works"? The Imperial Walkers needed mass and weight. If they were real (and not miniatures), what would they really sound like? In *Star Wars*, there is sound in space, which violates the law of physics. Objectively, sound will travel through any medium (air, water, gas), but not a vacuum, because sound needs a medium to travel. Silence can be used dramatically; however, a big, low rumble tends to feel more dramatic and emotional. In *2001: A Space Odyssey* (Kubrick, 1968), space was treated from a scientific perspective, but in discussing *Star Wars*, Lucas wanted impact and drama. He wanted the sound design to be emotionally right, as opposed to scientifically right, and adopted the position that they were using music and not justifying where the orchestra comes from, therefore did not need to justify the sound design. A slightly different approach was adopted on *Gravity* (Cuarón, 2013). Sound was designed so the audience would hear sound effects the same way the characters did. Space is silent except for when the characters are touching something and form a conduit. The

Varying approaches to sound design

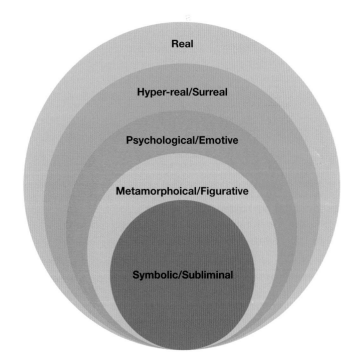

Gravity (2013, dir. Alfonso Cuarón)

simulated spacecraft, tools, and other objects needed to look and sound real, which involved recording similar types of machinery: robots that make cars at General Motors and air-conditioning units for inside the spacecraft. Guitars were submerged in water and their strings rubbed with various items, recorded with underwater and contact microphones to become the sounds for when Sandra Bullock's character is caught up in a parachute. The background radio chatter was not prewritten dialogue performed by voice actors but record-ings of a group of NASA employees.

Interesting to note is the recent debunking of the notion of silence in space. According to NASA, sound in the form of electromagnetic vibrations does exist in space, and they recently designed special instruments to record these vibrations as sound. The results are defined as complex interactions of charged electro-magnetic particles from the solar wind, ion-osphere, and planetary magnetosphere. The audible results sound like sound design tex-tures designed to emotively and dramatically accompany the corresponding visual images of planets. Planet Earth has its own eerie "voice," so the approach to sound in *Star Wars* (Lucas, 1977) might actually be more scientifically cor-rect than previously thought.

I usually first think, if these objects, places, or robots, or machines really existed, what would they sound like? How would they be powered? What would be the actual phys-ics of how they work, but if I find the sound isn't working within a scene I'll abandon the science and go with what works emotionally. (Burtt, 2008)

Design Duality—Audiovisual Synergy

Films that are held up as examples of creative sound and visual design tend to employ crea-tive audiovisual arrangements. For example, *Raging Bull* (Scorsese, 1980) is designed for the audience to "see" the world through the "eyes" of Jake LaMotta, a paranoid, possessive, violent boxer. The way the film was written and visual-ized, shot, and edited also opened the door for

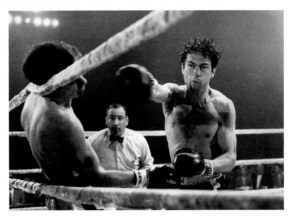

Raging Bull (1980, dir. Martin Scorsese)

hearing that world. When Jake LaMotta fights Sugar Ray Robinson, the sound design by Frank Warner combines silence, crowd noise, cheers, and groans with VO commentary, animal roars, bird shrieks, rumbles, punches, blood splatters, and gritty camera flashbulbs. The sequence is audiovisually stylized and visceral, which allows the audience to see-hear-feel the blows LaMotta delivers and receives in the ring (and outside of it). Similar techniques can be seen and heard in more recent films like *Snatch* and *Fight Club*.

As many filmmakers will agree, filmmaking is the blend of many interrelated and overlapping skills and processes. Most sound designers draw parallels between aural and visual disciplines. Sound Designer and Director, Gary Rydstrom likens sound design to production design and art direction, and sound mixing to cinematography and picture editing. There is a constructively "fluid" relationship between sound design and picture editing. On *Attack of the Clones* (Lucas, 2002), Ben Burtt was the sound designer and picture editor, working on both sound and pic-ture simultaneously. During picture editing, he got ideas for sound effects and made sure the pictures allowed sound ideas to be integrated. He spent a few hours to a few days working on sound design and then edited those designs with the pictures. Conversely, adding sound gave him ideas for picture edits. The process of working back and forth, between sound and image, also meant he was not distracted by sound that was unrealistic or lacked credibility.

I learned over many years of sound how to enhance drama with layers of sound. Now as a picture editor, I am asked to enhance drama with layers of images. The process of building up a complete dramatic sensation with sound is the same one I apply to picture editing. The key element in filmmaking is the juxtaposition of sound and picture elements to produce a desired emotional response in the audience. (Burtt, n.d.)

Thinking and working audiovisually is beneficial on a number of different levels. Ben Burtt adopted a similar approach to sound design and workflow on *WALL-E* (Stanton, 2008) by working alongside the visual artists. Burtt created voice and sound effect sets as auditions for Andrew Stanton, followed by montages from selected material. Sound design started early and developed through the use of rough reels and to a level that would normally occur in postproduction. Stanton wanted speech and sound effects to feel like they were coming

from their functions as machines, either a chip on board that synthesized the voice or a sound effect like the squeak of a motor to indicate how a character was feeling. Burtt blended human and synthesized elements to create their "voices" in a similar way to how he created R2-D2. He also drew from his experience designing sound effects for *Star Wars* in the creation of other effects. Striking a very long slinky made the sound of EVE's laser. The howling wind of Earth at the beginning of the film is a recording of Niagara Falls, reverb, with some feedback and filtering. WALL-E is "low tech" (analogue), therefore a combination of motors, squeaks, and metallic sounds, while EVE is "high tech" (digital), therefore a combination of more synthesized and sleek sounds. Burtt is the voice of WALL-E, Elissa Knight is EVE, Sigourney Weaver is the ship's computer, and the Macintosh text-to-speech engine "MacInTalk" is the voice of AUTO. The robots speak in sound effects and processed word fragments. Subtle aural-visual intonations add layers of meaning, which communicate character, story, and emotion. A mixture of song and score from composer Thomas Newman enhances the film's distinct narrative aesthetic.

TIPS AND TRICKS

There is no definitive path to designing a soundtrack, but there are parallels with visual disciplines, and part of the sound designer's skill set is the ability to visualize. While it isn't common to be working on both sound and picture simultaneously, *thinking* about sound and picture simultaneously will generate ideas that can then be incorporated into a script.

Sound is editorial; it affects story, but sound design involves more than just determining what to hear and when; it also shapes the emotional content of a scene. How something should sound from a "real-world"

perspective could be relatively obvious. How something should sound from a psychological, intellectual, and emotional perspective tends to involve a lot more trial and error.

The audio palette is extensive and the possibilities endless. Having a good understanding of the narrative and the intended aesthetics is vital, but emotional responses also come into play. It's important to talk about sound and picture, and it's important to experiment and try different things. Having meaningful conversations and exchanges is how creative collaborations evolve.

THE SOUND DESIGNER'S TOOL KIT

Sound as a Medium

Audio theory is often thought of as abstract and overly technical, but there are a few core principles that need to be realized in order to understand sound design within the wider context of recording, editing, processing, and mixing. Sound is both art and science. Most film sound designers have a background in engineering, music, film, design, but the core concern is always story. The material sound designers work with is sound, while conceptual ideas define approaches to sound design. Like in other design disciplines, tools are meaningless without a designer and a design concept. It helps to have a good understanding of the different film disciplines, but it's incredibly rare for a director to be well versed in all areas. Directors need to be good at communicating what they're trying to achieve and collaborating with people who can deliver that in their own particular craft.

One of the main reasons audio theory appears complex is because of the language involved. However, certain expressions and terms often mean the same, or a similar thing, just from a different perspective. A sound with a high "pitch" is a sound with high "frequencies." "Pitch" is a subjective term, whereas "frequency" is an objective term. The difficulty in understanding sound as a medium is also due to its invisibility. Pictures we can see. Anything that moves has a vibration, and although invisible, the material world is constantly moving. Motion creates frequency, and while sometimes inaudible, frequencies make sound, and sounds resonate and affect one another.

Sound as Waves
Sound is often described as mechanical vibrations, or longitudinal waves transmitted by an elastic medium and defined by their frequency and amplitude. Sound is produced when an object (the source) vibrates and creates a disturbance in the surrounding medium. When a piano key is hit, the movement of the string disturbs the surrounding medium, which is air, and displaces the molecules within the air. A sound source can be anything: the vocal cords of a person talking, the diaphragm of an audio speaker, or the slamming of a door. Each particle of a medium is set in a back-and-forth motion, which propagates to neighboring particles. Energy is transferred from one molecule to the next until the energy created by the initial displacement decreases. Sound takes the form of waves, which are measured in cycles per second (hertz, or Hz). This periodicity is rhythmic, and each cycle of a wave can be thought of as a pulse of sound. A common analogy used for visualizing sound waves is the waves produced by dropping a stone in pool of water.

Visualizing sound waves

"Sound propagation" is the term commonly used to describe the process of passing sound energy as a series of compressions and rarefactions, which is air pressure above and below normal atmospheric pressure. The compressions (or depressions) are defined as peaks (+, an increase above normal atmospheric pressure), and the rarefactions are defined as troughs (-, a decrease below normal atmospheric pressure). The behavior of each particle is described by a sinusoid (sine wave) that maps the cyclical pattern against time. The speed of a wave is defined as the distance that a point on a wave (such as a compression or a rarefaction) travels per unit of time. It is often expressed in units of meters per second (abbreviated m/s) and depends on the properties of the medium through which the wave is traveling. The speed (or velocity) of a sound wave in air depends upon the properties of the air, mostly the temperature.

The amplitude (or intensity) of a wave is the maximum disturbance from its undisturbed position, which the human ear interprets as volume or loudness. The decibel (dB) is the unit used to measure the intensity of a sound. The dB scale is logarithmic, like the way the human ear perceives changes in sound pressure. The frequency of a wave is the number of waves each second and is measured as the number of complete back-and-forth vibrations or cycles. The unit for frequency is the hertz (Hz), and one hertz equals one cycle per second. If a particle of air undergoes 1,000 longitudinal vibrations in two seconds, then the frequency of the wave would be 500 vibrations per second, or 500 Hz. Frequency is directly related to wavelength and represented by the Greek lambda (λ). The wavelength is the distance required to complete a full cycle.

The sensation of a frequency is commonly referred to as the "pitch" of a sound. A high-pitch sound corresponds to a high-frequency sound wave and a low-pitch sound corresponds to a low-frequency sound wave. Sounds contain energy in different frequency ranges, or bands. If a sound has a lot of low-frequency energy, it is described as having a lot of "bass" or "bottom-end". The 250 Hz to 4,000 Hz frequency band, where humans hear best, is described as midrange. High-frequency energy above the midrange is sometimes called "treble". The simplest kind of sound wave is the sine wave and is known as a pure tone, a single frequency without harmonics or overtones. Pure sine waves rarely exist in the natural world, but they are useful for demonstrating the fundamental characteristics of a sound wave.

Sound as Frequency and Pitch

The human ear is capable of detecting sound waves with a wide range of frequencies, approximately 20 Hz to 20,000 Hz (or 20 kHz) and associates frequency with the pitch of a sound. The upper hearing limit tends to decrease with age, so most adults are unable to hear above 16 kHz. The ear itself does not respond to frequencies below 20 Hz, but they are *perceived* via the body's sense of touch. We *feel* them. Any sound with a frequency below the audible range of hearing (less than 20 Hz) is known as an infra-sound, and any sound with a frequency above the audible range of hearing (more than 20 kHz) is known as an ultrasound.

The human ear-brain system is nonlinear so not equally sensitive to all frequencies. We don't hear low and very high frequencies as well as we hear mid frequencies. We perceive higher frequencies as louder because we are more sensitive to them, and lower frequencies as quieter because we are less sensitive to them. Because we are nonlinear, to perceive 20 Hz (a low-frequency sound) as loud as 1 kHz (a high-frequency sound), the 20 Hz sound must be louder. We "amplify" sounds with frequencies in the range from 1,000 Hz to 5,000 Hz (1–5 kHz), which is why sounds in this range seem louder even when technically (objectively and scientifically) they are not. The high-sensitivity region around 2,000 to 5,000 Hz is important for the under- standing of speech, therefore dialogue in a film. The peak sensitivity of the ear is around 3,500 to 4,000 Hz and associated with the resonance of the auditory canal.

All audio equipment comes with a frequency response chart or graph, which details the audio capabilities or frequency response of a given device. A loudspeaker's frequency response specifications describe the range of frequencies a speaker can reproduce. The ideal loudspeaker will have a "flat frequency response," which means it reproduces all frequencies equally, without changing or coloring the sound in any way, so no frequencies are exaggerated or reduced. This is especially important for the monitoring and mixing of sound. A typical frequency response graph has frequency plotted along an X-axis (typically 20 Hz to 20 kHz because it is the range of human hearing) and amplitude or volume (dB) represented on the Y-axis. Microphones also have different frequency responses, which is why microphone selection is important for different sound sources, recording applications, and situations. A microphone that emphasizes certain frequencies in the human voice is suitable for recording dialogue, particularly when recording in noisy environments. The range of 3,000 to 7,000 Hz (or 3–7 kHz) is important for intelligibility of speech.

Any sound of finite length can be seen as a sum of sine waves, each with its own frequency, phase, and amplitude. If we could see sound, it would look like air molecules moving back and forth very quickly, but when we hear sound, we're experiencing sound in terms of its frequencies. Fourier transforms (FTs) take a signal and express it in terms of the frequencies of the waves that make up the signal. Sound can be "seen" throughout the various design and postproduction stages by using audio software or plug-ins, typically a frequency or spectrum analyzer, which depicts the frequency spread and corresponding levels. As with frequency response graphs, frequency is plotted along the X-axis at the bottom and intensity (dB) is represented on the Y-axis.

Seeing sound—frequency analysis on Waves' PAZ analyzer and iZotope, Inc.'s metering suite, Insight (www.izotope.com)

Equalization

Equalization (EQ) is one of the most common tools sound designers and mixers use to manipulate sound. EQ alters the quality and character of sound, either by boosting (increasing) or reducing (attenuating) the level of different frequencies. Sound designers use EQs to alter and color sound, whereas mixers use EQs to shape and control a mix. If a sound effect feels "too bright," chances are there is too much energy in the 7,000 to 14,000 Hz range, so reducing frequencies in that range will "soften" the sound effect. The human voice is mostly in the 250 Hz to 4 kHz range, so if the dialogue in a film is difficult to hear, the solution could be reducing the midrange frequencies of the non-dialogue material to create a "sonic space," allowing the dialogue to be heard more easily.

There are different types of equalizers that function differently. A basic three-band equalizer divides the frequency bands into low/bass (low range), mid (middle range), and high/treble (high range). A parametric equalizer allows control over several separate frequency bands. A graphic equalizer allows the user to "interface" graphically and control a number of different frequency bands. A paragraphic equalizer combines the user interface of a graphic equalizer with the functionality of a parametric. Digital

audio workstations (DAWs) generally come with a number of different EQ plug-ins, which can also be purchased as separate plug-ins.

Equalizers use different types of filters to alter frequencies. Common filters include the low pass filter (LPF), which attenuates frequencies above a certain frequency, allowing low frequencies to pass. A high pass filter (HPF) attenuates frequencies below a certain frequency, which means it allows high frequencies to pass. A notch filter attenuates or accentuates a narrow frequency band, whereas a band-pass filter passes frequencies within a certain range and attenuates frequencies outside that range. EQs also have a frequency control, which allows the user to select the center frequency area to be altered, and a "Q" control, which allows the user to alter the bandwidth of the frequencies to be reduced or boosted, which is the range on either side of the center frequency.

Pitch Shifting

Pitch shifting is another common technique in sound design, which raises or lowers the pitch

Paragraphic EQ
(Waves Q10)

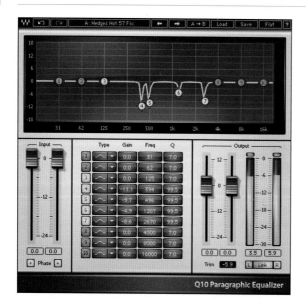

Common audio
filters

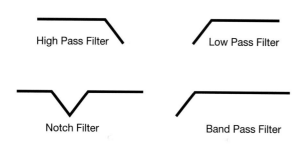

Pitch and time shifters (Waves'
Graphic SoundShifter / Avid
Technology's x-form)

of a sound. The simplest method increases pitch and reduces duration, or vice versa, lowers pitch and increases duration, but you can also pitch shift and retain the same duration of the original sound. Pitch shifting was accomplished on early reel-to-reel tape machines by changing the diameter of the capstan drive shaft or using a different motor. As technologies improved, "vari-speed" capstan motors allowed the speed change to be achieved more easily. Placing a finger on the turntable to retard it or giving it a "spin" to advance it achieves the same effect. Pitch and time shifters are a staple in the sound designer's tool kit and are used to alter and create different sounds.

Sound as Timbre

Musical instruments produce a range of frequencies that correspond to notes on the musical scale: A above middle C is 440 Hz, the next A is 880 Hz, and the previous is 220 Hz. A doubling of frequency is an octave. The first vibration is the fundamental and is usually the lowest, strongest part of the sound wave. It determines pitch and subsequent vibrations, which are generally higher and softer and known as harmonics. Harmonics are whole multiples of the fundamental frequency. So, if the fundamental frequency is 100 Hz, the harmonics will be 200 Hz, 300 Hz, 400 Hz, 500 Hz, and so on. These are not perceived as distinct pitches or separate tones, but as the timbre (or tone or color), which allows the ear to distinguish one instrument or voice from another, even when both are playing the same note at the same level. Some musical sound sources have overtones, which may or may not be harmonics of the fundamental. The term "overtone" refers to any resonant frequency: a natural frequency of vibration determined by the physical parameters of the vibrating object, above the fundamental frequency.

Musical sounds are more easily defined and "classified" than nonmusical sounds such as sound effects, which are many and varied and structurally complex. However, like musical sounds or notes, the combination of frequencies, or frequency spectrum, contributes to the timbre or tonal quality. Timbre is frequently described as the color, tone, or "feel" of a sound and characterizes emotional interpretations or responses to a sound. Timbre is also described with words such as "bright," "dark," "warm," and "harsh." When a sound feels "wrong," it could be because the sound is too bright/dark, too warm/cold, or too soft/harsh. Perceptual aspects that are often thought of as independent, such as timbre, volume, and pitch, are interrelated. If a sound feels "too harsh," it's often because of its level and/or specific frequencies. The envelope of the sound also determines timbre, which means "harshness" can relate to volume over time. A sound may have an *abrasive* "attack," and because of that it feels (and sounds) "too harsh." Altering a sound's envelope will change the "form" or "shape" of a sound.

Sound as an Envelope

In addition to overall volume, sounds have a "volume envelope," which is the rising and falling of volume over time. The envelope is defined as the amplitude structure of a sound, how the sound "fits" inside its envelope, which is what Pierre Schaeffer was experimenting with in his early work. He discovered that manipulating volume changes over time could alter sounds dramatically; musical sounds could become sound effects, or sound design effects and textures, and vice versa. Volume automation and fades are also used to manipulate a sound's envelope, and in sound synthesis, envelope generators are used to control and shape a sound's parameters. Some synthesizers add a "hold" stage between the attack and decay stages and are known as attack hold decay sustain release (AHDSR) envelope generators. Most commonly this is called an attack decay sustain release (ADSR) envelope. A rapid increase in loudness is the "attack," a subsequent fall in loudness is the "decay," the period during which the loudness remains relatively constant is the "sustain," and the period during which the loudness falls to zero is the "release."

Sound as Intensity, Amplitude, and Loudness

Amplitude is an objective and quantifiable measurement of the degree of change (positive or negative) in atmospheric pressure (the compression and rarefaction of air molecules) caused by sound waves. Intensity is amplitude over time, over an area, whereas loudness refers to the human perception of amplitude and intensity. A high-amplitude wave carries a large amount of energy; a low-amplitude wave carries a small amount of energy. As the amplitude of the sound wave increases, the intensity of the sound increases.

Shaping sound—iZotope's sample-based synthesizer Iris (www.izotope.com)

Sounds with higher intensities are perceived to be louder. Since the range of intensities that the human ear can detect is so large, the decibel (dB) scale, which is based on powers of ten, is used to measure intensity. The threshold of hearing is the faintest sound that a human ear can detect and is assigned a sound level of 0 dBSPL (sound pressure level). A sound that is ten times more intense is assigned a sound level of 10 dBSPL. A sound that is 100 times more intense is assigned a sound level of 20 dBSPL, and a sound that is 1,000 times more intense is assigned a sound level of 30 dBSPL.

The intensity of a signal can be measured, but loudness is subjective; it's perceptual, and perceptions vary between people and over time. Even the measuring of sound is not an exact or perfect science because there are so many factors involved. The mathematical relationship between intensity and distance is referred to as obeying the inverse square law. The intensity varies inversely with the square of the distance from the source. So if the distance from the source is doubled, the sound pressure is halved and results in a 6 dBSPL decrease. As waves expand, the sound pressure spreads over a larger area, which is why the farther you are away from a sound source, the quieter it sounds. This is only an approximation, as it assumes equal sound propagation in all directions in a "free field," whereas in the real world there are walls, reflective surfaces, obstacles, or barriers. Nonetheless, this is why the farther you move away from a sound source, the quieter it becomes, and why you would expect an audio "event" in the distance or background of a scene to be quieter than if it occurred in the foreground.

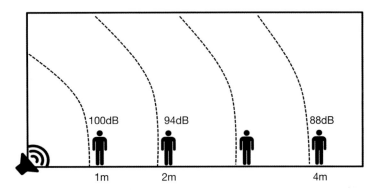

Inverse square
law

Phase

Phase denotes a particular point in the cycle of a waveform, measured as an angle in degrees, from 0 to 360, and compares the timing relationship between sound waves. At 0 degrees, two sounds are exactly in sync. When the time relationship is coincident, the sounds or signals are "in phase" and their amplitudes are additive, which makes an even stronger result. This is called constructive interference. At 180 degrees, the time relationship is not coincident; the sounds or signals are "out of phase," and their amplitudes are subtractive and cancel each other out, resulting in little or no sound. This is known as phase cancellation or destructive interference.

Phase cancellation can be a problem when recording and mixing very similar audio signals together, or when original and reflected sound waves interact. The resulting frequency cancellations depend on both the relative amplitude and phase of each wave. The amplitude of the

Phase
relationships

reflected signal (and phase rotation) varies according to the distance traveled by the wave, the wavelength, the angle of incidence with each reflective surface, and the absorbent nature of the room. Recording the same source with more than one microphone can cause phase-cancellation problems if the microphones are at different distances from the sound source. Even when recording with one microphone, phase cancellations can occur, because sound reflects from surfaces such as walls. In real-world environments, constructive and destructive interference occurs constantly, which alters the timbre of a sound. Production sound recordists and studio engineers are very aware of phase issues and will adjust microphones accordingly. Phase interactions are mostly known for destructively interfering with recorded signals, but they can also be used practically and creatively. Active noise-cancelling headphones employ the same principle through the addition of a miniature microphone in the earpiece that picks up ambient noise (such as traffic, AC). Noise-canceling circuitry creates a noise-cancelling wave that is 180 degrees out of phase with the ambient noise, which cancels it out.

Another effect of the ear's nonlinear response is that sounds that are close in frequency produce phantom "beats." When two sound waves of different frequency approach the ear, alternating constructive and destructive interference cause the sound to be alternatively soft and loud. Two sounds with a small difference in frequency may be perceived as a single sound, but as the waves evolve, they move slightly in and out of phase with each other, producing a pulsation of amplitude, which is known as "beating."

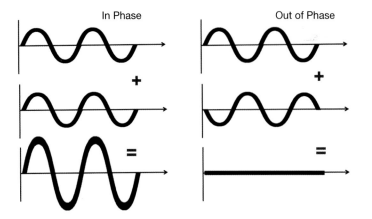

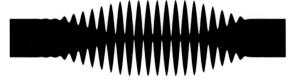

Beating

"Comb filtering" is the term used to describe what's happening when a sound is combined with a delayed version of itself, and the resulting cancellations of frequencies due to timing differences. Flanging is an effect produced by mixing two identical signals together. One signal is delayed by a small and gradually changing period, usually smaller than twenty milliseconds. This produces a swept comb filter effect: Peaks and notches are produced in the resulting frequency spectrum dependent on the duration of the delay. The term "flanging" comes from early methods of producing the effect by running two identical copies of the same recording on analogue recorders (usually in mono) and then summing the two outputs together via a mixer at exactly the same levels. The two recordings start together, but the speed of one of the machines is slowed slightly by using hand pressure on the tape reel to produce a comb filtering effect. Whichever machine is leading is then slowed down so that the delay decreases until the point where the other machine takes

Waves' Meta Flanger

the lead, so the two recordings drift in and out of phase with each other. One of the most common uses for these types of effects is in designing "robot" or synthetic-sounding voices and sound effects. Flanging tends to sound "metallic," and robots usually look metallic.

TIPS AND TRICKS

A sound in a film can have little or no relevance to its components, origins, or even the corresponding image. While this makes defining sound design and what exactly makes up a soundtrack difficult, it also provides tremendous scope for creating new sounds from raw recordings. In sound design, equalizers, filters and pitch shifters are some of the most common tools used to manipulate, alter, and "color" sound.

Frequency is the number of waves or vibrations produced by a source each second (an objective term), whereas pitch is the human ear's perception of frequency (a subjective term). So, the perceived pitch of a sound is our ear/mind's subjective interpretation of its frequency. In terms of communicating, most people will use the term

"pitch" (high-pitched/low-pitched) or describe something as too "sharp" or too "high" or too "bright," which is understood as another way of saying the pitch is too high, meaning the higher frequencies are either too pronounced or too loud.

Sounds interact with other sounds in unusual and unexpected ways. When layering two similar sounds, most people expect a "bigger" result, which is the case if the two sounds are exactly the same—the same frequency and amplitude. However, layering similar sound effects such as two explosions may not result in a bigger or louder sounding explosion. Layering a second explosion to a lower frequency explosion that has more "attack" and mid to higher frequencies will.

Sound as a Place

In addition to having parallels with visual design, sound design also has a connection with architecture. Creating soundtracks is a type of sonic architecture because it also involves the consideration and design of spaces. All spaces modify the sounds that occur within them, and sound can both physically and emotively define a space.

Sound tends to come in the back door, or sometimes even sneak in through the windows or through the floorboards. Remember, the ears point out the side of your head and take in a 360-degree spherical field. And while you're busy answering the front door, sound is sneaking in the back door. It's in the house as much as anyone who came in through the front door, but you're not as aware of it, and so its presence is more of a conditional presence—it tends to condition the things you are consciously aware of. The strange thing is that you take the emotional treatment that sound is giving, and you allow that to actually change how you see the image. You see a different image when it has been emotionally conditioned by the sound. So sometimes you will swear that you actually saw something that never, ever happened on the screen or in the soundtrack, but is the unique combination of the two inside your head. Also, for some reason that I don't fully understand, I am very emotionally moved by the space around a sound. I almost think that sometimes I am recording space with a sound in it, rather than sound in a space. (Walter Murch, n.d.)

Sound waves "spread" in unusual ways; they reflect off and diffract (bend) around obstacles, and they can also be absorbed by and transmitted into an obstacle or a new medium. Sound's behaviors inform us in a number of ways. Most people can roughly identify a space from listening to a recording. A hand clap recorded in a small bathroom will sound different from the same sound recorded in a large cathedral. Viewers/listeners can detect a sound and room reverb that doesn't correspond with the visuals. Understanding how sound behaves in a given space, and our perceptions of sound in spaces is necessary for recording, designing, and mixing soundtracks.

Reverb is another staple in the sound designer's tool kit and is defined as the perception of closely spaced and random multiple "echoes" reflected from one boundary to another within a determined space. In a reverberant environment, there is a long, diffuse sound tail consisting of all the late echoes interacting with each other, bouncing off surfaces, and slowly fading away. The more we hear the direct sound, in comparison to the later reverberations, the closer we assume something is. ADR (and most sound and Foley effects) are recorded "dry," (in an acoustically treated studio) and reverb is added to place dialogue and effects into a specific visual/acoustic space. Without the room reverb, and the right reverb, the dialogue and effects feel unnatural. Reverb gives us cues as to the size, density, and nature of a space and can be broken down into a number of components, which correspond with reverb plug-in parameters.

- The *direct* signal is the point at which the listener receives the original sound wave.
- Pre-delay is the delay between the original sound and the onset of the early reflections; large halls have long pre-delays, while small bathrooms have short pre-delays.
- *Early reflections* are the first few reflections from major boundaries within a determined space. Time elapsed between direct sound and early reflections tells us the size of the room; the farther the surfaces are away, the longer it takes for sound to reach and reflect back to us.
- Lower *reverb densities* give more space between the reverb's individual reflections; this would be the case in larger rooms and halls where walls are farther from each other. Higher densities place these reflections closer together, as would occur in smaller spaces.
- *Reverberations* are the last set of signal reflections that make up the reverb characteristic, the many random reflections that

travel from boundary to boundary in a room. They are closely spaced, so the brain cannot discern individual reflections and perceives a single decaying signal.

- *Diffusion* is sound energy spread in a given environment and relates to how flat or diffusive the walls of a room are. Increasing diffusion randomizes the reflections within the reverb tail, producing a smoother decay, whereas reducing diffusion produces a sound that tends more toward individual echoes.

Factors that affect a room's reverberation time include the size and shape of the enclosure as well as the materials used in the construction of the room. The initial time delay between the direct sound and the first reflected sound, and the initial reverberation consisting of the first few reflections, are very important in the perception of the acoustical quality of a room. Most reverb plug-ins will feature the same parameters (to a greater or lesser extent) and include an equalizer to filter the sound for a given room environment. Low-frequency reverb times will be longer, and high frequencies will be more diminished (especially in very large rooms). This is also known as "reverb damping," as higher frequencies are attenuated faster in large rooms.

Convolution reverb is a process for simulating the reverberation of a physical space by using an audio sample (impulse response) of the actual (real) space to model more natural sounding reverb. In live-action shoots, the production sound mixer can record impulse responses (IRs) of each location so that they can be used in postproduction for more accurate processing of ADR, Foley, and effects.

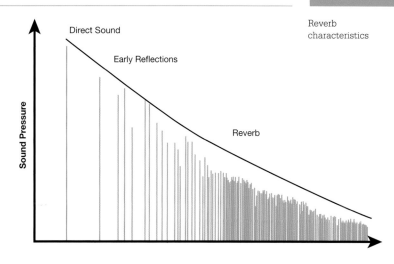

Reverb characteristics

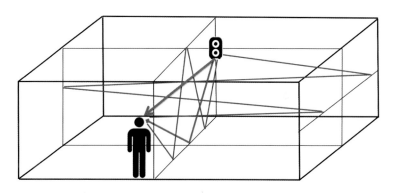

Perception of Space

The ear and brain combine to perceive distance and a sense of acoustic space when a sound occurs. When a sound is generated, it propagates away from the source in all directions. In nature, sound travels out from its source, diminishing in

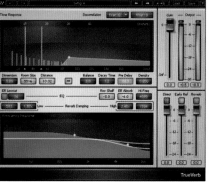

Reverb plug-ins—Waves' TrueVerb and Audio Ease's Altiverb Convolution Reverb

amplitude according to the inverse square law. The wave that travels in a straight line arrives first (the direct sound), whereas reflected sound travels farther (longer path lengths), so the ear hears the sound even after the source stops.

All surfaces absorb some energy, reflecting the remainder back into the space. Highly reflective surfaces absorb less of the wave energy, so the sound persists longer, and highly absorptive surfaces dissipate the wave energy. The amount being reflected or absorbed is determined by the physical properties and shape of surface materials. A hard surface will reflect most of the sound energy, whereas a soft or textured surface will absorb more of the energy. Irregularly shaped rooms will scatter reflections rather than reflecting them in a specific direction. So, the nature of reverb tells us a lot about the size, physicality, and design of a space.

Perception of Direction

We have two ears, but we can locate sounds in three dimensions because the brain, inner ear, and pinna work together to interpret a sound's location. The ability to localize sound sources is believed to have developed as an evolutionary necessity. Vision is limited, but we hear in all directions and in the dark. One ear cannot determine the direction a sound source originates from, but two ears can. This is called binaural localization and works by comparing the signals received by each ear. The term "binaural" means relating to two ears, and binaural recordings are recordings made specifically for listening to on headphones rather than loudspeakers. Recordings are made by placing two microphones in ear-like cavities on either side of a dummy head. The dummy head emulates the density and shape of a human head, so the microphones capture sound as human ears would hear it. The effect or illusion is three-dimensional audio. When reproduced through headphones the left earpiece of a pair of headphones is only audible to the left ear, whereas the left loudspeaker of a conventional stereo pair is audible to both ears, with a slight time delay and loudness difference.

People have been making binaural recordings for decades, but they were originally perceived as something of a novelty. The interest in binaural recordings has resurfaced due to VR (virtual reality). VR headsets integrate binaural technology with head tracking for complete audiovisual immersion.

Laterally localizing a sound is fairly easy because when a sound is closer to the left, the left ear hears it before the right ear hears it, and it sounds louder. When distance to each ear is the same, there are no differences in time or level and the sound is more centered. We can localize a sound based on the delay between the sound's arrival in both ears, which is called interaural time difference (ITD), and the difference in the sound's volume level in both ears, which is called interaural level difference (ILD).

Interaural time difference (ITD)—the difference in arrival time of a sound between two ears. When distance to each ear is the same, there are no differences in time, but when a source is to the side of the listener, the times will differ.

Interaural level difference (ILD)—level differences are frequency dependent and increase with increasing frequency. High-frequency sounds cannot diffract efficiently around a listener's head, which blocks acoustic energy and therefore produces interpretable intensity level differences. This difference is relatively insignificant at lower frequencies as wavelengths are larger (compared to the head) and therefore bend easily, but as the path is longer, the sound pressure sensed by the left ear is later and understood as a time difference. Sounds below a certain frequency (around 800 Hz) are harder to distinguish based on level differences. So, for low frequencies, ITD dominates judgment, and for high frequencies, ILD dominates judgment. There is a transitional zone between 800 Hz and 1500 Hz in which both are used for localization.

Front versus back localization is more difficult, and our brain uses spectral modifications of sounds caused by the head and body. Sounds from the front produce resonances created by the interior of the pinna, while sounds from the back are shadowed by the pinna. Sounds from above reflect off the shoulders, whereas the torso and shoulders shadow sounds from below. These reflections and shadowing create what is called a "direction selective filter" and underpin 3D sound spatialization techniques. Head motion also assists with localization; turning the head helps resolve any front/back ambiguities by making them lateral localization problems, which are easier to deal with.

Distance Localization

ILD, ITD, and head-related transfer function (HRTF) help determine the direction of a sound source, but to determine distance, we use a combination of factors, including volume, initial time delay, ratio of direct sound to reverberant sound, and motion parallax. Loudness is the most obvious distance cue, and for familiar sounds we are quite good at judging distance, but unfamiliar sounds can be misleading. Initial time delay describes the interval between the direct sound and its first reflection. The longer this gap, the closer we assume we are to the sound source. Motion parallax is a depth perception cue. Objects that are closer to you appear to move faster than objects that are farther away from you. So, if a sound source travels quickly relative to a stationary perspective, we perceive that sound as coming from nearby. High frequencies attenuate faster than low frequencies, so we also detect distance based on how attenuated those high frequencies are relative to the source.

Areas such as games, surround sound, and VR require a good understanding of sound spatialization, localization, and psychoacoustics. Psychoacoustics is a field in itself, and is defined as the study of sound perception; psychological and physiological responses associated with sound, and takes into account that both the ear and the brain are involved in the listening experience. In VR and 3D game audio HRTF algorithms mimic the effects of the pinna, the head, and listening environments to create immersive, realistic, 3D audio experiences through stereo headphones.

TIPS AND TRICKS

Different environments alter the sounds that occur in them, so having a good "sense of space" is important on two fronts. First, you want to record material as "clean" as possible, which means addressing any acoustic issues on set. Second, it can be difficult to get good production sound, so dialogue, Foley, and effects are rerecorded "clean", reverb is added where appropriate and individual sounds are treated spatially. In animation and games there is no shoot (principal photography), so everything needs to be treated to sit in the right visual-acoustical space.

The cinematic experience is largely aural. Most people, whether aware of it or not, go to the movies to experience a "big" or dramatic soundtrack. We say we're going to "see" a movie, but we're also going to hear it, and the more immersive the soundtrack, the greater the experience. In VR filmmaking consideration of space is paramount for creating immersive experiences. 3D audio immerses the user in a "virtual space," and individual elements anchor the user in that space.

As Walter Murch identified, people are also emotionally moved by the space around a sound. While space and treatment of sound in a space is too often considered "technical," think about how the visual aspects of your story world could influence the emotive-narrative dimensions of your film, and how that might "translate" sonically. Place your character/s in your story world, what do they hear?

Capturing Sound

Sound recording is like cinematography: A cinematographer needs to have a good eye, and a sound recordist needs a good ear (and eye). Cinematographers understand lenses in the same way sound recordists understand microphones. A cinematographer needs to be able to frame and recognize good shots; a sound recordist needs to be able to recognize and "frame" good sound. Understanding lighting is like understanding acoustics. Overexposure occurs when too much light is reflected into the camera, rendering an image that is brighter than normal exposure. Underexposure is the opposite. Checking exposure is analogous to checking sound levels. Light meters are used to help determine the exposure and were a necessity in early film because until the film was developed, nobody could be sure if the exposure was correct. With digital cameras, you can see the image in real time, and most cameras have light meters. Audio metering is just as important, and the much the same, except we can't see sound, which makes it more difficult to monitor.

Digital Audio Fundamentals

To understand sound recording requires a basic knowledge of digital audio. Pulse-code modulation (PCM) is the main method used to digitally represent analogue signals and was invented in 1937 by British scientist Alec Reeves. Reeves wanted to make higher-frequency radios that could carry several calls at the same time, but he found that they interfered with each other. He discovered that converting these waves, analogue representations of speech, into a digital form helped eliminate interference. However, due to limitations of technology at the time, there was no way of converting the digital signal back to an analogue signal for reproduction. Digital recording is data intensive so was somewhat impractical until the invention of the microprocessor. Nagra-brand tape recorders were the standard sound recording system for film production from the 1960s until the 1990s. During the 1990s, digital audio tape (DAT) recorders became reliable

enough to use in the field, and around the same time, Nagra released a four-channel PCM digital audio recorder.

A PCM stream has two basic elements that determine the fidelity of the original analogue signal being recorded. The sampling rate (or frequency) is the number of times per second that samples are taken, and the bit rate/depth determines the number of possible digital values that can be used to represent each sample. Common sampling frequencies are 48 kHz and 44.1 kHz, 44.1 kHz is the standard for compact discs (CDs), and 48 kHz the base standard for moving image and broadcast audio. Sampling is the method of converting an analogue signal to digital data— essentially the reduction of a continuous signal to a discrete signal. A useful analogy is animation; the human eye is fooled into seeing "lifelike" moving images when a succession of still images are presented at 24 or 25 frames per second (fps). Digital sampling takes snapshots (samples) of information at quick and regular intervals to recreate a constant waveform, a continuous line of information, which is represented numerically by a digital system at specified points in time. Subsequently, the quality of a digital recording increases with the number of samples taken.

The Nyquist theorem, also known as the sampling theorem, is the principle that underpins the digitization of audio. For analogue-to-digital conversion (ADC) to result in a faithful reproduction of the original waveform, samples must be taken frequently, at least twice the highest frequency contained in the original signal. If the sampling rate is less, some of the highest-frequency components in the analogue input signal will not be correctly represented in the digitized output. When a digital signal is converted back to analogue form by a digital-to-analogue converter (DAC), false frequency components can appear that were not in the original signal and result in a form of distortion called aliasing. As few people can hear above 20 kHz, the sampling rate for digital audio needs to be a least twice that frequency, or 40 kHz, hence the standard audio CD rate of 44.1 kHz. Dynamic range, the difference between the loudest sound and the quietest sound, is often described as a ratio and commonly notated in decibels. The human ear can perceive sound amplitude between 0 dB and 140 dB sound pressure level (SPL), which means the dynamic range of human hearing is roughly 140 dB. If a music track ranges between 10 and 100 dB SPL, then it yields a dynamic range of about 90 dB. Recordings at 16-bit resolution have a theoretical dynamic range of 98 dB, and 24-bit a dynamic range of 120 dB. Bit and sample rates are often debated. If the typical frequency range of human hearing is 20 Hz to 20 kHz, then why record at higher sample rates if nobody can hear it anyway? For most trained ears, there is actually an audible difference between rates. Additionally, the greater the dynamic range is, the lower the noise floor, which allows for the recording of very quiet passages without introducing any resolution-related noise. If you're down sampling and file converting, say in the case of creating/implementing game sound effects it's better to record raw material at a high/er sample/bit rate. Perceived quality is also influenced by other factors, such as the listening environment (ambient noise), hardware, software and audio equipment (such as sound cards, speakers, and headphones).

The PCM process includes three steps: sampling, quantization, and coding. The original signal is sampled to produce corresponding pulses and then quantized, which means a value from a given set of values is assigned to each sample of the discrete signal. The quantized forms of the samples are then converted to binary digits and are outputted in the form of 1's and 0's. Quantization errors occur when a digital audio sample does not exactly match the analogue signal strength it is supposed to represent (in other words, the digital audio sample is slightly higher or lower than the analogue signal). Quantization errors are also called rounding errors because imprecise numbers represent the original analogue audio.

Metering

One of the key areas of confusion is the difference between meters used for monitoring sound, specifically the difference between analogue and digital meters. Audio workflows begin with microphones and end with speakers, which are both analogue devices. The volume unit (VU) meter was originally developed in 1939 to measure complex audio signals. VU meters "average out" peaks and troughs of short duration (transients) and reflect the perceived loudness of audio material. Some practitioners prefer VU meters because they are closer to the human ear's perception of sound level, although they do not adequately reflect peak levels, which can be problematic. Depending on the amplitude and the duration of peaks in the signal, some transient sounds barely register and can cause overloads. On an analogue meter, 0 dB is the optimal recording or output level of a device. If the voltage is much higher, the signal may distort. If the voltage is much lower, the signal may be lost in any noise inherent in the recording chain.

VU meters are typically seen on standalone location audio mixers and analogue mixing desks. When a VU meter is reading 0 VU, there is around 20 dB of headroom (the safety zone) for any fast transient peaks. +4 dBu (a logarithmic voltage ratio) is the nominal operating level, and +24 dBu is the typical clipping point. Digital meters generally show transient peaks, and the clipping point is always 0 dBFS (full scale). This means to allow the same kind of headroom in a digital system (as

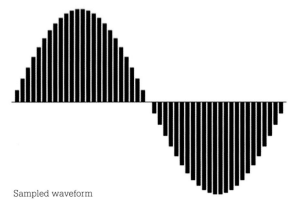

Sampled waveform

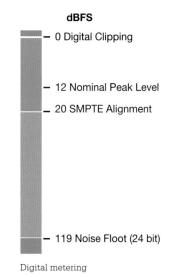

Digital metering

in an analogue system), the average signal level needs to be metering around –20 dBFS. Digital meters are always scaled so that the maximum quantization level is denoted as 0 dBFS, which is the maximum level a system will handle without clipping, and why the alignment level is always a negative value below this point, most commonly –20 dBFS in audio postproduction workflows.

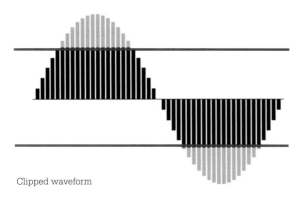

Clipped waveform

In digital audio systems, even a brief peak can cause clipping, so a basic rule of thumb is to allow 6 dBFS for transient peaks. Digital meters are easier to read because they show the entire headroom margin and have a red LED that serves as a clipping indicator, so if a level exceeds 0 dB, the LED will light up. "Clipping" is the term that refers to an overloaded signal path; when examined, it will appear as if the top of the waveform has been "clipped" off. Clipping is like overexposing a shot, and recording a low-level signal is like underexposing a shot. Clipping sounds harsh and cannot be fixed, so renders a recording unusable. The easiest way to avoid clipping is to make sure there is at least 6 dB of headroom, which means setting levels so that the loudest portion of a recording peaks at around –6 dB.

Dynamic Range and Signal-to-Noise Ratios

All audio material has a "dynamic range," which is the ratio between the maximum and minimum signal that can be recorded, depending on the system. While audio recorded at low levels can be raised throughout production, low-level recordings don't use all of the available bit depth so causes a loss of resolution, which cannot be recaptured by raising the level at a later stage. In audio, the signal-to-noise ratio (SNR) is a measure that compares the level of the desired signal against the level of noise in a system. In the days of recording to analogue tape, recording engineers had to be very aware of noise (induced by microphones, mixing consoles, and tape hiss) so recorded at high SNRs to minimize noise in the final product. Digital technology has minimal inherent noise, so it's less of an issue today, but when a signal is boosted at a later stage, any unwanted background sound (such as background traffic) is also boosted. In summary, not allowing sufficient "head-room" when recording causes clipping, while too much headroom reduces resolution, and therefore dynamic range.

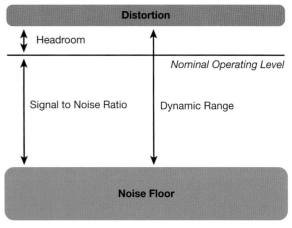

Dynamic range

The Recording Chain

In order to record quality sound, a number of factors must be considered. The easiest way to approach sound recording is to think of the entire audio path as a chain:

- The *sound* itself (*source*)
- The *microphone(s)* that capture the sound
- The *cables and connectors* that carry the signal from the microphone to the *mixer* and/or *recorder*
- The recorder itself (preamps /analogue to digital converter)

- The *monitoring circuit* of the recording device (*headphones*)

Like a physical chain, the audio path is only as strong as the weakest link. A high-quality recorder with a low-quality microphone will not be able to record anything better than what the microphone is capable of. A high-quality microphone paired with a low-quality recorder will only be able to record to the limitations of the recorder. *Gain structure* refers to the input and output levels of each stage of the path. *Gain* (volume) refers to the way that the volume of a sound will increase and decrease as it goes through the different stages of a recording or mixing path. *Changing gain* means decreasing it or increasing it, and *unity gain* means that a path has the same volume going out as it did coming in.

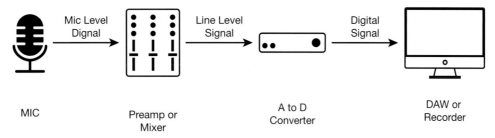

| MIC | Preamp or Mixer | A to D Converter | DAW or Recorder |

Signal flow (analogue to digital)

MICROPHONES

Microphone selection depends on the sound source to be recorded and the recording situation. There are a wide variety of microphones designed for different applications. The main factors that inform selection are the type, polar pattern, and frequency response of the microphone. Microphones are also called "transducers" because they change one form of energy into another—sound waves into an electrical signal. The most common types of microphones are dynamic, ribbon, and condensers.

Dynamic (or Moving Coil)

A dynamic, or moving, coil is a coil of wire attached to a diaphragm and suspended in a magnetic field. When sound waves vibrate the diaphragm, the coil vibrates in the field and generates an electrical signal.

- Rugged, reliable, and handle heat, cold, humidity
- Wire mesh shields/foam attenuate explosives
- Handle high volumes without distortion
- Less sensitive to handling
- Have tailored frequency responses for particular applications
- Do not need a power supply

Ribbon

An extremely thin, ultralight ribbon of aluminum is suspended in a magnetic field. When sound

Sound Waves   Mic   Electrical Waveform

waves vibrate the ribbon in the field, an electrical signal is generated.

- Considered warm and smooth
- Sensitive to handling
- Typically bidirectional
- Smooth at high frequencies, generally roll off above 14 kHz and below 40 Hz
- Do not need a power supply

Condenser (Capacitor)

In a condenser microphone a conductive diaphragm and a metal back plate are placed close together and charged with static electricity, forming two plates of a capacitor. When sound waves strike the diaphragm, it vibrates, varying the spacing between plates, which varies the capacitance and generates a signal. There are two types: true and electret condensers. In a true condenser, the diaphragm and back plate are charged from a built-in circuit. An electret material on the diaphragm or back plate charges electret condensers.

- Some come with switchable polar/pickup patterns
- Respond quickly to transients (rapidly changing waves), so attacks are sharp and clear
- Typically have a flatter frequency response than dynamic microphones
- Need powering via battery or phantom power, which is generally supplied by most mixing consoles, recorders, interfaces, and professional cameras.
- Good for detailed sound
- Need powering via battery or phantom power, which is generally supplied by most mixing consoles, recorders, interfaces, and professional cameras.

Polar Patterns

Microphones respond differently to sounds coming from different directions. They have different polar (or pickup) patterns. A polar pattern is depicted by a circular graph that shows how sensitive a microphone is in different directions. Some microphones have switchable patterns for different recording situations.

Omnidirectional microphones have a 360-degree, all-around pickup, which means they will pick up room acoustics, or reverberation,

which makes them useful for recording atmos but not dialogue or effects. They offer little isolation unless you place the microphone close to a source, they have a low sensitivity to pops (explosive breath sounds), and they have no up-close bass boost (proximity effect).

Bidirectional microphones (or figure-of-eight microphones) have a nearly equal front and rear pickup, with rejection of sound coming from the side of the microphone. They are useful for picking up two sources and when combined with a cardioid for recording "mid-side" stereo effects.

Unidirectional microphones have a selective pickup for sources in front of the microphone and rejection of sound behind the microphone so offer good isolation.

Supercardioids offer more difference between front and rear pickup, therefore more isolation compared to a *cardioid*.

Hypercardioids offer maximum isolation and therefore rejection of reverberation and background noise. Shotgun microphones are hypercardioids and used for recording dialogue because they isolate the dialogue from background sound. Shorter shotguns will usually pick up more sound from the sides compared to a longer shotgun.

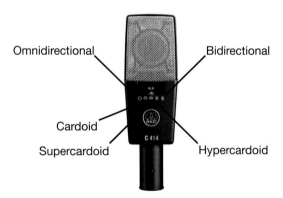

Multipattern AKG C414 condenser microphone

Frequency Response

Frequency response refers to the variation in output level or sensitivity of a microphone over its useable range from the lowest to the highest frequency. Microphone manufacturers specify frequency response in ranges, usually illustrated with a graph that indicates relative amplitude at each frequency. A microphone with peaks or dips at certain frequencies is said to have a

Schoeps CMIT5U
long shotgun

"shaped" response, designed to enhance a frequency range specific to a given sound source. For example, a microphone with a peak in the 2 to 10 kHz range will enhance the intelligibility or presence of voice.

A microphone's frequency response is not necessarily uniform at all angles, which is why microphone positioning is important. The most obvious example is using a boom (shotgun microphone) because it is highly directional and when positioned "off axis," the recording will lack higher frequencies (or "presence"), sound unnatural and "roomy" (off-axis coloration). *Proximity effect* describes an increase in bass or low-frequency response when a sound source is close to a microphone that has a directional polar pattern. This can also sound unnatural, so when close miking with a directional microphone, low frequencies may need to be rolled off either via a bass roll-off switch or EQ at a later stage. Bass roll-off (or lo cut) also helps reduce low-frequency content such as traffic and AC hum from being recorded. Some microphones also have a pad switch, which attenuates incoming signals and is used to prevent loud recordings from overloading.

Another important microphone characteristic is sensitivity, which is a measure of the electrical output (in volts) per incoming SPL. It is usually given in terms of a reference SPL. *Max SPL* is the point where the microphone distorts, or clips the waveform (higher SPL = better). *Self-noise* is the amount of noise the microphone creates all on its own. All microphones generate some noise (less = better). *Dynamic range* is the range between self-noise and max SPL (more = better). *Signal-to-noise ratio* (SNR or S/N) refers to the ratio of the nominal signal level to the undesired noise level (higher SNR = better).

Stereo Microphones

This use of two or more microphones to create a stereo image will give spatial depth to atmos recordings and certain sound effects such as car passes, however in film most sound effects are recorded mono and positioned (panned) in

postproduction. There are a number of different methods for stereo recordings. Three of the most popular are the spaced pair (A/B), the coincident or near-coincident pair (X-Y configuration), and the mid-side (M-S) technique. Commonly, stereo recording involves a matched pair of microphones, although there are custom design stereo microphones that employ various configurations like X-Y or mid-side arrangements. Mid-side offers the greatest control over the stereo image post-recording and is mono compatible. The technique combines a front-facing cardioid or super-cardioid "mid" microphone with a figure-of-eight "side" microphone. The mid microphone acts as a center channel, while the side microphone's channel creates ambience and directionality by adding or subtracting information from either side. The amount of direct sound from the mid microphone and the ambient sound from the side microphone can be individually controlled.

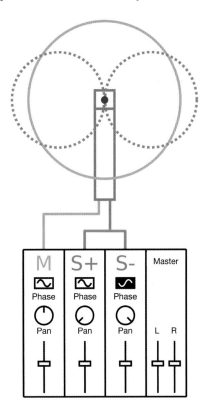

Mid-side
technique

Surround Microphones and Techniques

Surround recording is not that common in film soundtrack production; dialogue and most effects are recorded in mono. Surround soundtracks are created in postproduction; dialogue is placed center and effects are panned. However, there are surround microphones and specific techniques that can be used to capture surround material, typically atmos, and surround plug-ins for decoding recordings. "Double M/S" is "double" the M/S stereo recording technique. In addition to a front-facing cardioid or supercardioid "mid" microphone and a figure-of-eight "side" microphone, a rear-facing directional microphone is used, forming two complete, back-to-back M/S systems. One M/S system provides the three front channels (the center channel signal being provided directly by the mid microphone of the front system), while the other system provides the two surround channels. Increasingly, surround microphones are also being designed as "one" device, for both professional and pro-consumer recorders. Likewise, ambisonic microphones are being employed in VR filmmaking to capture full-sphere (3D) surround sound.

Digital Microphones

Digital microphones have been around for some time, but are not that prevalent, partly due to standards development being an ongoing process, cost, and the difficulty of interfacing with preexisting gear. They house an A/D converter that receives the signal directly from the capsule, which is optimized for the specific signal and parameters of the capsule. Analogue components such as preamplifiers and A/D converters are no longer required, and remotely controlled directional characteristics and features can be adapted for varying recording situations. The argument for digital microphones is a higher possible signal quality, which cannot be degraded by interferences (such as radio frequency, or RF) and losses that analogue signals are prone to.

Microphone Accessories

A *boom-pole* is an extendable lightweight pole that the operator/swinger uses to position the microphone during recording. While compact and lightweight, they can get surprisingly heavy when used for lengthy periods of time.

Mounts and pistol grips are used to mount microphones to the boom pole, cameras, and recording devices, and suspension mounts eliminate handling problems.

Windshield (blimp) and pistol grip

Shields, softies and socks (blimps), are protective enclosures that encapsulate a microphone to protect it from extraneous wind and AC air movement.

Headphones

Headphones are the last component in the chain and are used to assess what is being recorded. The importance of headphones is often overlooked, but they are crucial for critical listening. There are three types of headphones: (1) Full-sized headphones are known as *over-ear* (circumaural) models, which cover the ears and seal out external sound. (2) *On-ear* (supra-aural) headphones have pads that sit on top of the ears, rather than around them, and tend to be smaller and lighter but offer less attenuation of outside sound. Both over-ear and on-ear headphones can be further defined by the type of ear-cups: *Open-backed* leaks more sound out of the headphone and lets more ambient sounds into the headphone. *Closed-back* (or sealed) styles have the back of the ear-cups closed, which blocks ambient sound and gives the wearer the perception that the sound is coming from within his or her head. The third headphone type is called (3) *in-ear*, which extends into the ear canal and provides good isolation, but they also need to fit properly.

Portable Field Recorders

Aside from budget considerations, choice is dependent on the recording application and device characteristics:

- Built-in microphone(s) and/or microphone input(s)
- Microphone preamps
- Analogue-to-digital (AD) converters
- A range of recording file formats and resolutions

- Varying methods, formats, and capacities for storing and transferring audio data
- Audio output(s) and monitoring inputs (headphones)
- Meters
- Battery and phantom power

Microphones

Built-in microphones can be mono, stereo, surround and ambisonic, with varying pickup pattern(s), frequency responses, and quality levels, all influenced by their design. Built-in microphones can be limiting; useful for recording atmos and some effects, but generally not appropriate for recording dialogue, sound and Foley effects, which are recorded with higher quality external microphones. *Microphone inputs* for the connection of external microphones on consumer and prosumer recorders are TRS (tip-ring-sleeve) or minijack (3.5 mm). Professional microphones and recorders use balanced XLR's for each channel (L&R for left-right stereo), whereas surround recording requires a recorder with multiple XLR microphone inputs.

Preamps

A microphone preamp prepares a microphone signal to be processed by other equipment. Microphone signals are often too weak to be transmitted to recording devices and mixing consoles, so a preamplifier boosts the signal to a standard line level. Different preamps will offer varying degrees of sound quality, and generally the more expensive, the better the quality.

Automatic gain control

Automatic gain control (AGC) adjusts the audio levels for you. For example, when someone starts speaking, the AGC will turn the levels down to avoid peaking and distorting, and when the speaking stops, the AGC will turn the levels up, which makes the background sound louder. The result is very unnatural and unpredictable recordings. AGC should always be turned off and levels adjusted manually.

Meters

All recorders have meters, and it's important to keep an eye on meters during recording to avoid clipping or making low-level recordings. Most digital recorder meters will indicate dBs in steps, so it's easy to set, check and adjust levels, however some models are merely graphically marked, indicating the optimal recording level for the device.

Powering

Most field recorders come with a power supply and can also be powered by batteries for location recording. Professional recorders always supply phantom power for the use of condenser microphones.

Recording Formats

Field recorders offer a range of recording formats. Higher bit depth and sample rates give higher audio resolution and better quality but produce bigger files per minute of recording. Many recorders offer both uncompressed and compressed formats, most commonly WAV (BWF) on professional recorders and WAV and MP3 on consumer models. The Broadcast Wave Format (BWF) is the common recording format in film, radio, and television production. Audio is typically recorded at a 16- or 24-bit depth. 24-bit is the industry standard for most audio applications, and 48 kHz the standard audio sampling rate. Most professional recorders are also able to record at 96 to 192 kHz. Recording sound effects at higher sample rates is increasingly common for the creation of effect libraries. Some portable recorders also come with built-in time code generators capable of syncing with other devices.

Pre-Roll Buffer

A pre-roll buffer allows you to put the recorder in "record pause", so when you press "record," a few seconds before the record button was actually pressed is recorded. This function is useful in that it reduces the reaction time when noticing a record-worthy event is happening.

Headphone Inputs and Audio Outputs

Monitoring the recorded signal before and during capture is a critical step to getting the best quality recordings. Monitoring levels are separate from record levels and adjusted independently, so be aware of the difference between the two, and set headphone levels for accurate monitoring. Some recorders allow off "tape" monitoring and have additional audio outputs for connecting to other equipment.

File Storage

File storage mediums can take several forms: internal hard disc or solid-state memory, or removable media-like memory cards. The amount of storage space available (usually in gigabytes or GB) will determine the total number/length of recordings a storage medium can hold. All digital recorders allow you to transfer recordings to a computer, usually via USB or FireWire.

Signal Processing

Some recorders will have compressors, limiters, and filters. Compression and limiting compensate for fluctuations in input level. A compressor gradually reduces the signal level above a certain threshold, whereas a limiter completely prevents a signal from going over a specified setting. Generally, compressors and limiters are used sparingly during recording, if at all, in favor of manually adjusting levels. Many recorders will also feature a low-cut filter to eliminate wind, traffic, and other kinds of low-frequency rumble.

Accessories

Accessories include items such as a carrying case, microphone/tabletop stands and mounts, hot shoe mounts for DSLRs and camcorders. windshields, memory card(s), USB cable, external and additional microphone(s), headphones, and software.

Portable Field Mixers

A portable field mixer allows for the combining of signals from multiple microphones and other audio sources. The output of the portable mixer is connected into the audio inputs of another device, namely a recorder. Field mixers allow a sound person to quickly access various controls ("on the fly") and are typically used in film and television production. Unlike many recorders, mixers' gain controls are more easily accessible. Common controls found on portable field mixers include the following:

Gain and Level Controls

Like in audio recorders, the quality of preamp circuitry defines the overall quality of sound. The gain knob controls the preamp, which is the small amplifier that boosts the audio signal coming into the mixer's input. The level control determines how much of that boosted preamp signal gets to the main outputs of the mixer.

Field recorder—
sound devices 702

Headphone Monitoring (Tape Return / Fold Back)

In additional to standard headphone monitoring, some portable field mixers also allow off "tape" monitoring through the headphone output, which is useful for checking connections between the mixer and a recorder.

Pan

Panning is the ability to control the balance of an audio signal from left to right in the stereo spectrum. For example, if you were wearing headphones and you panned a signal all the way to the left, you would only hear the signal on the left side of the headphones.

Tone Generator

Portable field mixers generally include a tone generator (also referred to as an oscillator or slate). A tone generator's main function is to set the input level of a recording device with the output level of the mixer; it is also used for markers in postproduction. The tone creates a square block in the digital audio waveform, which helps editors sync sound with footage. Some mixers also feature a built-in microphone with the slate to record verbal identifications, and many include a time code generator for syncing with other devices.

Inputs/Outputs

Most portable audio mixers feature multiple inputs and outputs for microphones and connecting to recorders and cameras. Mixers always have a main output (usually two XLR jacks) to send the mixer's signal to the recorder. Many also have auxiliary sends to feed the mixer's signal to a second, backup recording device.

Cables and Connectors

Audio cables fall into two main categories: *unbalanced* or *balanced*. Unbalanced cables carry unbalanced signals, which means one of the conductors is carrying the signal voltage and the other conductor is grounded, or carrying no signal voltage, and therefore the conductors have different voltages on them. Unbalanced audio cables usually have two conductors, or wires, within the cable and also on each connector. Examples of unbalanced cables are the 3.5-mm "minijacks," RCAs, and 1/4'' TS (tip-sleeve) "phono."

Balanced audio cables carry balanced signals and are made up of two signal paths or

Production mixer—sound devices 302

wires, and usually a third conductor, which is a ground connection. The two signal-carrying conductors are referred to as *hot* and *cold*, or *positive* (+) and *negative* (–), with equal amounts of the same audio signal, or voltage, but the signal on the cold conductor is the opposite polarity of the signal on the hot conductor. These two signals are summed, and the resulting audio signal is the net difference with any noise introduced cancelled out. XLR "male" cables connect to various hardware *inputs*, XLR "female" cables connect to microphones and various hardware *outputs*, and TRS (tip-ring-sleeve) cables connect to both *inputs* and *outputs*. Most professional audio equipment uses balanced connection, whereas consumer devices tend to be unbalanced.

Audio cables and connectors (minijack, RCA, TS, TRS, XLR)

TIPS AND TRICKS

The complexity of sound as a medium and the way it affects us makes sound a difficult subject to understand and master. Many common recording problems encountered are technical, or due to acoustic issues, but solvable with due consideration.

When it comes to sound design, raw recordings are the "building blocks" of sound effects and sound design effects, which are then edited, layered and manipulated to achieve a desired effect/affect. Unlike live-action films, animation starts with a completely blank canvas, which is why having an understanding of acoustics and how we perceive spaces is particularly important for designing story environments. Conversely, live-action film involves recording in real spaces, which requires the same degree of understanding. Technical and acoustical aspects aside, it's the narrative, aesthetics, and emotion of a film, scene, or event that informs sound design. A story point is executed "technically", but the art and design is to make it work without seeming technical.

When a sound effect feels wrong, it's usually because it's disconnected from the story and visuals. Thinking about story, a character, a prop, an environment, and how a scene could sound or should feel leads to ideas for both sound and visual design. For example, a clock alarm could "ring," "beep," "buzz," or turn on the radio, depending on the clock design (visual aesthetic). If the alarm clock is electronic, it should probably "buzz" or "beep," so sound electronic. Depending on the narrative, perhaps it should "beep" insistently (timing/emotion), in an annoying fashion (harsh/high pitched), say if the lead character has been up all night finishing a presentation for an early morning client meeting that he/she is dreading (narrative/emotive/psychological).

The other key reason for something not feeling right or connected is sound aesthetics. Overly synthetic or artificially generated sound design effects and textures might suit certain elements of a science fiction film or specific effects in dream sequences and flashbacks, yet lack the degree of "organic realness" for many films. Regardless of the problem, the solution is generally found by thinking about sound within the context of the narrative, aesthetics, and emotion of a film.

4

Preproduction

There are three phases that constitute the creation of a film: preproduction, production, and postproduction. The preproduction stage is when a project is defined, refined, and each subsequent stage planned for. In live-action films, this involves scriptwriting; script breakdowns; concept art; story-boarding; shooting scripts; pre-vis; location scouting; hiring of crew, talent, and equipment; organizing props and wardrobe; budgeting; and scheduling. A production sound team is usually hired, and on medium to large-budget productions a sound designer or supervising sound editor is contracted during preproduction. Production involves principal photography (the shoot) and location sound recording, primarily dialogue recording for live-action film. Postproduction includes sound and picture editing, ADR, sound design, music, visual effects, compositing, grading, mixing, mastering, and encoding. In animation, a treatment is scripted, then storyboarded, scratch tracks are recorded, and story reels are created during preproduction. Animation production involves the design and creation of characters, sets, and props, which are animated, and in the case of 3D animation, virtual cameras capture shots. In postproduction, individual shots and scenes are edited together, compositing undertaken, visual effects added, sound design and music completed, and the final soundtrack is mixed, mastered, and encoded.

The Development Stage

In traditional live-action film, the preproduction and production phases focus primarily on the visual aspects of film production, but most industry professionals advocate for less of a division between production processes in general and greater sound-image collaboration throughout the entire creation process. Sound design has traditionally been perceived as a film postproduction discipline, but for sound and image to feel like a unified whole, the consideration of sound needs to be undertaken in preproduction. While some directors think creatively about sound, many leave any serious consideration until postproduction, which is too late in the production cycle for active participation. The same situation applies to music. Each phase of a production affects the next, and as a film begins with a script, the time to really start thinking about sound is during scriptwriting and development.

Identifying what a film should sound like requires having an understanding of the narrative, aesthetics, and emotive intent. These are the three key considerations for sound designers when taking on a new project. The word "story" is a synonym for "narrative" and refers to the interpretation of the sequence of events described in the script. The word "look" is a synonym for "aesthetics," which is often perceived as purely visual, but as film is audiovisual, aesthetic considerations incorporate the "sound" of a film. Narrative, aesthetics, and emotive devices can be any and all production elements, which includes sound. The approach to the narrative-aesthetic design of a film often defines the emotion, or "feel," of a film. The word "feel" is a synonym for "emotion," which relates to the characters, environments, and overall emotive impression, or effect, of a film.

Genre and Style

Action, adventure, comedy, crime, gangster, drama, thriller, historical, horror, musical, science fiction, coming of age, war, Western, and fantasy are all common genres for films, web series, television shows, and games. Defining a genre gives people an initial idea of the type of film or story being proposed. Certain genres are associated with specific approaches or sound sensibilities, although it largely depends on the treatment of the film. Films can be a mix of genres and a combination of ideas—realistic, synthetic, artificial, or stylized. *Fantastic Planet* and *THX 1138* are both science fiction films but are aesthetically very different; the sound design in *Fantastic Planet* is predominantly synthetic and stylized, whereas *THX 1138* is realistic, artificial, and stylized.

An expression like "film noir" describes the style, mood, or tone of a film, which also suggests an intended aesthetic. Hollywood's classical film noir period is generally regarded as starting in the early 1940s and is associated with crime or gangster genres and German expressionist cinematography. Also dominant in film noir is the use of narration and stylistic sound design. A contemporary example is *Sin City* (Miller, Rodriguez, and Tarantino, 2005). It has a "hyperreal-graphic" aesthetic, which is visually and aurally stylistic, and most visually stylistic films are aurally stylistic. Sound and image complement each other. Expressions like "abstract" or "experimental" normally relate to a more thematic approach to storytelling and audiovisual design. Many films are a mix of genre and style, but certain expressions

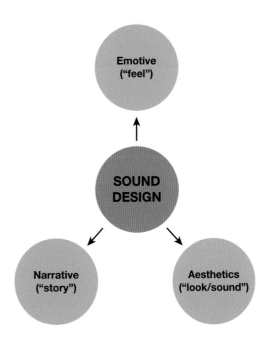

Fundamental considerations of sound design

Sin City (2005, dir. Frank Miller, Robert Rodriguez, and Quentin Tarantino)

will hint at a particular "vision," which is useful for sound designers in conceptualizing sound ideas.

Story and/or Theme(s)

A story or narrative comprises three acts, which in the most simplistic terms is a beginning (exposition), a middle (conflict), and an end (resolution). Characters drive the plot, while an underlying theme or themes hold the narrative together. Narrative scripts address a series of common questions that may not always apply to experimental or abstract works; however, a general theme and style can usually be identified regardless of the type of project. A theme is commonly understood as an idea that recurs and either encompasses or pervades a work of art. Experimental works are usually based around the exploration of something new, or a different way of presenting an idea, which opposes adherence to traditional or expected structures. *La Jetée* is a good example of an experimental film; it explores time, temporality, and movement through the editing of mainly still images and the use of sound. Despite the experimental aspect of the film, it still has a narrative. In experimental or abstract projects, there is usually an underlying theme or sense of narrative, which is also useful for thinking about sound design, particularly if there's also a specific or defined presentation method. In defining soundtrack direction, one of the key questions to debate as early as possible

is, *What kind of film am I making? What's the story? Who is the hero (protagonist), and what or who is in opposition (antagonist)? Whose point of view is the story being told from? Where and when is it set? What are the key themes? What is the intended visual style, and how might that transfer into an aural style?*

Story Development

Before a draft script is written, there are a number of story development stages an idea goes through before it's realized as a script. Each step of the script development process gives specific insights to the story, the story world, and the characters. A script is often defined as a map or a blueprint. They are not detailed documents so can be interpreted or "seen" differently by different people. While some writers are articulate about sound in their scripts, it's not that common. The traditional film script format doesn't lend itself to communicating sound—not in an obvious fashion. Unless you are the scriptwriter, and depending on how a script is written, the "psychology" or subtext of a film may not be initially apparent. Sometimes the materials generated through the script development process can be more "telling" than the actual script. A synopsis, story treatments, outlines, descriptions of characters, and environments all provide useful information for triggering ideas. Pitch, story, and writer bibles can be helpful because they outline the premise, story world and tone, locations, and genre, and they include character bios, descriptions and insights, full episodes or episode storylines, artwork, and sometimes a pilot episode. More recently, it's become common to create a teaser, pilot, or pitch-vis to introduce the premise, style, themes, locations, characters, key emotional relationships, and conflicts. These are all opportunities to explore potential ideas for sound.

Outlines and Treatments

The first step in any project is having or coming up with a good story idea. After deciding on the basic concept or premise, the next stage is creating the synopsis, outline, and treatment. Each phase of story development extends the opportunities for conceptualizing sound and visual ideas:

One-Line Synopsis (or Logline)
One sentence that gives the most concentrated version of the story or its key event.

One-Paragraph Synopsis
A one-paragraph synopsis that defines the essence of the story—WHO, WHAT, and HOW. It sets out whose story it is, what his or her problem is, what he or she does about it, and the outcome.

One-Page Synopsis
Like the one-paragraph synopsis, the one-page synopsis deals with the WHO, WHAT, and HOW, but also establishes other key characters, their conflicts, the setting in time and place, and major turning points of the story. The one-page synopsis gives a clearer indication of the narrative structure: how the story begins, develops, and ends. The one-page synopsis also includes the event, the decisions and actions the characters make in pursuit of their goals, the obstacles they encounter and what they do about them, whether they win or lose, and where they end up. It's still a brief and compressed document, but it does give the reader a sense of the characters and their key choices and actions, which generally defines the characters. It gives the reader some *emotive* insight to the story.

Story Outline
The outline expands on the one-page synopsis to include motive, cause and effect, and demonstrates the flow of the narrative—how it will be told on screen. Writers outline blocks of action, or plot points: the *opening/closing* (what is first/last seen/heard on the screen), the *inciting incident* (an event that changes the course of the main character's life/journey), the *first act break* (marks the end of the setup and key characters have been introduced), *the midpoint* (the middle of the second act and a direction change), *the point of commitment* (the main character reaffirms commitment to his or her goal or quest), *all is lost* (the main character has experienced an extreme setback, and generally the end of Act Two), *the climax* (the main character has gathered his or her resources), and the *resolution*. Not all films adhere to formula of course, but writing a story outline helps clarify the story, which in turn helps everyone involved understand how the narrative is going to play out.

Story Treatments
A treatment sets out the way a story is going to be dramatically and cinematically treated in terms of style and narrative. Like an outline, it's also a "selling" document, but the main goal is to convince the reader that the writer has a firm grip on the story and how it's going to be told. Treatments are widely used as a pitch document to outline story and character aspects of a proposed script, whereas outlines are produced as part of the development process. A treatment is usually a longer document that incorporates any subplots, indicating how they integrate and resonate with the main plot. Although the treatment is longer than the outline, it's still a prose summary of the film's story, but includes motive, thoughts, and emotions. So, a story treatment will give the reader *aesthetic* and *emotive* impressions, which are useful for generating sound ideas. Directors' treatments are also valuable documents for conceptualizing sound. They outline the director's vision or visual plan for animating or shooting a project, how the director envisages the sound design, and what kind of music he or she intends to use. Some are purely written treatments, and some include visual reference material such as illustrations and concept artwork. Alternatively, getting a sound designer to write an audio treatment is good way of gathering, exchanging, and clarifying sound ideas. An audio treatment functions in much the same way as a visual treatment, just from the perspective of sound. An audio treatment can also help a director gauge if a sound designer is on the same page, and can serve as the start point for sound design and preliminary aural sketching.

TIPS AND TRICKS

Documents generated throughout story development can help inform approaches to soundtrack design by elaborating on a film's narrative, aesthetic, and emotive dimensions, which may not be apparent in a script. Certain sound elements are evident (for example, "a dog barks in the distance"), but conceptual, psychological, and emotional aspects are not easily "seen." Engaging with and utilizing development materials gives both the director and sound designer the opportunity to get between, beyond, and beneath what's written on the page.

The sound designer's primary job is to assist the director in identifying what kind of soundtrack will suit the overall "personality" of the film. Defining the aural direction of a project starts with initial discussions concerning story, character, and environments. A script will go through a number of drafts before a final draft, which means there is plenty of scope for considering sound throughout story and script development.

Having an open dialogue between key people during development creates the opportunity to share sound-image ideas. The simple act of having a conversation about story and sound generates ideas, which can help inform the script. Most books on filmmaking concentrate on the process of visualizing a film, but film is audiovisual, so you also need to be able to auralize your film.

Sound in Script

Barton Fink (1991, dir. Joel Coen and Ethan Coen)

The way a script is written has a greater impact on sound than is generally appreciated. Most people don't think in sound terms, and there's never been a clear or common tradition for conceptualizing sound. There's also a tendency to lean on dialogue and overlook how sound and sound-image arrangements can contribute to the storytelling. Some writer/directors, like the multi-award-winning Coen Brothers, are known for being specific about sound in their scripts. They also have a highly collaborative working relationship with sound designer Skip Leivsay and composer Carter Burwell. In *Barton Fink* (1991), sound is used to express Barton's strange and apprehensive arrival at a hotel in Los Angeles. Fink is a New York playwright who accepts an offer to write B-movie scripts in L.A. but is suffering from writer's block. His neighbor tries to help, and a bizarre sequence of events unfolds. The Coen Brothers conceptualized the hotel like an abandoned ghost ship, centering the audience on Barton's point of view, and using sound to support and advance the narrative. There's a surreal encounter in the hotel lobby, which is accentuated by an excessively long and unnatural bell ring. A mosquito whines. We hear the wallpaper peeling off the wall. A picture of a woman on a beach coincides with the sound of surf and a gull. All these elements were written into the script, shot, and edited with sound in mind:

As Barton stops at the empty desk. He hits a small silver bell next to the register. Its ringout goes on and on without losing volume. After a long beat there is a dull scuffle of shoes on stairs. Barton, puzzled, looks around the empty lobby, then down at the floor behind the front desk.
A TRAP DOOR
It swings open and a young man in a faded maroon uniform,
holding a shoe brush and a shoe – not one of his own – climbs
up from the basement.
He closes the trap door, steps up to the desk and sticks his finger out to touch the small silver bell, finally muting it.
The lobby is now silent again.

In the film *Panic Room* (Fincher, 2002), a recently divorced woman and her daughter move into a new home in New York, which has a panic room. When three burglars break into their house, they take refuge in the panic room. The panic room is central to the film's narrative, so the atmosphere or ambience of the room was a key sound design element. The sound design was broken down into the "technical" (AC, electronics/TV monitors, lights) and the "emotive" (isolated, foreboding). One of the layers that made up the emotive dimensions was originally a choir, slowed down and filtered; another element was rain, treated with filters and delays. Through combining a number of different layers and textures, the panic room could be mixed and "controlled" to reflect what was happening with the characters (the emotive) and where they are in the room (the physical), and to support the action unfolding (the narrative).

The easiest way to start thinking about sound when writing or reviewing a script is by identifying key sound elements, ideas, or themes that have obvious or potential sound associations. By doing this, and considering the impact on the image, visual ideas will also surface, which helps inform cinematography, animation and editing.

Panic Room (2002, dir. David Fincher)

Scripts are formatted in a standard way, and generally there is an accepted norm, although there are some variations between writers and the type of projects. Film scripts usually include a scene heading, action, character name, dialogue, parenthetical, transitions, shots, and other elements such as montages. Each element suggests aural information, which is useful for auralizing, and can serve as a vehicle for discussing and defining what could or should be heard and how that might impact, underpin, or inform the intended visuals.

Scene Heading

The *scene heading* (or slugline) tells the reader where the scene takes place; it sets "the scene" in the reader's mind. The scene heading describes where we are: indoors—interior (INT), or outdoors—exterior (EXT). Following the scene heading is the name of the location, BEDROOM, CAFE, CITY PARK, and then the time of day—NIGHT, DAY, EARLY MORNING. While not obvious, the time of day will influence sound. A CAFÉ at lunchtime will probably be busier (and therefore sound busier) than it would be during late afternoon, and a CITY PARK will generally be quieter at night. Scenes take place in locations, which means scene headings suggest atmos, room tone, sound effects, Foley, and Walla.

> An interior (INT) = room tone, room reverbs, sound and Foley effects, walla
>
> A CAFÉ: small, large, quiet, or busy?
>
> An exterior (EXT) = atmos, sound effects, walla
>
> CITY PARK: distant traffic, birds, children playing?

Action

The *action* (description) sets the scene and describes the setting and staging. Action is written in real time and helps the reader form an idea about the setting and the action that is taking place. We know where we are, characters are introduced, and events unfold. Some writers will also highlight key or important moments in capital letters, which includes sound moments or references. In the following scene from *WALL-E* (Stanton, 2008), the script tells us where the scene takes place (exterior of the truck), what time of day it is (night), the event (a sandstorm is approaching), and how WALL-E is reacting (unfazed). It references atmos (wind, sand) and how that plays out temporally, while also indicating perspective (the wind picks up, the sandstorm rages and approaches). Key sound and Foley effects are identified: a play button, warning light, WALL-E raising the door, WALL-E whistling, the door shutting, and the impact of the storm. The script also implies other sound and Foley effects: WALL-E's motor, WALL-E turning over the cooler, WALL-E heading back to the truck. We also know there is source music, which comes from WALL-E, which would be treated and mixed to sound like it is coming from him. We know the storm is intense, because it obliterates everything in view. We also know that sandstorms are common in WALL-E's world, because he is unfazed. If sandstorms were an unexpected event, he would be panicking.

EXT. TRUCK - NIGHT

Wall-E motors outside
Turns over his Igloo cooler to clean it out.
Pauses to take in the night sky.
STARS struggle to be seen through the polluted haze.
Wall-E presses the "Play" button on his chest.
The newly sampled It Only Takes A Moment (IOTAM) plays.
The wind picks up.
A WARNING LIGHT sounds on Wall-E's chest.
He looks out into the night.
A RAGING SANDSTORM approaches off the bay. . .
Unfazed, Wall-E heads back in the truck.
IOTAM still gently playing.
. . .The massive wave of sand roars closer. . .
Wall-E raises the door.
Pauses.
WHISTLES for his cockroach to come inside.
The door shuts just as the storm hits.
Obliterates everything in view.

Character Name and Dialogue

Before a character speaks, writers insert a *character name* to indicate the character's dialogue follows. In the following scene from *Ratatouille* (Bird, 2007), the script tells us where we are (the French countryside), what time of day it is (late afternoon), the event (Remy is being "discovered"), and how Remy is reacting (frightened). It also makes a reference to atmos (rain, wind), room tone (kitchen), how the scene is shot (the camera tracks in from exterior to interior), and key sound effects (gunshot, furniture bumps, crash, window shattering, glass shards, and the "sounds of struggle"). We know there is the potential for silence (the action freezes) and that dialogue is a voice over (VO) from Remy. The writing defines character, his state, and a specific intent; Remy is scrawny, frightened, and comic, and the audience should feel sympathetic toward him.

FRENCH COUNTRYSIDE - LATE AFTERNOON

A light rain falls on a SMALL FARMHOUSE.
The last remaining dead leaves tremble in the gusts. The quiet is shattered by a LOUD GUNSHOT that lights up the inside of the cottage.
CAMERA pushes down and in toward a single window.

RATATOUILLE
As we move closer, we begin to hear muffled SOUNDS OF STRUGGLE; furniture being bumped, dishes breaking, an indescribable CRASH, followed by an OLD LADY'S SHRIEK.
We're close to the WINDOW now, when it is suddenly SHATTERED by a COOKBOOK.
Instantly the action FREEZES.
Underneath its splayed pages, shielding himself from the shards of splintering glass is, inexplicably, a RAT-
-REMY. He's scrawny, frightened, almost comic. It's hard not to feel sympathetic towards the little guy.
REMY (V.O.)
This is me. I think it's apparent I need to rethink my life a little bit. What's my problem? First of all—

Parenthetical

A *parenthetical* remark can be an attitude, verbal direction, or action direction for the actor or character (or animator) and indicates a corresponding action and/or emotive style of delivering dialogue. Parentheticals are short, to the point, and descriptive. They help clarify an action or a reaction. For example, a character could shudder, be stunned, or be elated, which would all look and sound different. In films like *WALL-E*, where there is an absence of spoken dialogue, the intent can be written along with sound effects in a parenthetical or brackets. This indicates what the sound effects or "vocalizations" need to "say." In the following scene, WALL-E is *inviting* EVE into his truck and then *panicking* as she starts unspooling his "Hello Dolly" tape.

INT. TRUCK - MOMENTS LATER

The back door lowers.
A rush of wind and sand.
Wally pulls Eve inside. Closes the door.
She coughs up dust.
Wally hits a switch. . .
Strings of CHRISTMAS LIGHTS fill the space.
His racks of oddities painted in colored light.
An air of enchantment.
Eve is taken aback.
WALLY
(beeps)
[Come on in.]

She drifts through the sea of knickknacks.
Becomes spooked by a SINGING BILLY BASS
FISH.
Threatens to shoot it, but Wally calms her
down.
He is compelled to show her everything.
Hands her an eggbeater. . .
. . .bubble wrap (so infectious to pop). . .
. . .a lightbulb (lights when she holds it). . .
. . .the Rubik's Cube (she solves it
immediately). . .
. . .his Hello Dolly tape.
Curious, she begins unspooling the tape.
WALLY
(loud beeps)
[My tape!!]

Transitions

Transitions are used when they are integral to
telling the story. A DISSOLVE TO indicates time
has passed, a MATCH CUT illustrates that there
is a correlation between something we just saw
and something in the new scene, and a FADE
OUT suggests transitioning to a new scene, time,
or place. Visual transitions often accompany
sound transitions; a MATCH CUT could result in
transitioning between two sounds with similar sound properties, a DISSOLVE TO is like a
CROSSFADE between two sounds, and a visual
FADE OUT is much the same as an audio fade
out (or fade down).

Shots

A *shot* tells us the focal point within a scene has
changed. Not many scriptwriters write shots
into a script unless they are important to the
story. Adding shots can interrupt the flow of a
script and is generally seen as the territory of the
director. For sound, defining shots gives a clear
sense of the sound perspective. An EXTREME
CLOSE-UP (ECU or XCU) often involves a close
perspective, present and detailed sound association, whereas a WIDE SHOT (WS) suggests establishing sound, typically sound that establishes a
location, such as atmos.

Abbreviations

Some writers will use abbreviations in the action/
descriptive part of their scripts.

b.g. = background, which means action is
taking place in the background

f.g. = foreground, which means action is
taking place in the foreground

CGI = computer-generated image

SPFX = special effects (that do not require
CGI)

SFX = sound effects

POV = point of view

Detailing shot composition is comparable
to detailing the positioning and mix of sound(s).
Sounds in the foreground are generally louder
(usually dialogue if there is dialogue and spot
effects); sounds in the middle ground are quieter,
but still present and often contextual; and sounds
in the background may be audible but are often
location orientated and/or functioning on a more
subconscious level. Point of view (POV) shots
are more subjective and therefore emotive; we're
seeing/hearing the world from a character's POV,
and SPFX and CGI generally dictate the need for
specific sound and sound design effects.

Montages and Series of Shots

"Montage" as a term is generally associated
with the juxtaposition of images. Many film
directors believe the montage is what distin-
guishes cinema from other mediums. In contemporary cinema, a montage is commonly
understood as a series of shots or sequences
designed to provoke emotional or intellectual
responses. The connecting of images allows
for complex ideas or emotions to be created
and extracted by the audience. In other words,
the editing of shots constitutes the intent of
a sequence, as opposed to the content of an
individual shot. In scripts, they are usually
numbered or lettered 1, 2, 3 or A, B, C. A series
of shots is similar to a montage, and written
the same way, but it usually takes place in one
location and concerns the same event or action.
Montages are often conceived with and edited
to music, but they can also be conceptualized
creatively with sound and sound design effects.
Film trailers are basically montage sequences
accompanied by key dialogue and/or VO, music,
and spot effects.

Intercuts

Intercuts concern the cutting back and forth between two or more scenes, which are often occurring at the same time. In scripts, instead of repeating the scene heading for each scene, an INTERCUT is used to tell the reader the scene is moving back and forth between locations. In the same way that montage sequences are often "held together" by sound and music, intercuts often follow the same formula.

Superimpose, Title, and Credits

SUPERIMPOSE or TITLE/TITLE OVER is used when text or an image is placed over footage, typically for information like the place or time. Text for sound is generally only relevant if it implies associated sound effects or design. For example, motion graphics and computer-generated text is often punctuated with sound effects in science fiction films. Film credits and text within trailers can also be approached creatively, which can determine the need for sound design.

Emphasis

As readers tend to skim-read a script, sometimes writers will emphasize words in capital letters, which draws the eye (and/or ear) to important or key elements, details, and actions that might otherwise be overlooked.

Marking Up and SFX Lists

Marking up a script is a simple and effective way of focusing on sound, and can serve as the basis for further discussions. Scripts are loaded with references to sound, and simply highlighting them can trigger ideas. An SFX list can also be created quite early in the process, which is helpful for considering each sound and how it could be sourced or created. Is it literal or not? Is it a sound effect or a sound design effect? An SFX list can be devised as a spreadsheet with columns for individual elements: room tone, atmos, Foley, sound effects, and sound design effects. Ideas for music or specific music cues can also be added. Some scripts don't adhere to a traditional script format and are written more like a story outline or a series of events. Regardless of the format, any text-based document can be "heard." For example, a rough outline for *Steamboat Willy* might read as follows:

The film begins with Mickey **piloting** the Steamboat Willie **riverboat** down a **river** and **whistling** to the **tune** of "Steamboat Bill." He **pulls a rope** to **sound** the boat's **three whistles**. The tall and medium **whistle sound** off in sync but the shortest one stays **quiet** until it receives a good **hit** from the medium one. A **growling** Captain Peg Leg Pete appears behind him and **grabs** Mickey's torso, **stretching** it in the process. Mickey **screeches** and retrieves his **innards**. Captain Peg Leg Pete **yells** at Mickey and Mickey **blows a raspberry**. Pete turns around angrily and **kicks** Mickey but **misses** and **hits** himself instead while Mickey **tumbles** down some **stairs**, **slips** on a bar of **soap**, and **lands in a bucket of water**. A parrot nearby by **mocks and laughs** at him, which provokes Mickey to **throw the bucket of water** on the parrot, who **squawks** for help. Pete, who has been watching this whole time, **pulls** out a **slab** of chewing tobacco, **sighs**, and **bites off** half of it. He **chews**, then **spits** in front of him, and the **spit circles** around and **hits the bell** behind him, causing it to **ring**. He **laughs** and attempts to **do it again**. He **spits** and **turns around** to watch it **hit the bell** but gets **hit in the face** instead. He **wipes** off the spit and **grumbles**. The film then cuts to a shot of a dock landing with two chickens **clucking**; a duck **quacks** and a cow **moos**. Steamboat Willie **makes its way around a bend**, and with **whistles tooting**, it **backs up** into the dock. Mickey is **lowered down to the dock** by a **crane** near the **cow**. He fastens a belt around the **cow**, which is **lifted up** to the ship. However, the belt is far too big and the cow far too skinny. Mickey attempts to bring the cow back down by **grabbing his tail** and is **sprayed** by the udder. The cow is **lowered** back to the **dock** and Mickey, **squeaking**, attempts to **tighten the belt**. He **grunts** in frustration. He looks distraught until he sees a wagon of hay and grabs **a big fork load to feed to the cow**. The cow happily **swallows** the entire ball and easily **fills out** to the size of the belt and is r**aised to the ship**. Just then, Minnie Mouse appears **running** to catch up to Steamboat Willie. Mickey **jumps aboard the ship** and takes off, leaving Minnie **yelling** at the dock. She **calls** out. Steamboat Willie **disembarks and toots**. Minnie Mouse, wailing, **jumps up and down**. She proceeds to **run** alongside the **river** after the **whistling** steamboat, calling for help. Mickey hears her and decides to **lower the crane** to catch her. The crane hook **lifts up her dress** and, grabbing hold of her bloomers, **transports her onto the ship**. As she is lowered, Minnie **drops her fiddle** and "Turkey in the Straw" **sheet music**, which bounces and **lands** by the goat. The goat sees it, makes an **appreciative utterance**, and begins to **eat the sheet music**. Minnie is **lowered to the ship** and the hook **pulls her dress back down**. Minnie is happy to see Mickey and turns shyly away to see the goat **eating her sheet music**. She **screeches** in alarm. The goat then starts on the fiddle and Mickey attempts to **yank it out of his mouth**. Mickey struggles but can't pull it out and falls on the ground, launching the fiddle into the goat, which proceeds to **bounce around**, **causing music notes to sound**. Mickey hears this and gets the idea to use the goat as a phonograph. He opens the goat's mouth and calls Minnie over. Minnie gets the idea and begins to **"crank"** the goat's tail and **"Turkey in the Straw" begins to play**. Mickey then starts to join in and play along with the tune. He uses a **barrel** and **garbage can** as drums, **bangs on pots and pans**, **strokes a washboard**, **pulls on a cat's tail to make it sing** and swings it around his head, uses a **duck as a makeshift bagpipe**, **pulls on piglets' tails to make squeaks**, and finally uses the **cow's teeth as a makeshift xylophone**. After the song, Mickey takes a bow and finds Peg Leg Pete scowling at him. Pete **growls menacingly**. Mickey

sighs and attempts to walk away, but Pete **grabs** him and **dumps him** below deck to **peel** potatoes. Mickey **sighs** again and **grabs a potato**. He grabs a large knife and starts **cutting the potato** and **throws it in a bucket**. The annoying parrot flies through the window and begins to **mock and laugh** at him again, provoking Mickey to **throw a potato at him**, sending the **squawking** parrot **splashing** into the water. Triumphant, Mickey begins to **laugh** and the film concludes.

Script Breakdowns

After a script has gone through revisions and a final draft is locked, the script is broken down. In film and television, a script breakdown is defined as (1) an analysis in which all of the production elements are reduced to lists in order to schedule and budget the production and (2) the director's creative analysis of the dramatic action and design elements. The process is repeated for each scene and information is compiled into a table with columns listing the scene number, location, atmosphere, characters, backgrounds, props, VFX, dialogue, SFX, music, production notes, and comments. This helps in the creation of dialogue recording scripts, SFX, and music cue lists, which further defines ideas raised during development. The process of breaking down the script usually occurs after the producer and director review the script and mark certain elements that need to be taken care of before production, or even before preproduction can begin.

TIPS AND TRICKS

The ongoing debate surrounding the dialogue-centric nature of mainstream films reflects concerns raised in 1928. A preoccupation with dialogue, being the most obvious sound orientated element in a script can be detrimental to other elements, both sound and image. It's always worth questioning the "weighting" of a script. Sometimes as visual and sound design ideas become more developed, dialogue, particularly in animated films, can be dropped or "thinned out."

Contemplating sound in script is especially important when working on low-budget projects. If you think about it in terms of radio (mental imagery) and limited animation (illustrated radio), we can hear and imagine something without necessarily needing to see it, which can help reduce the need for complex and costly setups, CGI, and VFX.

A script will elicit both sound and imagery, but often overlooked is how sound design can impact, support, and inform the visuals. There isn't a formal or definitive process; it requires the capacity to "hear" a script, and not just dialogue or references to music. Adopting an inclusive and collaborative preproduction methodology provides the opportunity to identify narrative, aesthetic, and emotive possibilities for creative sound design.

AUDIOVISUAL DEVELOPMENT

Concept Art

Concept art explores, conceptualizes, and artic-ulates the visual elements of a film. While sound has no formal equivalent, concept art can serve as a means for exploring the look, feel, and sound of a film. Aural sketches can be created from view-ing visual sketches, mood boards, visual treat-ments, illustrations, and photographs. While static images are rarely associated with sound, they do offer aural information. Images can provide acoustical information about environments and physical information about props. In animation, if the intention is for authentic and real-sounding environments, then real rooms and locations with the same or similar acoustic properties can be sourced and recorded. Depending on the level of detail, concept art can translate into sound ideas and serve as a starting point for sourcing and creating sound and sound design effects.

- Casting and character design = dialogue, sound, and Foley effects
- Props = Foley and sound effects
- Backgrounds and environments = atmos, sound effects, sound design effects, walla
- Rooms and interiors = room tone, sound design effects

Aural sketches can also be used to commu-nicate ideas in reverse. On the short film *Lifted* (2006), writer, director, and sound designer Gary Rydstrom created a temporary soundtrack before animation, as a way of articulating what he wanted to the animators. In the film, an overly con-fident young alien (Stu) is taking an examination in alien abduction inside a spaceship. Confronted with a large console with a large number of iden-tical switches (much like a sound mixing console), he must abduct a sleeping farmer from his bed with the ship's tractor beam. Every time he selects the wrong switch, he causes the sleeping farmer to bump into the walls and ceiling. He finally suc-ceeds in maneuvering the farmer out of a window

and up into the ship, but then he shuts off the trac-tor beam without closing the cargo hatch, and the farmer plunges toward the ground. The examiner (Mr. B) takes over the controls and puts the farmer back in his bed. Upset at his failed examination, Stu struggles to hold back tears, causing the now sympathetic Mr. B to let him resume control of the spaceship. Stu grabs the controls and accidently slams the ship into the ground, crushing the famer's house. When it lifts off, all that remains is the crater and pillar of dirt, with the farmer still asleep on top. As the end credits run, the sound of an alarm clock is heard, followed by a yawn, a scream, and a thud, indicating the farmer has fallen "out of bed" and into the crater.

When watching/listening to the opening scene, you see/hear how a temporary soundtrack or aural sketch can help inform the rhythm, tim-ing, pacing, and design of a scene, sequence, or entire short film. *Lifted* is science fiction and com-edy, and in comedy films "comic timing" is espe-cially important. The use of rhythm, tempo, and "beats" (pauses) enhances the humor and allows the audience time to recognize and respond to jokes and gags. The film opens with a *tranquil night atmos*, followed by the arrival of the space-ship, which is indicated by *rising wind* and a *rum-ble* causing a wooden swing chair and a weather vane to *creak*. It cuts to an interior of the house, where the sleeping farmer *snores*. A flash of light from the ship's tractor beam lights the room, which is punctuated with music and an *electronic sound design effect*, both of which intensify as the farmer is elevated out of bed and transported toward a window. The music and sound effect cuts out as he *hits* his head on the side of the window and *snores*. The beam attempts to trans-port him through the window but misses again, and again the famer *hits* his head and *snores*. We then cut to the *interior of the spaceship* and Stu attempting to *flick* the right switch. A *hologram* of the house and position of the farmer *alerts* him that he has failed. With a *click* of a pen, Mr. B starts *writing*, noting Stu's failure.

Storyboards

While scripts serve as a starting point for pro-duction, many directors rely more heavily on storyboards to communicate their vision for a film, especially complex scenes. A film script is a text-based document and is often dominated by dialogue, whereas film is audiovisual "text," so reimagining a script in visual form makes sense for the medium. Martin Scorsese uses storyboards to visualize and plan entire films. Some of the scenes in Alfred Hitchcock's films were so complicated that storyboarding became the most appropriate way to communicate them to others.

Storyboards are visual breakdowns of the script and indicate how a film will be seen through the perspective of a camera lens. They allow production teams to see what certain shots will look like before shooting or animating them. Storyboards describe framing, camera shot sizes (close-up, medium, wide), and camera movement, so are valuable tools for identifying audio requirements, problem solving, and exploring aesthetic possibilities. As animation is an expensive and time-consuming process, creating shots or scenes that could eventually be edited out of the completed film is impractical. Storyboarding isn't limited to animation. For *Mad Max: Fury Road* (2015), George Miller devised the film as storyboards before writing the script. Ridley Scott (*Bladerunner, Aliens, Gladiator, The Martian*) is another director known for storyboarding entire films. Storyboards are a cost-effective way of aural-visualizing a project, through adding sound, given the relative ease of creating moving storyboards or story reels.

Shot Lists

A shot list is created after storyboarding and is a document that lists and describes the shots to be filmed during principal photography for a live-action film. It takes into account characters in the shot, type of shot, camera movement, action, and any important props. The main purpose of the shot list is to make sure that every part of the script is assigned a shot. Once completed, a shooting schedule is created, which takes into consideration locations, budget, time restrictions, weather, complexity of shots, pickups, on-set logistics, and actors' availability to create a schedule. In animation, shot lists are also used to determine the complexity of shots by taking into account how many characters are involved, props, backgrounds, and camera movement. In both situations, they can also be used to plan for production sound and further isolate ideas for sound.

Story Reels

Once a storyboard is completed, shots and scenes are timed to make sure the correct or proposed duration is maintained. The most effective way to do this is to create a story reel (or animatic), which consists of images from the storyboard synchronized with a soundtrack. An animatic is essentially an animated storyboard. The term is used in both film and animation, although more commonly in animation production. Storyboards, or panels are brought into a picture editing program and cut together. Today, editing software packages make it easy to time panels, add motion and camera moves, integrate sound, and export reels. Story reels help inform the picture edit and can reduce expensive postproduction time, which extends to sound design and audio postproduction. The integration of sound assists in timing and pacing, developing or clarifying the narrative, and identifying aesthetic opportunities.

Pre-Auralvis

Pre-visualization processes are becoming common in the film and digital media industries. The concept is optimization of preproduction before production begins, particularly for complex live-action scenes. Increasingly, 3D animation and virtual environments are created to block shots and camera movement, which helps establish the look of a film. This allows the director to conceptualize and test complicated scenes before production. The same information can also be used to establish the sound of film. The concept of pre-auralvis is the consideration and incorporation of sound design in early stages of development. Pre-visualization, like the creation of story reels, takes a script into an audiovisual medium. Throughout early development processes, there are pivotal "points" where hearing sound with pictures helps inform the story, the edit, and the mix. As securing funding is highly competitive, polished pitch materials can give a project an edge. Film-funding bodies are increasingly expecting more extensive pitch materials. Dedicated companies have emerged that specialize in creating pitch and pre-vis material to communicate ideas to potential investors. On *Gravity*, sound designer Glenn Freemantle sound designed a forty-five-minute pre-visualization for studio executives.

Animation studios such as Pixar and Dream-Works use "iterative/agile design" models, which incorporate editorial into pre-vis and production phases. Integrating an inclusive audiovisual editorial phase affords sound the opportunity to "update" the soundtrack against and visual changes and new edits. In turn, the director has the opportunity to evaluate how sound and image are working together. Active collaboration also helps illuminate anything that's been misinterpreted or overlooked within the story development stage. In live action, the same principle can apply, starting with concept art, storyboards, reels, or pre-vis for development of sound design, and continuing throughout the picture edit phase for finalizing sound and music prior to the final mix.

Scratch Tracks

The use of "scratch tracks" (or temp tracks) is common in animation production and refers to a preliminary dialogue track, or vocal songs in the case of musicals, so that the animation can be timed, which usually starts at the story reel stage. Using dialogue, temporary music, and sound effects is a more precise way of synchronizing animation to a soundtrack. It's generally easier to synchronize animation to a preexisting soundtrack than it is to synchronize a soundtrack to preexisting animation. Some directors also prefer recording dialogue before storyboarding, which is useful for artists to storyboard with. A cost-effective scenario is doing a "scratch recording" of dialogue using in-house personnel. The performance may not be professional or "right," but it will give the director ideas in terms of timings and performance direction. The process also helps to work out how long recording sessions are likely to take, which makes scheduling and budgeting voice recording sessions and dialogue editing easier.

The degree to which sound is able to participate in storytelling is largely determined by the use of time, space, and point of view, which means scratch tracks can be used to help clarify, define, and lock shots. Once visuals are complete, some sound elements may no longer be necessary and/or need to be revised, but having "place holder" sound makes it easier to get a sense of how a scene is working or not. Without

hearing sound, it's fairly common to overlook how sound affects image and vice versa. A shot could be depicted as a wide shot (WS), but the script and story may call for a particular sound effect that dictates a tighter shot. Sound is temporal, and certain sound elements, such as atmos and sound design effects, need time to "work." If a scene calls for rain to start and get heavier, the scene may need to be timed for that to happen. Rain generally starts slowly, with a few spots, and then builds and gets heavier. As sound design effects often function psychologically and subconsciously, audiences need time to cognize in order to engage with the intent. In addition, a storyboard or reel may not contain VFX information, and it's very easy to miss subtle details and opportunities for sound when not seeing everything that's going to be in a shot. A montage scene may have been devised with music in mind; while this might be the best direction for the sequence, it might work even better with spot sound effects and music. Once you start hearing sound with pictures, you're in a better position to assess how the final scene will feel.

Temp Music

A temp music track is an already existing piece of music that serves as a guideline, or a means of communicating a certain mood or style, emotion, pace, rhythm, progression, and instrumentation for a project. Music can come from a variety of sources, from production music libraries, film soundtracks, and CD's/albums. Without a temp track or some form of reference, composers can be left guessing as to what a director wants from the music. Temp tracks are a starting point and should only be used during preproduction. A specially hired composer will later replace the track with original music. Temp tracks can save time and money by avoiding the composing of countless tracks, because the composer has gone down a completely different path from what the director envisioned. Music can be difficult to articulate, and temp tracks can help bring a film to life while conveying the music's desired effect more efficiently than a brief, especially if the director has no musical experience.

There are a number of pitfalls when using temp tracks, and the way they are used needs to be defined before any work is undertaken. If a composer is asked to create something similar to another composer's work, there is the risk of plagiarism. Composers often feel creatively limited by having to follow a temp track, especially scores by well-known composers. If a composer is directed to adhere to the temp track, his or her creative input will also be stifled. A composer could have completely different ideas, which might be better than the temp track. A director might also select a number of tracks, or sections from many different temp tracks, and inadvertently confuse the musical direction. The use of temp tracks throughout production can also result in the rejection of original music because the temp track is heard so often anything new feels wrong or not as good. The "attachment problem" also occurs with sound effects and design; if a director has used stock effects, an attachment to them can form. Temp tracks are useful for communicating ideas and guiding a story reel or rough edit, but they should be removed as soon as possible. The alternative, and a better route, is hiring a composer early and working alongside him or her to create completely original music.

Research and Referencing

As it's difficult to articulate sound and musical ideas, using other forms of media as reference material can be helpful as a communication tool. Alongside preproduction documentation, music, archival footage and sound, illustrations, photographs, and books often function as audio research and reference tools, particularly in the case of period and historical films. To create the sound design for *Master and Commander: The Far Side of the World* (Weir, 2003), sound designer Richard King and director Peter Weir reviewed Patrick O'Brian's novels for inspiration. The film is based on O'Brian's books, specifically about naval life during the Napoleonic era, and Weir wanted both the visual and sound design to be as authentic to the period as possible. Most film projects will involve some form of audio-based research, whether it's for the purpose of creating authentic and localized soundtracks or merely reviewing and considering other materials for inspiration. *Mad Max: Fury Road's* (Miller, 2015) sound designer Mark Mangini was inspired by *Moby Dick*, drawing a parallel between the truck and Moby Dick. The truck was "personified" as a giant, growling, breathing, roaring beast through

combining truck sounds with whale sounds. At the end of the film, the truck is being fired at by harpoons, which adds to the metaphor. There's the sound of metal and deep, whale-like groans. Films are also often adapted from novels. *Coraline* (Selick, 2009), for example, was based on a Neil Gaiman novella with the same title. While there are obvious differences between film versions of novels, reading a novel introduces the story, characters, and general themes in a different way from reading a script, which can elicit ideas. *Coraline* the novella is described as a horror/fantasy tale of a young girl who finds a portal into an alternate reality. Even a simple description of the genre and brief synopsis lends itself to sound ideas, specifically the real versus the alternate reality, which is fundamental to the narrative. Sound designers Ron Eng and Steve Tushar split their roles in a similar way; one role involved creating the real-world sound effects such as impacts, doors, hits, bangs, and squeaks, while in contrast the other role was focused on creating the otherworldly sounds for the alternative world, such as a haunting mirror squeak.

Coraline (2009, dir. Henry Selick)

Design Direction

Depending on the degree of preproduction undertaken, the first step in audio production is further assessing soundtrack requirements. Materials generated throughout preproduction assist with identifying audio direction, while visual information created during production further defines soundtrack design. Dialogue and other vocal material such as walla need to be recorded or rerecorded; sound, Foley, and sound design effects need to be sourced, recorded, or generated; and music needs to be sourced, licensed, or composed.

The start point for sound design is the collecting of raw sounds. Sound designers source and record anything that could prove useful for creating sounds. Films often have specific or key environments and elements that are unique to the film, like the helicopters in *Apocalypse Now* (Vietnam War), or the truck in *Mad Max* (postapocalyptic Australia). Dialogue, music, and certain sound effects are often specified within a script, whereas nonliteral and psychological sound is implied, which entails experimentation. The process of recording, generating, and editing sound is when emotional responses to sound are identified. Even the "simplest" of sounds evoke emotion; doors can creak in numerous ways, from annoyingly to spookily. However, it's not until you start hearing sound with pictures that you can really gauge the effect.

Something magical happens when a sound effect is added to picture—and it's not predictable. After all my years of doing it, I still depend on experimenting, putting sounds against image and seeing what happens. First time I did this, as a film student, it amazed me how sound could "open up" a movie, how the combination of sound and visual could create something greater than the sum parts. Having a great sound library is essential, but the real secret is how one uses it. (Rydstrom in Milani and Placidi, 2011, para. 16)

Digital recording and manipulation has enabled the potential for greater complexity in sound design; however, attaching sound to every visual event can be problematic. Too much sound can "crush" the visuals and result in narrative incoherence, which can de-emotionalize a film. On *Coraline* (2009), director Henry Selick avoided complex background sound in certain scenes so the audience was presented with only what they needed to hear. In the film, Coraline and her parents move to an old house. Her parents are so tied up with their work that she feels neglected. While exploring the house, she finds a hidden door to a parallel world with seemingly more caring parents who spoil her. Her "other mother" invites her to stay, but she refuses after discovering that the alternate reality is a trap. The house is wooden, with many floors, so it could "authentically"

have creaked and groaned in the way that old wooden houses do, which would have made the house creepier. Instead, the house is quiet, which accentuates Coraline's feeling of alienation. The audience hears sound associated with or caused by Coraline, but not the house itself. As the film unfolds, the "other mother's" evil side is exposed and the story takes on a darker tone, visually and sonically. If the house was dark and creepy and creaky from the onset, the impact of Coraline's discoveries and the change in tone would be diminished; the dynamics of the soundtrack and the impact on the narrative would be different.

A film like *Bolt* (Howard and Williams, 2008) has a more dense and multilayered soundtrack. The plot centers on a dog named Bolt, who, having spent his entire life unknowingly isolated in a TV studio, believes that the fictional world of the TV series he plays a lead role in is real. When his costar and owner Penny is "kidnapped," Bolt escapes from the studio to rescue her. After Bolt escapes from the studio, he accidently ends up in New York and must make his way across the country, back to Los Angeles. In the fictional TV series, Bolt possesses superpowers, but once he enters the real world he becomes an ordinary dog. His "real world" journey is set in real-world locations, so the fictitious television world and the "real" world environments have different visual and sonic aesthetics. The TV action show is "shot" and sounds like a Hollywood action series, a story within a story, which contrasts with Bolt's "real" journey, which looks and sounds more naturalistic. *Blue Velvet* (Lynch 1986), is described as psychological horror meets film noir, and operates on a number of thematic levels. Alan Splet divided the film into two distinct worlds of sound: the bright, ordinary world inhabited by Jeffrey, a college student, and the dark and twisted underworld inhabited by the psychopathic Frank.

Aside from production sound, there are few differences between live action and animation for sound design, except the relative ease of integrating sound earlier in animation. Contemporary animated films hardly ever adopt the classic "cartoon" (*boing*, *kapow*, *ziiiip*) approach to sound. The goal is usually "realism," but it is frequently a different kind of realism from that in most live-action films. In animation, sound can be more easily exaggerated. We know animation isn't "real." Live-action films are trickier; realism needs to feel very real, but as most films are sound designed in postproduction, it's still a fabricated reality. The lines between animation and live action are diminishing. *Lord of the Rings* (Jackson, 2001) is set in Middle Earth, which is based on Earth, but with a number of mythical elements and creatures. *Avatar* (Cameron, 2009) was predominantly CG animation and VFX; Pandora and the Na'vi are fictional. Regardless of production format or style, through considering how something should or could sound, various directions will naturally come under discussion.

SPOTLIGHT ON: Peter Miller, Sound Designer

Sound designer Peter Miller went to film school in the late 1970s and specialized in sound. After a period of working in television, he formed production company Meaningful Eye Contact with director Alex Provas, producing music videos, commercials, and films. He later set up a music and sound design company, Perpetual Ocean, and recently Scribbletronics to focus more on self-generated audiovisual projects. His earlier friendship with film editor Craig Wood, and Gore Verbinski's interest in creating a creative "trio" (director, editor, sound), led to Miller working with Wood and Verbinski on *The Ring* (2002) and later *Rango* (2011). *The Ring* is a supernatural psychological horror film and a remake of the 1998 Japanese horror film of the same title, based on the novel by Koji Suzuki. The film centers around a strange and haunting videotape; after viewing it, the viewer dies seven days later. The videotape plays a montage of disturbing images, with sound design, which serves as the clues to its origins. A journalist decides to investigate following the unexplained death of her niece. She acquires the tape and after viewing it, finds herself with only seven days to prevent her own death, as well as that of her son and ex-partner. Horror as a genre lends itself to sound design, but it needs to feel real, and scary. Watch a horror film without sound, and generally it's not very frightening.

Doing *The Ring* was fantastic because Gore was so receptive to the kinds of ideas Craig and I were putting together, and we had a lot of contribution to the whole soundtrack, including the direction of music, the selection of temporary tracks, which made Hans Zimmer interested in the project. There comes a point, and certainly in *The Ring*, where we were very much in intellectual land. You're not scared by it anymore, so you have to make decisions about what you're doing—will it scare the audience? You can never tell how an audience is going to react to something.

  In *The Ring*, there were times when we were not sure whether something was scary or not, and it's very hard to make an assessment. There's a sequence where the mother of the girl pushes her down the well. At one stage I suggested to Gore that the scene might be much more powerful if we did it without any sound. Initially he was skeptical and then we tried it and he was amazed. We put it to test screening and it just freaked the audience out, so in the end we had to pull back because it was too strong. It also made the mother, who was callous enough pushing her down the well, seem harder—it just made the whole scene so black.

The Ring (2002, dir. Gore Verbinski)

Certain things don't translate well to test screenings, especially for sound, if it doesn't have some of the things in it you're intending to do. A good example of that was when the horse gets spooked and jumps off the side of the boat. It went to a test screening and was fine, and then we had another test screening about a week and a half later, and people were freaked out by it. We couldn't understand why there was such a big difference considering the first audience made no comment about it. There were questions about the horse, was it a real horse, but no, it's a digital horse. The difference was, we put a sound effect in for when the horse falls and hits the side of the boat on the way down, and that's what was doing it. Suddenly it felt real, and we decided that was a good thing.

Mystery/thriller *In the Cut* (Campion, 2003) tells the story of Frannie Avery, a New York City high school teacher who has an affair with a local detective, even though she suspects him of murdering a woman. As the relationship develops, she discovers more and more evidence pointing to him being a serial killer. After her half-sister is murdered, Frannie fears she might be his next victim.

In the Cut (2003, dir. Jane Campion)

One of the things we noticed straight away was that it was a psychological story, which led to the possibility of internal sound, sound that directly taps into your emotions, not literal sound which taps into a location. We realized the story was easily dividable into a vertical structure. The character spent some time downstairs; there's several scenes in the subway and a basement bar. The writer had written them in such a way that they represented the subconscious, her subconscious. Then there's the street level, the realistic element. She's on the street, talking to people, and it's all very real. Then there's upstairs, which represented her safe places. Her apartment was upstairs and her friend's apartment was upstairs. Each of those scenes plays out with her feeling like she's secure. Straight away we had a perfect sound structure. So it's sitting with the script and realizing there's a sonic environment there, it's a literal environment, and it's a psychological environment. We decided when she's downstairs, when she's underground, we'd lose all the high frequencies material, so there's lots of rumble and it's quite muffled, like the music from the club upstairs. Everything downstairs we take away the definition of reality. In the middle, we're in reality, so everything is hyper-real, we're using all the sounds of traffic, and more high frequencies, and when she's upstairs we go into a place of comfort, so we take away all the bottom frequencies, we let it feel like it's light, add some air in there. You don't notice it when you watch the film, but it really affects the way you relate to the story and her character. It's a very important way to be able to see films. It's the great thing about sound; it transmits right across reality, through the psychological to the emotional. Sound is really powerful like that. It's a direct conduit into someone's emotion. We can go in, push that emotion button right inside their brain, and they don't even know we're doing it. You can sneak up behind someone and tap them on the shoulder, which visuals can't do. Some sound works psychologically on an audience; it's nothing to do with its literality.

If I was a writer and I didn't have any sound knowledge I'd go to a sound person and say I'm going to write this script about this story, give me some thoughts. Sound people always have thoughts about things. Say it's a story about vampires and set in New Orleans—a sound person will say, you know there's swamps, there's alligators, so immediately you're getting a sound picture, and that's what you need as a writer, you need that sound picture put in your head. You might know that as a writer, that there's swamps there, but as soon as somebody says, think about the frogs, think about all the sound that's going on in a place like that, and then think about what you can do by taking it all away and having silence. Straight away you're seeing the drama of the sound develop, suddenly there's a dramatic landscape in your sound. As you start to type and think, in this scene we could have no sound, all the sound of the swamp could disappear. That's going to inform how you set that scene up, and what you do with it. For me it would be great if when a writer sits down to write a script they go, okay, here's my story, these are the locations, and here is the sound I imagine. It's about finding the sound inside the story. Every story is set somewhere and every place has its own sound environment, and it doesn't have to be a literal environment; it can be an internal environment (Spotlight with Peter).

In devising the Academy Award–winning *Rango* (2011), Verbinski and a number of artists spent more than a year creating the film as sketches with a dialogue track. Verbinski then pitched the project to Paramount and Industrial Light & Magic. He later filmed scenes of recording sessions with the actors, which were cut together and used as reference by ILM. Due to his background as a live-action director, he wanted what was later termed "emotion capture"—the actors performing together as they would in a live-action film to capture the live-ness of their vocal performances. The filmed material also became useful for the referencing of the characters' reactions and interactions, which is not usually captured during typical voice recording sessions. Verbinski wanted emotional realism rather than photore-alism, and for the animation to be "ultra/super

realistic," which entailed thinking about it as a "movie," as opposed to an "animated movie."

Rango is a lonely pet chameleon living in a terrarium, which accidently falls off the back of a car, leaving him stranded in the middle of the Mojave Desert. After an exchange with a philosophical armadillo, he sets off to find water and himself. Surviving an attack from a malicious hawk, he meets a female chameleon named Beans. She drops him on the outskirts of a town called Dirt, where he ends up in a bar pretending he's a dangerous gunslinger from way out West. Another attack from the hawk results in Rango accidently killing the bird. In the process, he becomes the sheriff of Dirt, which is presided over by an old tortoise who controls the thirsty town's water supply. Rango starts to suspect the mayor is behind the water shortage, but before he can do anything, the mayor's henchman, Rattlesnake Jake, exposes him as a fraud and Rango is cast out of the town. He walks back to the road, encountering the "Spirit of the West," who convinces him to return to save the townspeople.

I first got an email from Gore, and he said I'm doing this Western. It's kind of like a combination of Sergio Leone, Carlos Castaneda, and Miyazaki, and that's what *Rango* turned out to be. *Rango* was great; it's the best thing I've ever done. The whole experience was fantastic—the working experience was great and the movie is great. It's the most unaffected movie I've ever worked on. What you see on the screen is Gore's total vision. He was able to do what he wanted on the film, and we were

Rango on the main street of Dirt in *Rango* (2011, dir. Gore Verbinski)

able to do what we wanted on that film. It's the purest Hollywood film I've ever been involved with. He had some good producers, he also had contacts in ILM, and they hadn't done a full feature animation, and particularly the kind of animation Gore had in mind, super realistic, so they were very keen to do it. He had all the right things at the right time. It was storyboarded from the first frame to the end frame, immaculately, so the studio knew exactly what kind of movie they were going to get.

I worked on *Rango* for two years, starting when the storyboard edit was almost complete. The first thing they did after they had a working storyboard was to photograph the storyboard. They photographed every single frame of the storyboard, put it into FCP and then they started animating it in a very basic way. So you'd have a shot of Rango and they would animate a head move, just two frames, to give it some feeling of movement. Occasionally they would have Rango move across a frame. It was very basic, pencil drawings, the whole film moving like that. That's when I came onto the movie and started putting sounds in. We started building a soundtrack in full surround soundtrack, laying sound up, and working out ideas and all kinds of things. I was still in Australia at that time, but Craig was cutting and he would send me little snippets and say, "Can we do something here, for that?" He'd then lay that back into the edit as he progressed. So we literally built up a working model of the film. It ran 100 minutes, which was the contractual length of the film. It had every single frame that was going to be in the film. When they started doing animation, they were literally popping that out and popping in the wireframes, and then they'd pop that out and pop in the first renders. As we went, the sound would get refined because things were moving, so suddenly it would be different.

I also went across to Universal and did a whole lot of temp things for the big musical numbers. There was no composer at that stage, but Gore wanted some structure. There's a scene, which we call "metaphor," which is where Rango meets the Armadillo

character, and he tells him about the road—it's a metaphor. Rango goes through this process being thrown from car to car and under the truck, so I built up a rhythmic piece. Later there's a scene where the villagers are doing a weird water dance so I did something for that. None of it ended up in the movie, but the animators were told to animate to that piece so by the time Hans came on he had a fairly tightly structured rhythmic scene he could work to. We built the sound alongside everything else and a lot came out of that. Gore has great ideas for working with teams of people. We were all in the Universal lot, in a big two-story building with a theater, offices, and a whole floor, which were the cutting and sound rooms. So we set up all together, I had a sound room, and there were production people, the animators, people doing pre-vis, and the cutting rooms. So we were all together. Gore would literally walk around the rooms and sit in and listen to what we were doing, or he'd be in the cutting room. It was fantastic, because all the time you're seeing what everyone else is doing. It was unparalleled, a really fantastic way of working. I was also working with sound designer Tim Neilson, a really good sound designer. There's a sequence when Rango walks across the road after he gets thrown out of the town—we called it "the suicide walk." He did beautiful work there, which stayed all the way through the movie, so ended up on the screen at the end because it was so perfect. It's beautiful and ghostly; the cars are not heavy, just swishes. It was lovely.

There were many cases where we would put in sound and it would inform what was going on in the story. Early on we put a wind sequence in and Gore really liked it and said we should leave space for that because it really helps. It's when Rango finds himself in the desert, where he's talking to the Armadillo character, from there all the way through until he gets to Dirt. Aside from the chase sequence, it slowed it down from what it would've been. After his terrarium falls out and he's standing there, there's a slow development; he walks across to where the fish is, and looks up at the sun—there's lots of space in there. The storyboard was a still so it could be extended longer, which made it feel better, to feel the tempo along with the sound. If you're cutting a film mute and not spending time with sound, you tend to tighten everything up because you think, it's boring now, so let's get out of that scene really quickly. Your brain, quite rightly, doesn't have any information coming in so it wants to go on to the next thing. If you give it some sound, there's some space, and your brain's got something to work with (Miller, 2016).

Project Planning

Projects need to be evaluated (and often reevaluated) in order to prepare and maintain a realistic production plan. Creative opportunities, complexities, and potential issues need to be discussed by key people involved. At least 50 percent of a film is audio, and many argue that good sound is at least, if not more important than the visuals. Given today's technology, it's easier to get your film to look good than in the past, but bad sound is still the telltale sign of a low-budget film. Films with poor sound rarely get selected for film festivals or distribution. This makes it especially important to focus on getting good production sound and preparing for post-postproduction. One of the first steps is hiring a sound designer or supervising sound editor; someone capable of ascertaining requirements and working alongside the producer, director, and postproduction supervisor. The planning stage also involves establishing roles, responsibilities and relationships, budgets and schedules.

Budgets and Scheduling

Hollywood feature film sound budgets are approximately 3 to 5 percent of the total production budget. Medium-sized film budgets have decreased, and on the other side of the spectrum, independent production budgets can range from a few thousand to a few million dollars in total. A number of film directors have migrated to working in television, with budgets similar to those of medium-sized and independent films. Shorts, micro and Web-based films are a way for filmmakers to cut their teeth, often on very limited budgets, so allocating 3 to 5 percent of a total budget for sound is usually inadequate. A sound designer/supervising sound editor will be able to review materials and devise a more realistic budget, relative to available resources.

Typically, a location sound mixer will hire a boom operator and utility person, or in the case of very low budgets will handle all three jobs. The location sound team captures the dialogue, room tone, and atmos. Preparation and attention to detail ensures quality production sound, which will reduce postproduction costs. In the United States, basic budget requirements for a location sound mixer are approximately $300 to $500 per day and $150 to $250 per day for a boom operator/utility person. Sound studios generally have "rate cards" and charge either by the hour, day, or week, depending on the type of service they offer. Some studios will offer a variety of services, whereas some may specialize in a particular area, such as ADR. Media and entertainment organizations and unions provide local salary rates, which, depending on the specific role, type, and scale of the project, are normally per hour, day, or week. In the United States, rates for sound editors, designers, rerecording mixers, Foley artists, and other associated roles can be found on the Motion Picture Editors Guild website. Depending on the project scale, fees can range from $2,000 to $4,000 per day for talent. Music is always a separate budget. Musician rates are normally by the hour or number of lines in a score, conductors by the session, and composers by the minute, episode, or project. A current trend in composing is toward the "self-contained" composer, predominantly MIDI-based compositions, especially for low- and medium-budget projects.

An audio postproduction budget covers sound supervision, dialogue/ADR, sound effects design and editorial, Foley, re-recording mix, and deliverables. Sound supervision includes previewing, fixes, and client correspondence. Each stage of production should be broken down and budgeted for and the appropriate facilities scheduled and booked. As with visual elements, when working with small budgets and short production schedules, expectations need to be managed. If the budget is too low, it may be inadequate for hiring Foley artists, commissioning a composer, using music tracks from an established artist, or undergoing a Dolby-certified surround sound mix. One of the first things to establish is the final output. Is it for the Web, broadcast, DVD, or theatrical release? Most low-budget independent features and short films have limited budgets so may only be able to afford a stereo mix, whereas medium and higher film budgets include a 5.1, 7.1, or Dolby Atmos® mix. Sometimes studios have "down time," so if a project is flexible, it's possible to get reduced rates in between bigger commercial projects.

It can be difficult to schedule and budget for sound design. Estimating how long rerecording dialogue will take or the cost of licensing a music track is easier to ascertain. Certain requirements might be clear, but time for recording and experimentation needs to be built into schedules. It also varies with workflow and the size of the sound department. Each project needs to be evaluated based on the length, scope, and overall budget. Obviously, a one-minute short animation for the Internet will not require as much time as a full-length action feature film. As a guideline, sound should at the very least approximate picture editorial and post schedules; for example, six weeks of picture editorial equal six weeks of sound editorial, and two weeks of picture finish equal two weeks of mixing (re-recording). Also, if the production sound is poor, the postproduction schedule and budget will increase. As animation dialogue is usually recorded in studios, therefore controlled, a basic rule is to allocate eight to twelve hours per minute of animation for sound design, but if a scene involves a lot of action and visual effects, then usually both sound design and mixing will take longer.

Once the project and delivery date have been defined, the script broken down, and budgets allocated, the overall schedule can be created. An ever-increasing number of tools and apps are being developed for creating and managing breakdowns, shot lists, storyboards, schedules, and associated production information so it can be easily shared, revised, and updated as production unfolds. As with other areas of production, the sound schedule needs to be realistic. Scheduling is always difficult and dependent on a number of factors: the type of project; delivery dates for picture edits, animation, and VFX; and the final deadline. Scheduling will also affect the budget; if the project has a tight deadline, a bigger sound team will be needed to meet any deadlines. Other issues are availability of talent, facilities, music clearance issues, and any test screenings. Schedules will also change if there are rendering or picture issues that need to be addressed, which may require rescheduling talent and facilities.

As technology has evolved and become more affordable, it is possible to design a soundtrack without needing a full-scale commercial studio facility, especially for short films, Web-based projects, mobile games, and other smaller-scale productions. However, dedicated facilities are usually required for voice and Foley recording and mixing. A Dolby surround mix must be undertaken in a Dolby-approved mix studio and will incur mastering and Dolby licensing fees. As mobile entertainment becomes more standardized around the globe, the audio experience is becoming more a "focal point". New tablets and devices are available with Dolby Atmos(R), which means cinematic and immersive experiences can be created for home, Web, and mobile entertainment. VR, AR and 360 video is also an expanding market. But if a soundtrack is poorly planned and not budgeted adequately for, it will not take advantage of the technology and opportunities that are available.

Tech, Format, Length, and Deliverables

Deliverables affect budgets and schedules, which in turn affect quality and outcomes. Frame rates, file types, and sample/bit rates need to be defined as well as a protocol for transferring files, sessions, and outputting material across sound and picture departments. When arranging and scheduling projects, it is important to identify and clarify any issues that could affect sound and workflows. In the case of games and interactive projects, there could be engine limitations, and the platform will influence the sound design and the mix. Games sound designers need to know how software or hardware processors will treat sound effects, and if certain sound effects or voice commands have priority. The viewing/listening audience should always be considered when a project is devised and a distribution plan defined accordingly. VR and 360 film projects are listened to on headphones so need to sound good on different headphones. Increasingly, festival submissions include a digital cinema package (DCP), and most cinemas have or are installing DCP servers and 2k or 4k digital cinema projectors. This necessitates a multichannel surround sound or up-mix, which will need to be planned, scheduled, and budgeted for. More and more projects are, or are likely to be, cross-platform so require multiple mixes and music and effects mixes (M&Es). Archiving is the final stage in the production cycle and involves the backing up of a project in various formats and mediums to make sure nothing is lost or destroyed. Often projects are re-released at later stages, which involves revising and remixing the soundtrack in line with current standards. Again, a sound designer/supervising sound editor or audio director will be able to work through project requirements and identify what needs to be done and when.

Ancillary and Marketing Materials

The preproduction stage is also a good time to start thinking about and planning ancillary materials such as teasers and trailers, which will affect budgets and schedules. Trailers are frequently thematic, which means deciding on what shots and shot arrangements are going to be used. Narration, key dialogue lines, music, and spot effects usually drive trailers, so selecting visuals and doing a visual edit is problematic without sound. Increasingly common is the production of other materials such as teasers or "behind the scenes" clips, which also involve sound. With the advent of VR filmmakers are also creating VR experiences to compliment marketing materials. All additional content requires sound so needs to be considered alongside the main project.

Voice Casting

Aside from vocal-oriented sound design, sound designers are not usually involved in casting for film or animation unless the project is low budget and they possess the necessary skills. Conversely, it's not uncommon for sound designers to have experience in selecting and directing voice talent, dialogue recording, and editing, but it should not be assumed. Voice casting for animation and games is another dedicated and specialized role and is generally handled by the director and/or a casting director. If an experienced sound designer or supervising sound editor is formally involved, then he or she will be responsible for overseeing, managing, and guiding the process in collaboration with the director and producer.

The first step in voice casting is defining the types of voices that are needed through character designs/models and descriptions, references, and other development materials. Human characters tend to be a little easier to define in terms of gender and age, but as animated characters can be anything from aliens to lamps, deciding on gender and age is not always clear. Props can also speak. Does the character have feminine qualities or masculine qualities? Should he or she have an older or younger voice? Does he or she have an accent or specific speech requirements such as lisps, stammers, or stutters? If a character is large and menacing, should he or she have a voice to match, or perhaps the opposite if the genre is comedy and/or the character has specific personality traits that conflict with appearances? Most talent and voice agencies have voice samples online, and listening to artist demos is a good way to get a clearer idea or ideas. If working with an agency, they will review any information and make recommendations. After talent is selected, recording materials (cast list, character descriptions, models, reels and recording scripts for the voice talent, recording engineers, and director) are compiled and sessions scheduled. Casting sessions are usually recorded so that the director can select the preferred voice(s) to be contracted. Countries have different rates and fees, and territorial rights need to be negotiated, ideally worldwide rights. Sometimes a voice actor will play a number of characters, which can be a little cheaper if there are small or many incidental characters. This needs to be checked against any union regulations because some countries have regulations regarding how many parts an artist can perform in a given project. Before recording rehearsals are conducted, allow time for actors to get into character and address any script issues, which reduces the time spent in recording studios.

Recording

In animation and games, once a script is locked, a recording script is prepared. A common way to do this is to number each line with even numbers and use odd numbers for alternative and offscreen lines and additional vocal material such as grunts and groans. All recordings need to be named as per the project "naming convention" as they are recorded (to a DAW), or recorded on separate tracks that are named as per the character. When the dialogue is broken down, the dialogue editor can number each take with the same character, scene, and line (e.g., BOB_sc1_0010_tk1; for an alt, BOB_sc1_0011_alt1; and for a grunt, BOB_sc1_0011a_grunt1). Not identifying recordings slows the dialogue breakdown process and makes it difficult to track files. A large-scale project can involve hundreds to thousands of dialogue lines/files, and anything that slows a project down costs money.

Animation scripts can then be stripped of everything but dialogue or just left as is, with each character highlighted for the corresponding actor. Creating a dialogue recording script makes it easy to mark off what has been recorded so that nothing is missed. A full script should always accompany a recording script in case anything needs to be double-checked. During recording sessions, the director or voice talent may make changes, which should be noted and added to the final script.

It's important to record any offscreen dialogue and vocal elements such as grunts, groans, breathing, sighs, inhales/exhales, exertions, laughs, screams, and any other voice-related sounds that a character is likely to make, which also applies to live-action films. A useful tactic is to go through the script before recording and add these to the recording script. Additionally, if there is any debate over particular dialogue lines, "alts" (alternatives) can be added to the recording script. Scenes that require walla should also be noted. Voice actors can then be grouped to perform walla such as crowd noises and background conversations. Recording multiple takes of even a small group of people can be layered to create a large group. If any background conversations need to be "audible" in the mix, they should be scripted and added to the recording script. Doing this early on will prevent the need for additional recording sessions due to oversights and missing information.

Commonly, actors are recorded separately, although some directors prefer actors performing scenes together. Gore Verbinski opted for recording the actors together on *Rango* (2011) because he wanted to avoid performances that were unnatural and lifeless. Instead of reading lines to match animated characters, the cast was filmed so animators had reference material to inform the characters. If characters are running, you expect them to be out of breath when they stop and start talking. The downside to this approach is when lines overlap, it can cause difficulties for dialogue editing, which is something to be aware of when directing group recording sessions unless planning to do ADR at a later stage. The solution is using multiple microphones, which means a bigger recording team. The upside is a more realistic, energetic, and "animated" performance. Work out a strategy that suits the film, and organize and prepare the appropriate documentation and materials.

- Cast list
- Numbered script
- Recording script/ADR cue sheets
- Character descriptions
- Model sheets/illustrations
- Storyboards/reels/animatics

Copyright

Licensing music and songs can be expensive, time-consuming, and complicated. One of the big mistakes people make is assuming they can use a commercial track and writing it into a script without budgeting for it. Another oversight is not writing it into the script so copyright and licensing is overlooked. Copyright owners have exclusive rights over the music, and using music in a film is not considered fair use. To avoid legal issues, filmmakers need to acquire the necessary licenses before including any music in their films. If a project relies on particular music tracks or is musically oriented, the budget needs to factor in rights; otherwise, music requirements will need to be reassessed if cost-prohibitive.

Music is unique to copyright law because it has two copyrights, one for the song or track (synchronization) and one for the actual recording of the song or track (master), which means a specific recording of a track will often require separate licenses. When a filmmaker wants to use a song in a film, he or she must acquire a synchronization license, which only applies to the musical composition. It allows for the reproduction of the musical composition and synchronization with the visual images. The downside is the track needs to be rerecorded, which can also be expensive. If a filmmaker wants to use a specific recording of a song, he or she needs a master use license. If a filmmaker wants to release a film soundtrack, then he or she must also obtain a "mechanical license," which grants the right to reproduce and distribute the composition.

In order to obtain a license, a filmmaker must find out who owns the copyright. This information can usually be found on CD packaging or through the record label, artist websites, and organizations like the Music Publishers Association of the United States, the Australasian Music Publishers Association, and the Music Publishers Association (UK). Artists generally assign the copyright of the musical composition to a publishing company that administers licenses and distributes royalties to the artist. The copyright of the sound recording is usually owned by the record company, which administers the master use license and distributes royalties to the artist. To acquire the master use license, the filmmaker should contact the record label itself. Most media companies have online systems and music supervisors or rights clearance people who deal with licensing. Music supervisors are responsible for overseeing all music-related aspects and have specialized knowledge of music licensing and negotiation. Music licensing costs also depend on duration, which needs to be specified; the territory (United States, United Kingdom, Europe, the world); the type of media, (TV, DVD, theatrical, online); and the term, (one year, five years, perpetuity). The most common and cheapest is a limited-term festival license, and the most expensive is worldwide all media in perpetuity. Music cue sheets and accompanying song titles, which will include the duration of the cue, the artists performing the music, and the publisher(s), are also required for commercial distribution.

The other options for music are:

- Composers
- Unsigned/independent acts/bands
- Library music
- Sound design (as score)

Composers

A key factor in getting great music is getting a composer involved in a project as early as possible. Discussing requirements and ideas early can also eliminate the need for and reliance on temp tracks. A composer can provide rough ideas or sketch tracks, which can be used for reels, in animatics, and in the rough edit. The composer chosen for a project needs to be skilled in the intended genre as well. If a composer specializes in composing orchestral scores and the project needs hardcore dub, the results could be alarming. Music can be difficult to budget for, but an experienced composer or music supervisor will have a good idea of the work each cue involves. In the case of musicals or films involving song and dance, animators need the music tracks, or at least temp tracks, to work with as early as possible. In *Strange Magic* (Rydstrom, 2015), the intention was to tell a story with popular songs from the last six decades, matching the words with the story line. The film was inspired by William Shakespeare's *A Midsummer Night's Dream*, mixing fantasy and adventure to tell the tale of a group of elves, goblins, imps, and fairies battling over a mysterious potion. Music producer Marius de Vries served as both musical director and composer and collaborated with music supervisor Steven Gizicki to create new cast performances of the selected songs.

Chico & Rita (Trueba, Mariscal, and Errando, 2010) tells the story of a lifelong romance between two Cuban musicians; music and music history are the greater part of the narrative. The film is dedicated to Cuban pianist, arranger, and bandleader Bebo Valdés, who was also responsible for the original music, and a number of other pioneering Cuban musicians from the 1940s. Trueba had selected tracks rerecorded by three different bands in Havana, New York, and Madrid. The film also includes cameos by jazz icons such as Dizzy Gillespie, Charlie Parker, and Nat "King" Cole, interpreted by living musicians "playing" in character. Some films are not musicals but feature music being played. In *The Conversation* (Coppola, 1974), surveillance expert Harry Caul plays the saxophone in the film, and the music was also recorded before principal photography. When music is integral to the narrative, it must be addressed as early as possible.

The Conversation (1974, dir. Francis Ford Coppola)

Chico & Rita (2010, dir. Tono Errando, Javier Mariscal, and Fernando Trueba)

Library Music and Unsigned Artists

The easiest and most cost-effective kind of music to access is library music. In the case of period music, there are websites where music out of copyright can be downloaded for free. Stock library music is usually classified by genres and available for a nominal fee. There are still license agreements, and producers of library music earn fees when their music is broadcast; broadcasters pay a local collection society when a piece of music is used. Library music can work if all that's required is relatively generic tracks for source cues, such as background music in a bar. The downside to using stock music is that the track may feature in numerous other projects. A visual equivalent is using stock footage, templates, and clip art instead of original and custom-designed material. Library and preexisting tracks are also rarely a perfect fit, so need editing. There can also be issues regarding the quality of the actual recording. Unsigned bands and musicians are another alternative for sourcing music. It's still advisable to devise a licensing contract and specify the terms of use, even if no money changes hands.

Sound Design as Score

As sound design can have a musicality, it can function, and be perceived as, music, but unless a sound designer defines his or her work as music, it's not normally treated as a copyright concern, which can be a really cost-effective alternative to music. This type of approach still needs to suit the scene and film so should be discussed as early as possible. The Coen Brothers initially conceived *Barton Fink* without music, just dialogue and sound design, but without music, the film would've felt quite different. Always think about what's important for the film and keep in mind any budget limitations or implications.

TIPS AND TRICKS

A successful outcome hinges on considering sound and story. The right time to start the process is when writing a script, before the script is finalized. Once a film has been shot or animated, the creative options are reduced. The absence of attention to sound in preproduction has a flow-on effect into production, postproduction, and distribution. To compete internationally, independently produced films need to be of a certain "quality." Distributors and festival selectors are unlikely to select films with "bad" sound. If sound practitioners spend increasingly limited time on problem solving, then creativity is marginalized. A film might look great, but audiences do not engage with "poor" soundtracks.

Paramount to collaboration is communication, the ability to communicate ideas, which starts with the script. Preproduction materials contain a wealth of information, and solidifying production relationships and responsibilities ensures that everyone involved is "in tune" with what needs to happen, when, and why. Available resources can be assessed and an appropriate workflow defined. Arrange a meeting with the production mixer, sound designer and/or supervising sound, and the film editor to sort out a workflow, and any project dependent specifications or requirements.

For live-action films, hiring a good production sound team is essential. The costs associated with audio postproduction can be prohibitive for independent producers and directors working with low budgets. Engaging a sound designer or supervising sound editor in preproduction means budgeting can be addressed to maximize available resources. Music can be expensive, so music requirements need to be addressed very early on. Short films can also pose difficulties for composers. A very short scene hinging on music can be challenging, abrupt changes can feel abrasive, and too much music can make a short film feel more like a music video.

Another key issue to be mindful of is having sound designers and composers working on the same scene unaware of each other, which can cause mix problems. Ideally, the sound designer and composer are collaborating throughout production, for the benefit of the final mix. Production problems will always arise, but having an overarching production ethos helps isolate creative opportunities and address problems common to most projects.

5

Production

Once a script, storyboards or reels, and shot lists are approved, a project enters the production phase. Production is a coordinated process with personnel working together, utilizing resources, to achieve a set goal within a specified budget and time frame. In live-action, production centers around the shoot and production sound, whereas in animation there is more of an overlap between the production and postproduction processes. However, different studios and production companies customize pipelines relative to the project and available resources. For sound, the production stage can involve everything from recording, to sound editing and design, through to premixing. Some sound designers work in-house, which means they are employed by a studio full time, while many are contracted in as projects arise. Freelance sound designers working on smaller films are frequently asked for a "package deal," which generally means combining services and often managing the entire project, effectively functioning as a supervising sound editor or audio director. This can involve hiring a production sound mixer for live-action shoots and booking talent, recording, and mix facilities. While most sound designers will have a background in production sound, sound design is a specialist role, and most sound designers do not undertake production sound. Sound effects recording is usually a separate task from production sound, and the territory of sound designers. On large-budget productions, a dedicated separate sound effect recording team is often hired, particularly if there are specific effects such as vehicles or certain props that need to be recorded.

Production Sound

While most sound designers and supervising sound editors are not physically involved in film production sound, they often coordinate with production sound teams because of the impact production sound has on the quality of the soundtrack. Production sound is sometimes referred to as location sound because live-action films are recorded on locations or sound stages. Production sound is recorded at the same time as the recording of image (or principal photography). A production sound mixer is responsible for recording dialogue, room tone, atmos, and sometimes sound effects. The main priority is capturing good quality dialogue and separate recordings of room tone and atmos. Production sound can also include the recording of "wild tracks," which refers to additional atmos, sound effects, or extra takes of lines performed for audio only. Recording extra dialogue lines is a cost-effective way of undertaking ADR on set. Problem lines are recorded "wild" while actors are still in character, and in the acoustic environment of the scene. Production sound recording is either "single system," which means audio is recorded directly to a camera, or "double system," which means audio is recorded to a separate recorder. The recorded production sound is then later combined with Foley, effects, music, narration/ VO, walla and rerecorded dialogue (ADR).

Production Sound Mixer

The sound mixer is considered a department head and is responsible for all aspects of production sound, which includes the hiring of a boom operator and utility person, preparing and testing the sound equipment to be used on the set, planning the recording setup, determining which microphones are used for each scene, deciding on sound perspective, operating the sound recorder, alerting the director to any sound problems, keeping sound levels consistent, watching for boom shadows, and maintaining the sound report. Sound reports are the production reports and notes created to keep track of everything recorded. They inform everyone as to what was recorded (scene/ takes), how it was recorded (how many tracks, mono or stereo, "safety" tracks, track assignment, sample/bit rates, microphone selection), and general notes, which incorporate any issues.

Boom Operator

The boom operator assists the production sound mixer and operates the boom microphone, which is either handheld on a boom pole or dolly mounted on a moving platform. If lavalier (or lapel) microphones are required, the boom operator will position them correctly, either on sets or on actors. Boom operators are also responsible for testing the sound equipment and making sure it's in good working order.

Utilities Person

A utility or cable person assists both the production sound mixer and the boom operator on set. He or she helps with setting up equipment, running cables, and adjusting microphones and will sometimes function as a second boom operator when required.

On Location

Production sound practitioners encounter a wide array of challenges during a production shoot. Issues range from needing to record multiple moving actors, difficult locations, and tight schedules, to crewmembers adding unwanted sound. Location and crew problems are never intentional and sometimes unavoidable; however, there is a tendency to confuse not being seen (on camera) with not being heard (on microphone). What is being shot is the priority, not what is being recorded, which can create issues for audio postproduction. If dialogue recordings are problematic, then dialogue needs to be rerecorded and the process becomes much like creating an animation soundtrack. Many emerging and independent filmmakers overlook the magnitude of this.

Sound and Foley effects are usually recorded in dedicated sound studios, whereas atmos and room tones are typically created from production (or field) recordings. Sound effects that cannot be practically recorded in a studio, such as gunshots, are recorded on location. Eliminating background, reflections, and other sounds (unless recording atmos, which is essentially background sound) is one of the main problems encountered when recording on location. If a scene requires footsteps on concrete, it's difficult to isolate footsteps from background sound, even in a quiet location with a highly directional microphone. While certain frequencies such as AC or a low-end distant traffic rumble can be rolled off (filtered), it's difficult and often impossible to completely remove unwanted background sound. More often than not, you're removing part of the sound you want to record in the process. Most production mixers will avoid using any EQ or filtering during filming, especially when recording dialogue.

For animated films, certain locations can provide the perfect atmos and room tones if they match the visuals. In an "INT. City Apartment, Kitchen," you would expect to hear a fridge hum and background traffic. If a scene were set in a kitchen, in an isolated country cottage, prior to the invention of the fridge, then the background traffic and the fridge hum would need to be removed. As it's difficult to effectively remove elements without altering the sound, it's important to be aware of how different environments sound. It's also easy to "overlook" subtle and short duration sounds that become more apparent when atmos or room tone is looped (i.e., repeated). It's also important to be aware of environments like shopping malls with music playing as this can pose a potential copyright issue. Music can always be added but not removed from a recording.

Doing "a recce" is a filmmaking term used to describe a pre-shoot location visit to assess its suitability for shooting. A recce involves ascertaining likely or potential problems, including sound issues such as unwanted background sound. Doing a recce is an opportunity to listen to and assess a particular environment. It's also worth taking a recorder to record, for reference, which could even suffice for atmos and room tones, potentially eliminating the need for further SFX recording sessions for animated films, and as a way of building up sound libraries for use at a later date. Other factors to consider are the time of day/night, the season/weather, and the need for additional equipment such as microphone windshields and sound blankets for dampening. There are a number of common problems location sound people encounter, which can often be solved before recording.

Common Problems

- Background sound: traffic, people, dogs, birds, cicadas, sirens, cars, aircraft, trains
- Building/machinery: AC units, fans, elevators, clocks, lighting fixtures, computers/monitors, fridges, freezers
- Excessive reverb: overly reflective rooms/surfaces
- Weather: wind, rain, lightning and thunder
- Human error: microphone handling, noisy clothing/shoes, mobile phones ringing in the middle of a recording, clipping (distortion)

Common Solutions

- Reposition the microphone and/or sound source *(to eliminate/reduce background sound)*.
- Avoid recording in overly reflective rooms/within opposing flat surfaces; reposition the microphone and/or sound source *(to avoid excessive reverberation)*.

- Shut doors/windows (to eliminate/reduce background sound).
- Wait until the unwanted sound disappears (such as cars, trains, planes).
- Record at night (a quieter period).
- Disable, turn off, or remove any noisy equipment.
- Use a windshield (or record on a less windy day).
- Use a boom or microphone stand (to eliminate microphone handling noise).

- Do not wear noisy clothes/jewelry/shoes (to avoid unwanted sound).
- Always monitor audio levels (to avoid clipping or recording at too low a level).
- Employ a mike attenuator (when recording extremely loud sounds).
- Always use headphones (so you know what is being recorded).
- Record multiple takes (so there is plenty of leeway for editing).

TIPS AND TRICKS

Conduct a sound recce, allow ample time for the sound team to select and place microphones, and collaborate with other members of the crew. Do not take onboard the "fix it in post" mentality. Getting great production sound will not only save money, it will elevate the quality of your film. If you're planning to record dialogue on location for an animation film, make sure you are very aware of the potential implications.

Before a recording session, always double-check recorder and/or camera settings to make sure they are set to the correct file format, sample, and bit depth, and to ensure equipment is working properly. Be aware of the room or location and how that affects microphone placement. If you put a microphone too far away from a source, you will probably need to turn up the microphone gain, which will increase the degree of room reverb and background sound. Close miking reduces room reverb and background sound, but miking too close can "color" the recording, depending on microphone choice. A few inches from a sound source will give you a tight and more present sound, whereas farther away will give you a more "roomy," live, and distant sound, which is generally unacceptable for dialogue. When recording in a "live" environment, dampen hard surfaces, place talent away from walls to reduce reflections, and try to eliminate all background sounds. When recording on

location for animation, even if the acoustic environment is a good visual match, the dialogue needs to be as clean as possible.

A shotgun microphone is highly directional, which will help reduce unwanted background sound as long as it's on axis. Overhead miking is the most favored boom technique because it produces the most natural-sounding dialogue, whereas booming from underneath produces a slightly more bassy sound because it picks up more of the chest cavity. Shock mounts help to insulate the microphone from vibrations, but make sure the boom operator does not move his or her hands along the boom pole during takes as the sound can be conducted by the pole to the microphone. Lavalier microphones are common in broadcast work and are generally attached to an actor's or presenter's lapel. When an actor is moving, the microphone can pick up excessive clothing rustles and other unwanted sounds. Lavaliers are also sometimes used as "plant" microphones, which means they are hidden on sets.

Always be conscious of issues like leakage from headphones, squeaking floorboards, or the rustling of a script during dialogue recording sessions. Unwanted sound can be difficult to impossible and time-consuming to edit out. If there are problems, record multiple takes (wild tracks) so the dialogue editor(s) have enough material to cut together clean lines of dialogue. Listen for anything that should not be there and address it; turn fridges off and remove batteries from clocks. Think about corresponding camera angles and vary the microphone position to vary the perspective of room tones and atmos. Record multiple takes and more than you anticipate needing, so that any unwanted noncontinuous elements can be edited out later.

It's important to always do a level check before recording a take, but be aware that at times actors will talk louder or softer during a sound check. Inexperienced actors are often not aware of this, so explain that you need a few lines delivered as if it were a "real" take to make sure levels are set correctly.

Audio recorders and cameras have at least two channels, but if there are more than two actors to be recorded at the same time, then more microphone inputs are needed. One microphone can capture most of the dialogue, but it is difficult to boom a number of actors even if they are performing "static." One microphone also means each actor is recorded on the same track, which can cause edit and mix issues. If two actors are arguing over each other, and one actor is louder than the other, reducing the level of the louder actor will also reduce

the level of the lower-level actor. In this situation, two matched microphones are needed. DAWs have some advantages over recording to a field recorder. If there is an issue with a line, it's quick and easy to loop a problem take and rerecord the line while the actor wears headphones. If possible, review recordings early on in a project to check the quality, preferably in a studio or controlled environment.

When planning a recording session, consider other elements such as effects that could be recorded during the same sessions(s). Always record separate room tones and atmos, and record more than you think you need, a minimum of at least two minutes. Do not call "cut" too soon and potentially ruin a good recording.

Material such as narration and voice-overs (VOs) are usually recorded in "dead" rooms, and therefore hiring a studio is generally the best option. Voice-overs are non-diegetic, which means they are not part of a room, or the screen world, so they tend to be confusing for an audience if they hear a VO with room tone or room reverb. If recording dialogue on location that is likely to be used as VO, make sure that it is as clean as possible, but also prepare for needing to rerecord it at a later stage.

Recording Dialogue for Animated Films

Animation dialogue is usually recorded in a dedicated studio, although recording dialogue on location has become a popular alternative. When actors are employing the full range of movement, their vocal performances can sound more natural and realistic compared to standing in front of a stationary microphone in a studio. Recording dialogue on location can also reduce the amount of postproduction work required; there's no need to add room tone, reverb, or atmos. This can work, but only if the acoustic environment matches the visual, or intended visual environment, and the acoustic environment is controlled. On the stop-motion animated feature film *Fantastic Mr. Fox* (2009), director Wes Anderson opted for recording the cast on similar locations instead of using the traditional studio method. The recording sessions were treated like a live-action shoot.

In live action, the boom operator (or swinger) is always limited by the framing of a shot. For animation dialogue recording, the microphone can be positioned closer than is typical for live-action shoots because there is no principal photography. *Fantastic Mr. Fox*, based on the children's book by Roald Dahl, is about a fox who steals food from three wealthy farmers. The farmers retaliate and try to kill him, his family, and the other animals that live near the farms. Interior scenes were recorded in similar farm interiors, such a makeshift chicken house and a horse trailer. Exterior scenes were recorded outside, by a river, or in the woods to correspond with the visual locations.

Recording dialogue on a sound stage concurrently with motion-capture is also becoming a popular method for animation and games projects. Actors wear lavalier microphones on their foreheads or motion capture helmet, plus a boom

Fantastic Mr. Fox (2009, dir. Wes Anderson)

can be used to capture different perspectives and serve as a backup. Recording dialogue on sound stages means the sound team needs to be very conscious of reflections and other sounds. Empty soundstages can sound quite "live," which is not ideal for recording dialogue. Motion capture suits, head-cams, computer servers, and props can also create unwanted sound. Baffles, heavy drapes, and matting are used to reduce reverb, and installing any servers in treated boxes or off set helps reduce unwanted sound and reflections.

On *Rango*, production mixer Lee Orloff and a recording team spent three weeks on Universal's Stage 42 soundstage to record the cast performances. It was shot like a live action film, with a number of cameras, to provide the animators with the actors' facial expressions as a reference, while also documenting spatial relationships and blocking. The sets were mostly "virtual," with some physical elements such as an oak bar, a wagon, and a wheelchair. The production remit for sound was to capture the highest-quality production material so that it could serve as the entire dialogue recording for the film. Preproduction tests were conducted to work out how to control the acoustics of a large, and largely empty space. The recording team silenced props, installed portable sound walls, and used both fixed and portable

baffles to dampen sound reflections and lower the ambient noise floor. Portable rigs were used for referencing playback, video storyboards, sound effects and music cues that Verbinksi wanted to enhance the on-set experience for the cast.

It was huge fun. They got them all together and gave them costumes, not much, but a waistcoat, a gun holster, a hat, just to get them in the mood, and they played the scene out just as if it was a live action scene. The animators got shots of each of their characters. So there was a camera trained on Rango, and the animators would look at Johnny's (Depp's) performance and take aspects of his performance. Bill Nighy who did Jake the Snake, a snake, which doesn't look like a human at all, but you can see Bill moving his head and performing, and they really looked at what he did and took that into the character. It really was quite astonishing. The real advantage was Lee could put microphones on everyone because the image wasn't going to be used, so he got terrific close recordings of the cast. We had to do some ADR, but very little, it was purely to change lines that they didn't get in the shoot, because all the sound was immaculate. One particular scene I remember very vividly was the scene between Jake and Rango where Jake says "where are your pals now," which they did together and that performance really came out of them being together. There are a lot of sequences like that. The scenes with the Mayor and Rango were very much informed by the two of them playing off one another. Gore didn't want it to be hilariously funny; he wanted it to be unsettlingly humorous and weird and I think he hit the exact note of what he was trying to do. (Miller, from Spotlight on Peter Miller, 2016)

Recording Sound and Foley Effects

Recording sound and Foley effects on location, unless controlled, is difficult, because sound and Foley effects are typically detailed and "quiet" sounds, and therefore easier to record in acoustically controlled studios. Foley and effects need to be clean. Recording a Foley effect like a door shutting or slamming from an interior is easier than recording it from an exterior perspective. Exteriors are more difficult to control. Sound designers and effects editors will collaborate with Foley artists to recreate Foley sounds, usually on a Foley stage, performed to picture (video projection), and synchronized with the visual action.

Sound effects are also diverse in terms of loudness and dynamic range. Capturing loud sounds is always challenging. A door *slamming* is a loud sound with a fairly sharp attack, which poses a potential level problem, especially for sensitive condenser microphones. Decreasing the microphone gain may prevent the signal from clipping, or alternatively, using a dynamic microphone. Increasing the distance between the microphone and the door will decrease the level but increase the level of reflections and background sound. A door *shutting* is a lower-level sound, which can be close miked to reduce excessive background sound.

Sound effects such as gunshots are known for being one of the hardest categories of sound effects to record. Most assume a gunshot is one sound effect, but it's actually a number of different recordings assembled, edited, and layered. Aside from the shot, there are also the quieter elements such as gun handling and metallic clicks, which means multiple microphones and microphone placements.

SFX Lists

It can be difficult to remember what was recorded at a later stage, so all recordings should be slated, documented, and reported on. The fastest way to do this is to record a vocal ID (description/slate) at the head of each recording, while noting down any problems on the recording list (or sound report sheet), even if it's just "G" (good) or "NG" (No good). This can seem time-consuming, but having documentation and reports will reduce time, costs, and problems. Devising an appropriate naming convention also makes it easier to track and audition material.

Description

Character name, scene, line number, take (as per recording/ADR script for dialogue)

Footsteps, male, sneakers, EXT, wooden stairs (walk, stomp, run—slow/fast)

Door, wooden, INT, kitchen, open/shut (softly to a hard slam)

Car pass, make/model/year, speed, dirt road, rural (doors, trunk, keys)

Distant traffic, EXT, night, balcony/high-rise apartment

Large basement, INT, concrete, RT (room tone)

Reports/Notes

ID, date, location, microphone(s) used/distance, channel(s), sample/bit, format, problems

Transfer, Edit, Name, and Backup

After each recording session, transfer the raw material to a computer and a separate hard drive to back it up. Review, edit, and name or rename sooner rather than later because if material wasn't adequately documented during recording, some details may not be obvious when listening back. This process can also be helpful as a review period, to "rehear" what was recorded and "rethink" how elements could be treated. Sometimes just the "essential quality" of a sound recording is "abstracted," which may not be apparent during the actual recording session. Set up a library structure that makes sense for the project, such as individual folders for dialogue, Foley, sound effects, room tones, and atmos, and subcategories for specific material. This prevents valuable studio, production, and design time being wasted on additional file management tasks.

TIPS AND TRICKS

Assess the sound effects list and break down each effect into its components to ensure you have the right microphones to capture each individual sound.

Vary the length, speed, timing, and impact of events, for example pulling curtains across a curtain rail slowly and quickly, closing a door softly to a hard slam, walking, stumbling, scuffling, jumping, skipping, stomping, and running. Record each cue from different "shot" perspectives and the perspective (POV) of the character/s.

If a project is in early stages, factor in the possibility of script, shot, and perspective changes, and always record more material than you think is required.

Sound Effect Libraries

There are two options for the creation of sound effect libraries: produce your own or purchase existing stock sound effect libraries, either as collections on CD, DVD, and HD (hard drives) or purchased online as individual sound effects. Online sound effects come in various file formats, commonly .WAV, and can usually be previewed (auditioned) as an MP3. Libraries are arranged in categories to make it easier and faster to locate appropriate files. Most license agreements are standard and grant the rights to synchronize and reproduce sound effects for any media production; however, distributing, lending, assigning, transferring, or selling copies to any third party is an infringement. Purchasing existing libraries can be time-effective, but it can become expensive if a lot of effects are needed. Additionally, at the time of auditioning and purchasing a sound effect, it could sound "right" but then sound "wrong" when heard with pictures.

The advantage of creating custom libraries is that the material is original; everyone has the same sound effect libraries. Relying solely on stock or preexisting sound effect material can result in a "canned" sounding soundtrack. It's also very rare for even a "simple" sounding effect to be one "unaffected" sound. Most sound effects are a number of sounds that have been edited, layered, and treated in some way. Sound designers record, create, collate, and own their own libraries, which is ongoing because individual projects always require the creation of unique effects. Material can also be recorded or generated at higher sample rates than many preexisting libraries. On smaller budget projects, this is not always possible, so effects are created from a combination of libraries, existing and new recordings.

Creating an effects list during preproduction illuminates any potential issues surrounding the recording or sourcing of sound effects. At times, recording a particular sound effect is problematic, for example, the sound of a car from the 1930s. A similar motor could be replicated and recorded in a studio, but the result may not sound authentic. Hiring a vintage vehicle is costly and poses recording challenges; the recording location would need to be controlled so that no modern content is captured with the recording. Unless there is the time and budget for difficult or costly recording session(s), it is generally more practical to source preexisting sound effects. Stock sound effects are often "older" recordings and sometimes have been originally recorded on tape and later digitized, which can present a quality compromise. Often projects also require "localized" sounds, which are sounds distinct to a particular geographical or regional location, such as native birds that are unique to a country, or the sound of pedestrian crossings that are unique to a specific city. If authenticity is important, then these types of sounds need to be sourced unless there is the budget for travel and recording sessions. In scripts, references to effects can also be vague, for example, "a gunshot." There are numerous types and models of guns, and an M16 sounds (and looks) different from an AK-47, even though they are both classified as assault rifles.

Studio Recording

When planning a production, it's important not to underestimate what needs to be done, when, and where. In audio production, there is often confusion as to the differences between music production studios and studios designed for screen sound production. Studios are acoustically designed and equipped for specific areas and aspects of production. Depending on the type of music and scale of a project, music can be recorded and mixed in project studios, whereas full-scale orchestral performances are recorded in specially designed rooms by specially trained recording teams. While project studios can be cost-effective for various aspects of production, this can be a double-edged sword. Studio equipment, the room(s) that house the equipment, and experienced staff are important considerations. Using custom-designed recording studios may cost more, but the results are usually superior to "DIY" approaches. This also applies to the final mix; if a film or show is going to be broadcast or theatrically released, the final mix is always best undertaken in a dedicated and certified mix facility, whereas sound design, editing, and premixing can be carried out in reasonable project studios.

It can be a daunting task to ascertain appropriate facilities, which is why a supervising sound editor, sound designer or audio director should be hired during preproduction. On low-budget films, sound designers are increasingly taking on more roles, such as ADR, dialogue editing, and mixing, but this needs to be clarified. It's important to make sure roles and responsibilities are clearly defined, relative to the project and associated tasks, so that appropriate facilities can be booked.

Studio equipment and DAWs have become less expensive, but there are a lot of "bits" to the audio chain, digital technology is always changing and the media landscape forever evolving. High-end production facilities are expensive for a reason, but there are "staples," and it has become more affordable to build good project studios to undertake the editing and design aspects of soundtrack production.

Digital Audio Workstations (DAWs)

DAWs are now commonplace in studios and are essentially a computer software application for recording, editing, processing, mixing, and mastering audio. Most sound-for-picture studios migrated to digital during the 1990s, and one of the most common systems is Avid's Pro Tools. Professional DAWs have a fairly standard layout: an editor, a mixer, transport controls (play, rewind, record), and track controls. Most support multiple sample rates, bit depths, frame rates, and the importing of various audio and video file types. DAWs support multiple tracks, and as with a mixing console, each track can be adjusted individually. Most DAWs also feature automation for volume and panning plus the automation of plug-ins for altering, processing, mixing and mastering sound. Musical instrument digital interface (MIDI), a common data protocol for transferring and communicating information, is also incorporated into most DAWs. MIDI information can be recorded, edited, and played back. DAWs like

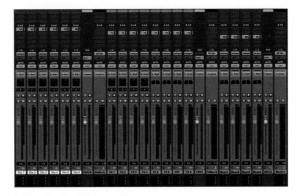

DAWs (Pro Tools) Mix and Edit windows

Pro Tools are used for various professional audio applications, particularly sound-for-picture, whereas some DAWs are geared more toward music production.

Audio Interfaces

An audio interface allows for the recording of external sounds to a computer. Interfaces are analogue-to-digital convertors (ADCs), which means they convert analogue sound to a digital format, and vice versa, they convert digital to analogue (DAC) for playback from amplifiers, monitors, and headphones. There is an extensive range of audio interfaces available, each of which is designed for various applications. Most film dubbing stages use Pro Tools HD or HDX systems, whereas design, editing, and premixing is often done on less expensive Pro Tools systems and then transferred to another system for the final mix. The key considerations are DAW compatibility, interface connectors, and the number of inputs/outputs (I/O). The number of I/Os relates to the number of tracks (inputs) that need to be recorded and monitored (outputs) at the same time. An audio interface can have anywhere from two to twenty-plus I/Os. Recording an orchestra requires a number of I/Os, whereas two I/Os will suffice for recording ADR, Foley, and sound effects. USB or FireWire connections are typical for small and project studio interfaces, while newer equipment employs Thunderbolt connections. The most cost-effective option for a project-recording studio is an audio interface with microphone preamps built in, as opposed to the addition of more sophisticated (and usually better sounding) stand-alone preamps.

Control Surfaces

Control surfaces are designed for DAWs and bridge the gap between old style analogue mixing desks (consoles) and DAWs by providing physical controls. They are a necessity for feature film mixes because of the number of tracks and re-recording mixers involved. Control surfaces are varied, ranging from basic iPad applications to large-format consoles used in film dubbing theaters. As DAWs have been more predominant, premixing and sometimes mixing small projects is undertaken "in the box," without the use of control surfaces or mixing consoles.

Plug-Ins

Plug-ins are the virtual alternative to physical "outboard" and have largely replaced what was racks and racks of physical "black boxes." Today there's pretty much a plug-in for anything: equalizers, reverb, compressors, limiters, gates, and various other effects. All DAWs come with their own set of plug-ins, which can handle most production requirements, but dedicated plug-ins and plug-in bundles are used for certain tasks such as ADR, mixing, and mastering.

Monitors

Studio monitors are an important part of the audio chain because without good monitors, it's impossible to accurately assess sound. In the same way that a microphone is designed to capture particular frequencies, speakers reproduce specific frequencies. If you compare the built-in speakers on a laptop to even a reasonable consumer stereo system, there is a notable difference. The ideal monitor has a flat frequency response, which means all frequencies are reproduced equally. One of the main issues in speaker design is bass response; most studio monitors will reproduce mid and high frequencies relatively well, but a good bass response usually requires an additional subwoofer. Monitors are "active" or "passive." Active monitors can be connected to line-outs of an audio interface, whereas passive monitors require a separate amplifier.

Headphones

Even with a high-quality speaker system, monitoring in an acoustically poor room will pose a problem for accurately assessing sound. Studios are acoustically treated so that the room itself does not color the sound. While headphones can be restrictive on long sessions, if monitors are inaccurate and/or a room problematic, a high-quality pair of studio headphones can be a better option, at least up to the premixing stage. It's also important to note that when mixing projects that are going to be heard on headphones, as opposed to speakers, re-recording mixers will test the final mix on various headphones.

Video

Video playback is obviously a necessity in sound-for-picture work, and most if not all DAWs have the ability to import and play back video. Sound designers and editors will use dual monitors, one for their DAW and one for video, and/or an external video monitor. When conducting ADR and Foley recording and re-recording sessions, talent and other staff need to see video, so studios use additional video monitors and projectors for picture playback.

Hard Drives

DAWs have recommended or supported internal and external hard drives, which are separate from the main system drive, where the operating system, programs/applications, and plug-ins are installed. Most DAWs perform best with approved and dedicated external audio drives, particularly for recording and mixing. Sound effect libraries and archival backups are less of an issue. Libraries can be stored and accessed from generic drives, servers, and networks, and session backups can be transferred to a formatted "work" drive if a session needs to be revisited.

Transfer Formats

Sharing and exchanging media across sound and picture departments is conducted through various methods. Open media framework interchanges (OMFIs) and advanced authoring formats (AAFs) are commonly used to transfer information from one application to another, including common audio/video editing systems such as Final Cut, AVID, and Pro Tools. AAF is a newer format that supports the exporting and importing of additional information such as volume automation. The more recent material eXchange format (MXF), supplies full-time code and metadata support for video and audio applications.

ADR

The primary goal when recording ADR is to obtain a clean "dead" recording so that the dialogue can be "placed" in the appropriate acoustical space. The performance needs to sound good, sync, and match the visual performance. In live-action films, ADR is conducted after production, whereas in animation and games ADR is sometimes recorded before or during the production phase. In early stages of animation production, when lip-sync is not an issue, re-recording provides the scope for improving on a temporary scratch track. If the initial dialogue was a "rough record" for pitching an idea or general timing purposes, then the script, dialogue, and intended performance can be revised. Aside from background sound and potential editing issues common in location recordings, there are some common dialogue problems that occur even in controlled environments, which are easily prevented.

Distortion

Voice-overs (VOs) are relatively easy to manage in terms of sound levels; it's rare for a VO to go from a whisper to a shout. General dialogue is more varied; an argument can start at an average speaking level and finish in a shouting match. If levels are set for average speaking, the shouting is likely to clip, and if they are set for the shouting, the speaking will be low level. There are a number of ways of dealing with variations in volume: adjusting the gain on the microphone preamp as the shouting starts; recording the line twice and setting levels to capture the average speaking on one take and the shouting in another, then editing the two takes together; using an attenuating pad on the microphone; getting the talent to move back as he or she starts shouting; and using a compressor or limiter to control levels. Most sound practitioners avoid the use of compressors and limiters when recording, preferring to "ride the faders." Adjusting gain during the performance is a manageable solution as long as the change is well-timed, and a number of takes are recorded to make sure lines can be edited together if there are problems.

Plosives

Plosives are words that start with the letters b, d, g, k, p, and t, which produce a quick burst of air, causing the microphone diaphragm to "pop" and often clip (distort). Some plosives can be edited out of a dialogue line, but a faster solution is using a pop filter, which is placed in front of the microphone or attached to the microphone stand. A typical pop filter has one or more layers of acoustically semitransparent material such as woven nylon stretched over a frame. Another solution is repositioning the microphone so the voice is slightly off-axis, though this can compromise the quality of the recording.

Phase Issues

Phase issues result from the voice reflecting off walls and other surfaces; when combined with the direct sound, it results in a "hollow"-sounding recording. In acoustically treated ADR studios, this is unlikely, but sometimes voice can reflect off a script or script stand. Covering stands with absorbent material and/or repositioning the script stand will minimize or eliminate any reflections.

Sibilance

Sibilance is a common problem in the recording of dialogue. It sounds "shrill" or like "hissing" and is made by directing a stream of air with the tongue toward the sharp edges of teeth. Words beginning with s, z, t, and d are the most problematic.

Pop filter

Moving the microphone slightly above or to the side of an actor's mouth (off-axis) will minimize sibilance but can also compromise (color) the recording. In postproduction, a de-esser is used to reduce sibilance. De-essers are essentially a compressor with a filter in the sidechain, which changes the compressor's behavior so it only reduces gain when sibilance is present. Sibilance is often centered between 5 kHz and 8 kHz, but depending on the voice can be anywhere between 2 kHz and 10 kHz.

Waves DeEsser

Performance and Direction

ADR was originally called looping and involved recording an actor in sync to film "loops" of the image that were played repeatedly with matching lengths of recording tape. The actor would watch the image while listening to the original dialogue on headphones, and then reperform each line to match the wording and lip movements. ADR involves two types of looping, *visual* looping and *audio* looping. With visual looping, the actor listens to the original line several times to get a feel for the delivery before recording. When recording, the talent doesn't hear the line but watches the pictures to match lip-sync. In their headphones, they hear the new line they're delivering. Audio looping is performed the same way as visual looping, just without pictures. The line is looped so that an actor hears the line a number of times and then

"mimics" it, which is easier for some people than the visual method.

The impact of body language and context on the performance of dialogue is often underestimated and the reason why some directors are averse to recording dialogue in the traditional fashion. When directing dialogue recording sessions, it can be easy to forget that a character is talking to someone on the other side of a room (not to the microphone in front of him or her) or that the character has just run up a flight of stairs (and should be a little breathless) or is anxious and paranoid (so will probably talk faster than if he or she were feeling relaxed). When ADR "fails," it's usually because it feels "flat" and there's a "mismatch" between sound and image. The dialogue might synchronize, but the performance lacks the degree of energy and emotion of the original or intended performance.

The key to capturing a quality performance is working with the talent. Actors and voice talent can get fatigued when having to do multiple takes of the same line. There's a point when the performance starts to suffer and even ordinary words can start to sound strange. With preparation and good direction, it's possible to limit the number of takes. If an actor is struggling with a line, it can be advantageous to move on and come back to the problematic line. There is also dedicated ADR and dubbing software to help speed up the process and make it easier for actors. VoiceQ, for example, is multi-language synchronization software that integrates with Pro Tools and other DAWs. Dialogue is projected below the screen in text and waveform, with words stretched or compressed to give visual cues about how the phrasing will best match the lip movements. Scripts can also be imported and edited "on the fly" and reporting documents such as ADR cue sheets generated.

Dialogue Editing

In animation and games, dialogue recordings are broken down and named or renamed so that the director can select his or her preferred take(s). ADR recordings for live action films can be handled the same way, although generally the director is always in attendance and will usually select takes during the sessions. In the same way that voice talent can suffer fatigue, so can directors

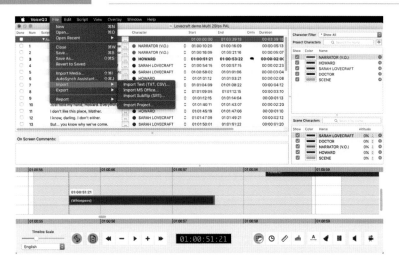

KIWA's VoiceQ
(www.voiceq.com)

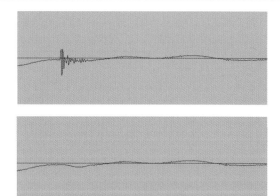

Removing clicks: before and after

when hearing numerous takes of the same line. Dialogue editors are highly skilled at ascertaining the best performances and quality of recording, which means they can select, edit, and deliver the best takes for review. During editing, dialogue is also "cleaned up." Mouth clicks and clacks are a common problem encountered by dialogue editors and caused by lips and tongues "sticking" to the inside of the mouth. Clicks can be very audible (and visible), especially when close miking. It's recommended that voice talent avoid drinking tea or coffee before a recording session. Drinking water can also help, and some swear that eating green apples minimizes the problem. Clicks can be manually removed by "drawing" the click out of the waveform with a pencil tool, which is time-consuming but often necessary. Dedicated software like iZotope's Noise Reduction & Audio Repair Software can also be used to address many of the problems sound editors encounter.

Foley and Sound Effects

Foley and sound effects add "realism." Audiences rarely notice sound and Foley effects because they appear to belong to the visual action. In live-action films, there has been an assumption that all the sound was recorded with the pictures. Film sets are fabricated; props are made of plastic and floors are often painted or treated plywood to look like another texture. The addition of Foley and sound effects make a scene feel real. Footsteps ground a character in an environment (shoes, texture, weight).

The traditional Foley recording stage includes a number of pits built into the floor. The pits are filled with different materials, such as gravel, and different-sounding surfaces, such as tiles for the recording of footsteps. The DIY approach is improvising using large trays or containers. The job is more difficult than it appears and requires a good sense of timing and rhythm. Every step is unique; the pace and weighting changes, so the sound of each step is always different.

Dedicated Foley studios also house Foley and sound effect prop rooms, which helps eliminate needing to source and collect sound props. Aside from footsteps, any "human"-generated sounds, such as clothing rustles, doors, windows, drawers opening/closing, typing, or sitting in a chair, are considered Foley. Sometimes a character is associated with a particular sound, which can be suggested by his or her clothing and is a subtle way of giving a character a "real" sense of presence.

Foley and sound effects are generally close miked and recorded in isolation, free of reverb and room tone. Subtle and detailed Foley effects are recorded with either a condenser or a ribbon microphone, while louder Foley and effects are recorded with condensers that can handle high SPLs and sometimes a dynamic microphone.

The Foley team includes the artist or "walker," who perform sound in time to projected visuals, and a Foley recording engineer. In the case of more complex scenes, like a fight or a larger dinner party scene, two or more Foley artists may perform. Sound effects and elements that need to be recorded in a studio are usually recorded in separate sessions from Foley, typically by sound designers/editors. For short or low budget films, with minimal effects, recording session are often combined, whereas on larger budget feature films Foley effects are recorded during dedicated Foley sessions.

An alternative to Foley recording sessions is the use of Foley effect libraries, although most film projects will require some original Foley recording. A Foley library combined with a sampler like Kontact 5 allows you to choose from a variety of different footsteps and "play" them back on a MIDI keyboard. Libraries come with a range of shoes for men or women—a right, left, and scuff—and by automating the tuning and velocity layers, you can alter each footstep to mimic the way people walk. Playing a footstep harder makes the footstep heavier, to reflect a character's weight.

SPOTLIGHT ON: John Simpson, Foley Artist

John Simpson has worked on numerous films over the last thirty years, which includes *Mad Max: Fury Road* (2015), *The Hobbit: The Battle of the Five Armies* (2014), *The Desolation of Smaug* (2013), *An Unexpected Journey* (2012), *The Lego Movie* (2014), *The Great Gatsby* (2013), *Les Misérables* (2012), *The Adventures of Tin Tin* (2011), *Happy Feet* and *Happy Feet 2* (2006/2011), and *King Kong* (2005). Simpson built up industry contacts after working as a projectionist at the South Australian Film Corporation at the beginning of his career. He initially wanted to be a cinematographer but met a sound recordist while doing work experience on location, which led to an interest in post-production. Simpson now runs FeetnFrames, a Foley studio on a 300-acre property in remote rural South Australia, which records, edits, and mixes Foley track for a wide range of film projects. The remote setting also enables him to record location based Foley and effect recordings such as gunshots. He is licensed to record shots from almost any type of weapon and has access to hundreds of modern and antique firearms.

I love to create and try new things, so getting into Foley was just perfect for me. It took me five years to become a Foley artist. To begin with I was doing things like sound transfers, running the projection room, loading the magnetic dubbers—back in the day that's all we used. In 1982 when I started to record foley, it was only over three tracks, feet on one, fx on another, and then the cloth track. We have up to five people in the studio at times, all doing feet together. With digital technology, it's mostly one artist doing everything, and we have gone from three tracks to over 100 on some large-scale films. The greatest advancement today is the digital recording platforms, such as Fairlight (my preferred system) as well as Pro Tools, which is a real time saver, and we need it, mostly because the budgets are just getting smaller. My rate for standard type feature drama has not changed since 1997. In fact, we've had to go cheaper to fit into current budgets, plus with advancement in film now, where it's all shot on digital camera and the editing process is such that a director can swap shots and recut so easily, that then affects us down the line to try and make things we have recorded work with the new cut, or try and get extra funds to rerecord, with the latter hardly ever happening these days.

I think one of the main things for filmmakers from all areas to look out for is props—give an actor a prop and they will do stuff with it, then whatever that is, I have to make its sound! I've done plenty of indie films and on most of them a lot of favors are pulled in from actor friends etc. to really make a low-budget film look amazing for little cost, but just remember that all that nice cheap action has to have a Foley track, at least for M&E purposes, plus the rest of the soundtrack, so keep a bit of money aside.

Foley really is the sprinkle of icing on an indie film; it will add great detail to those delicate shots, and just that alone can change the shot mood. If your location is a noisy one, then it's very hard to get any detailed sound from the location sound. In the sound editing process all the gaps between words will be taken out, leaving only the clean dialogue, and that's where Foley comes in, to fill any cloth moves, jewelry tinkles, etc.

Lastly, if on set you have a prop with a particular sound, then look at sending that to the Foley team, just so they can get a match on sound—it certainly makes things a lot easier.

Animation is a bit different, there's a much wider scope to play with sound, especially in a creature-type or magical-type film, whereas in live-action you can only go so far before it sounds ridiculous. I really enjoy animation, like the Lego films; I am currently doing Lego Batman, which is so much fun. (Simpson, 2016)

Sound Design Effects

While sound design effects (or elements/textures) are often defined as nonorganic, fabricated or as "special effects", frequently the origin(s) are ordinary real-world, organic sounds, and/or a combination of the "real" and generated sound. Synthesizers are typically used for creating sci-fi sound effects, drones, pads and textures, and samplers for creating stylized sound design effects, but there are no hard and fast rules as to how a synthesizer or sampler is used.

Kontakt softsampler (Native Instruments)

Synthesizer and Samplers

A synthesizer is an electronic or a virtual instrument that uses oscillators and filters to create waveforms, which are processed to generate sound. Some synthesizers can closely reproduce the sound of musical instruments so can be used to create "organic"-sounding material. Synthesizers are controlled with a piano-style keyboard, called a MIDI controller, which acts as an interface between the user and software. MIDI is an industry-standard protocol established in the early 1980s to enable electronic musical instruments to control, communicate, and synchronize with each other. MIDI does not transmit an actual audio signal; it transmits event messages such as pitch, intensity, and vibrato. Most DAWs are MIDI capable and come packaged with virtual instruments. MIDI can be integrated into sessions, edited alongside audio, and rerecorded as audio. There is a wide variety of virtual studio software and synthesizers, which use different technologies to generate an infinite number of new and unique sounds.

Subtractive and Additive Synthesis

Subtractive synthesis in its most simplistic form consists of an oscillator (sound source) running through a filter, which is then sent to an amplifier and envelope (ADSR) control. The subtractive synthesizer was initially designed to mimic instruments, but then developed into its own "instrument." The basic principle of subtractive synthesis is to start with a simple waveform (such as a square, triangle, or sawtooth) generated by

an oscillator, remove (subtract) certain frequencies with a filter, and manipulate the envelope response. The filter selectively removes certain harmonics or frequencies, altering the spectral content of the original waveform, and the envelope alters the "shape" of the waveform. Additive synthesis is similar except it "adds" instead of subtracting; multiple waves of varying levels and frequencies are combined to build different harmonic structures.

Frequency Modulation Synthesis

Frequency modulation (FM) synthesis employs a modulator oscillator that varies the frequency of a simple waveform, resulting in a more complex waveform and differing tones. FM synthesis is not effective at refabricating acoustic instruments and is generally used to create the more "synthetic" and electronic type of sound effects.

Physical Modeling Synthesis

Physical modeling synthesis uses algorithms to define the harmonic and acoustic characteristics of the sound being generated to simulate a more physical source of sound, usually a musical instrument. Synthesizers can be programmed to make distinctions between specific principles and design aspects of different instruments such as materials, size, and dimensions.

Wavetable and Vector Synthesis

Wavetable synthesis employs a table with various switchable frequencies played in certain orders (or wavetables). When a key is pressed, the sound moves smoothly in order through the wavetable, changing its shape into the various waves in the table. Wavetable synthesis is used for creating effects, textures, and pads. Vector synthesis employs the same method, except it uses a two-dimensional grid, which is considered smoother sounding.

Phase Distortion Synthesis

Phase distortion synthesizers are subtractive synthesizers that employ the waveform flexibility of wavetable synthesis in the oscillator, which allows for the control of waveforms between set shapes. The oscillator produces a periodic signal (sine, square, saw, triangle), and the fundamental frequency of the oscillator is determined by how fast the shape is repeated.

Samplers and Sample-Based Synthesis

A sampler is similar to a synthesizer, but instead of generating sounds, it uses audio recordings (or "samples") of sounds that are loaded or recorded by the user and then played back by a keyboard, sequencer, or other triggering device. Most samplers have filters, modulation via low-frequency oscillation, and other processes to modify the sample in many different ways. Samples can be assigned to a keyboard in different zones and played back at different pitches/speeds. Samples can be anything from recordings of real instruments to sound effects. For example, a recording of a helicopter blade swooshing could be played back at a lower pitch and slower speed, and depending on the processing (reverb, flanger, etc.), could sound like the helicopter blades in *Apocalypse Now*. Real sounds can be altered and stylized to blur the line between "real" and "surreal." Like with synthesizers, there is a variety of options, from simple apps to more complex programs.

Granular Synthesis

Granular synthesis works on the principles of wavetable synthesis and sampling, except on a micro-sound time scale. Instead of an oscillator providing the original waveform, sound samples (or fragments of sound) are used, which are split into small pieces of around 1 to 50 ms, called "grains." Multiple grains can be layered and played at different speeds, phases, volume, and frequency. Granular synthesizers can create complex waveforms and are used to design sound effects, sound design elements, and textures.

These forms of synthesis are present in numerous different programs and full software programs that combine synthesizers, samplers, signal processors, sequencers, and mixers. Increasingly, synth apps and app versions of popular programs are being released, which is a cost-effective way of experimenting with different models. Packages such as Reaktor also allow users to custom design and build their own custom synths, samplers, effects, and sound design tools.

Graphical modular software studio Reaktor (Native Instruments)

TIPS AND TRICKS

The options for creating sounds are endless, and in the same way that microphones are applicable to specific recording applications, there is not one option for all occasions. Real sounds are complex, and currently there isn't the technology to generate truly organic sounds. Overly synthesized sound effects tend to feel machinelike, artificial, and electronic, and therefore out of place in many film genres, aside from sci-fi. A laser is an obvious synth-generated effect, however synthesizers designed to emulate real instruments can be used to create interesting, unique, and organic-sounding sound and sound design textures.

It boils down to selecting the right "source," tools, and process. A single bass guitar note, or a kick (acoustic or electronic) drum sample repeated, filtered, and effected, could provide the basis for "depicting" a pounding headache or serve as a texture to underscore and add tension to a scene. A wild recording of a jackhammer, equalized and played at a lower pitch, could also provide a convincing alternative. Most of the sound design textures heard in contemporary films are a combination of real, generated, and processed sounds.

Unlike sound effects, many sound design effects and textures are not sync dependent, which means they can be created during preproduction and production. On *A.I.* (Spielberg, 2001), sound designer Gary Rydstrom looked at design work to get a sense of what the cities, characters, and vehicles were going to look like. It's helpful for sound designers to get a sense of what might work for particular environments, moods, themes, scenes, props, and visual aesthetics, which can be via artwork, production stills, and footage from the shoot. This can spark ideas for recording and/or generating material as a 'start point' and "tooling up" in terms of sound design technology and processes.

SPOTLIGHT ON: Hweiling Ow, Filmmaker

Hweiling Ow is an independent writer, producer, and director who creates short films and Web series with writer/director and partner Peter Haynes. Ow and Haynes' first Web series, *Jungle Fever*, won Best Web Series in the LA New Media Web Festival (2011), their second crowd funded series, *AFK (Away from Keyboard): The Web Series*, was awarded Best Web Series at the New Zealand Web Fest Awards (2016), which led to funding for a second series. On the strength of these successes, the pair were also awarded Web series funding from *Skip Ahead*, a joint initiative from Google/YouTube and NZ On Air. The aim of the fund is to support online storytellers to expand their vision and create new narratives for online audiences. Ow discovered her affinity with the horror genre through writing T Is for Talk (2012), a short film made for The ABCs of Death, and has recently been awarded funding to direct a short as part of women-led horror anthology.

I'm currently working on a web series horror anthology for the H2Ow Channel on YouTube. The web series horror anthology will be six short films based in New Zealand. It's called Ao-terror-roa, which is a play on Aotearoa, which is the Māori name for the New Zealand. I'm also working on a couple of short shorts for web-based Crypt TV in USA, who specialize in short-form horror content.

Sound is definitely a massive element when it comes to horror, so we're thinking about sound for each short film, as each film will require different sound design to tell the story. Sound often gets overlooked in the preproduction stages of a lot of films, but I think if it was given more thought beforehand, the impact on a film would be immeasurable. A lot of the scenes I write, and I don't usually realize it at the time, but the scenes always have an element of sound design in them as a form of character, and in a way that adds tension to the

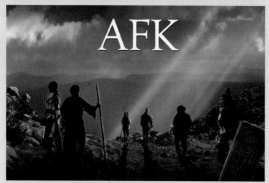

overall story. I usually think about the type of emotion I am going for, and if you work with the right sound designer, they can bring that emotion in, through sound design, and when that happens, it's magic! The whole story just takes on another level of depth.

Indie filmmaking is challenging. We always try to keep things simple, to make sure we all have enough time to do the work, but other things will always pop up in life, which can take precedence over a project, purely because we all have bills to pay. I endeavor to keep communication channels open, but always factor in deadlines along the way, otherwise a project could go on forever. I also think you need to be inclusive with your discussions, as with any creative project it's a collaboration of many creatives, on many levels. Firstly, you've got to gel. It's like finding a personal relationship, but on a creative level. Secondly, you've got to like their work. Be honest with each other but also be kind. Don't be afraid to face the fact that certain friendships will last, but some working relationships won't, and hopefully your friend and colleague can and will see things the same way. Get an amazing sound designer who loves your projects, and when you find that special someone, hold on to them! (Ow, 2017)

(a) Anzel Greyling in *T Is for Talk* (b) *AFK: The Web Series* (c) *JF2: Primal Fury*

Aoterroroa, series launch (H2Ow, 2017)

Development

Spotting Sessions

The traditional film "spotting" session entails the director and sound team getting together to watch a cut and decide where music and sound effects should be and why. During spotting sessions, SMPTE time code is used for identifying sound and image sync points, and the entry and exit points for music cues, which are all noted. Picture edits are typically exported with burned-in time code along with other materials such as effect cue sheets and edit decision lists (EDLs). Film spotting sessions are normally conducted after a rough cut and attended by the producer, director, supervising sound editor, sound designer(s), composer and sometimes the picture editor. Sometimes "physical" spotting sessions are not always possible or practical because work is undertaken in different countries or the director is tied up on other projects. In some situations, there are no sound effect spotting sessions; the sound designer(s) spot as they design, without any direction, and the director assesses the pre or final mix.

In animation, spotting can occur in pre-production and throughout production. Earlier audio "sketches" are further developed, revised, and experimented with. Often there are alternatives; for example, a number of sound effects could work for a given visual cue or effect. Sound designers/editors frequently leave "muted" material in a session and revisit alternatives prior to the final mix. Deciding what could be dropped or kept can be counter-productive, especially without a locked edit. On the other hand, too much material can cause mix problems.

Working with Animatics

In animation, as production advances, animatics or works in progress (WIPs) are updated. Working with animatics means the soundtrack is being designed and revised alongside visuals, which helps with story, pacing, and shaping the rough cut.

The first mixing task is the preparation of a temp soundtrack for audience test screenings and studio or client previews. This puts an additional demand on sound editors and designers to create at least the major effects and resolve any sound-image problems. Most directors are opposed to screening a film unless it has a relatively complete soundtrack. A temp mix is a preliminary mixing of dialogue, music, and sound effects, so that pre-vis, storyreels, animatics, and picture edits can reviewed with all of these elements incorporated.

SPOTLIGHT ON: Adam Elliot, Animation Director

Harvie Krumpet (2003), a surprising Academy win, at least for director Adam Elliot, utilizes Claymation to tell Harvie's unfortunate biography. Elliot made his first short film, *Uncle* (1996), about an anonymous uncle, narrated by an anonymous nephew, while a student. His second film, *Cousin* (1998), explored the childhood relationship he had with his cousin, followed by *Brother* (1999), which explored childhood memories of his brother. As a writer, director, and animator, Elliot has a distinct storytelling style and an aesthetic approach that he's carried through and developed in subsequent films.

Harvie Krumpet, a more complex and larger-budget short film, tells the story of a man cursed with bad luck. Born in Poland in 1922, Harvie is brought up by a lumberjack father and a lead-poisoned mother who works in a mine. Suffering from peculiarities and odd twitches, Harvie is diagnosed with Tourette's syndrome. The other children at school tease

Uncle (1996), *Cousin* (1998), and *Brother* (1999)

him, so his illiterate mother with a thing for "fakts" homeschools Harvie. The film contains a number of these "fakts" as Harvie carries on the tradition of gathering them. As he grows older, his mother gets crazier, often mistaking him for an intruder. Longing for change, Harvie discovers his house burned to the ground and his naked parents frozen to death on a bicycle. While attending their funeral, the Germans invade. Harvie flees to Australia, where he ends up living in suburbia with eleven other migrants. He gets a job at the local dump and tries to make friends, which results in a punch in the head from a coworker. His skull is split in two, requiring a steel plate. After lint picking and selling pencils, he gets a job collecting golf balls and is struck by lightning. Harvie survives, but his habit of smoking twenty-eight cigarettes a day gives him asthma, and the plate in his head has turned him into a human magnet. While he is sitting in a park feeling sorry for himself, a statue of a Roman poet tells him to "seize the day." This strikes a chord with Harvie; he decides to stop believing in fate and start living. He joins a nudist group, becomes a vegetarian, and liberates chickens. Despite being enlightened, he loses a testicle, but meets Nurse Valerie and gets married. After Harvie is found sterile, they adopt a thalidomide girl they call Ruby. Harvie quits working to teach "fakts" to Ruby, who excels at school, becomes a lawyer, and moves to the USA to champion the rights of the disabled. On Harvie's sixty-fifth birthday, Valerie's brain clots and she dies. Harvie becomes a hermit and slips into senility. After trying to withdraw money from his microwave, he is sent to a nursing home for Alzheimer's patients. At the home, nudity is banned when Harvie is found

naked and passed out on the floor after performing a drunken finger puppet show with his roommate. As Harvie's Alzheimer's gets worse, he slips in and out of dream worlds, most notably when the local church group visits. Suffering depression, he's put on Prozac, but missing Ruby, he decides to overdose on morphine instead. During the suicide attempt, he meets another patient who does commit suicide, and Harvie decides to just enjoy the time he has left. He gets naked, sits in the nursing home's "pretend bus stop," and waits for a bus that will never come.

In 2005, *Harvie Krumpet* was named one of the top 100 animated films of all time by the Annecy Animation Festival board. The film's success helped Elliot create his first feature,

Harvie Krumpet (2003)

Mary and Max, winning the award for Best Animated Feature at the Stuttgart Animation Festival, the Audience Award at the World Festival of Animated Film in Zagreb, and a shared Grand Crystal Best Feature Award with Henry Selick's *Coraline* (2009) at the Annecy International Animation Festival. The film tells the tale of an unlikely twenty-year friendship between pen pals—Mary, a lonely and odd eight-year-old girl living in the suburbs of Melbourne, and Max, a middle-aged, overweight man living in New York suffering from Asperger's syndrome.

Mary is the only child of an alcoholic mother and a distracted father. One day at the post office, Mary decides to write to a person picked at random from one of the international phone books. She accidently tears out a page during an incident with her "klepto" mother and later writes a letter to Max. Max is initially distraught by the letter, but finds the courage to write back. Despite their differences, they share a lot in common: a love of chocolate and a TV show called *The Noblets*. As the exchange progresses, Mary's curious questions disturb Max, and his sporadic correspondence causes anxiety for Mary, who is growing up and experiencing her own problems. As she learns more about Max's condition, she decides to study psychology at college, and writes a book on Asperger's. When she sends Max an advanced copy, feeling betrayed, he loses it and sends her the typewriter key for the letter "M," which causes Mary to lose it. She shreds all the book copies and sends him a can of condensed milk, her favorite food, as an apology. Max eventually overcomes his anger and writes back to Mary. He sends her his entire collection of Noblet

figures to say he's forgiven her. The gift prevents the distraught and now-pregnant Mary from hanging herself. Later, with her new baby, she travels to New York and finds Max leaning back on his sofa, having just passed away. As she sits beside him, following his gaze, she sees that Max had pasted her letters all over his ceiling.

The film involved more than 200 puppets, 130 sets, and nearly 500 miniature props. A larger budget allowed for a bigger team and higher production values. In keeping with Elliot's previous works, narration drives the story, with sync dialogue, sound design, and music. The sound design is often subtle: Saturday afternoon suburban atmos, contrasting with the more prominent New York City sounds, gunshots included. Music further supports the two differing environments, drives key emotive scenes, and supports the comical events. However bleak the storyline, it's loaded with comic moments that could almost be missed if they weren't punctuated with sound effects. There's Grand Poppy Ralph's erect nipples, the counting of sheep, babies in the bottom of beer glasses, and the wobbly mother who bakes drunk mistaking the dishwasher for the oven. Sound draws the eye, enhancing visual details, character traits, and the two differing environments the lead characters inhabit.

Elliot's most recent film, *Ernie Biscuit* (2015), explores the life of a deaf Parisian taxidermist and marks a return to short form. As an independent filmmaker and someone intent on telling his own stories, in his own way, Elliot has also used *Ernie Biscuit* as a vehicle for exploring new technology and

Max in *Mary and Max* (2009)

Mary in *Mary and Max* (2009)

ways of reducing production costs in preparation for his next independent feature film.

Uncle (1996), Cousin (1999), and Brother (2000) are very minimal with the sound. They were also shot on film and sound was done the old-fashioned analog way. You didn't have the luxury of complex soundtracks, but now you do; with computers you can have many tracks and hundreds of layers. Right from day one I've always known that sound is crucial. As my films are driven by narration, it's important to have very good voice recordings, particularly with my first three films, because there's no music at all. The narration is what's driving the film. I agree with criticism about the use of narration: it's often seen as a lazy way of telling a story, and it certainly can be, but I've always argued that my budgets don't allow for a lot of lip-sync. Stop-motion animation is incredibly slow and therefore expensive to do, so having a narrator saves money. I also love the anonymous narrator, guiding and telling you what's happening. There's something very intimate about narration that I've always loved. There's that quote, "Don't say it, show it," and I always apply that principle when I'm writing and doing the storyboard. I try to keep my narration to an absolute minimum and pair it right back. The award for Harvie Krumpet was unexpected. I was just glad when it was completed. We didn't have very high expectations. It's a very long short—festivals hate long shorts—it doesn't have a plot, and it's quite linear. So Melanie and I were shocked when it happened, but then quickly realized that an Oscar was going to allow us to make a feature film.

I do a lot of drafts of the screenplay and once that's locked off I hand-draw all my own storyboards. I've never

Max in Mary and Max (2009)

employed a storyboard artist. I've only ever had one animatic and that was on Mary and Max, because it was a feature and there was so many other people I had to work with. It was easier to have an animatic. My storyboards were scanned and then put into an Avid. They weren't overly complex, but the good thing about having an animatic was being able to insert the music very early on in preproduction. It helped the animators understand why I was using certain pieces of music and how crucial they were. I often choose music at script stage and it's the impetus for a certain scene or moment. So music often comes first, even before the characters. I'm writing a new screenplay at the moment and the whole film has a signature piece of music I chose even before I came up with plot. Music in my later career has actually become a wonderful way of conveying emotion, mood, humor, and pathos. That's why I use a lot of very emotive classical music juxtaposed with quirky, cheesy music. It's a bit of a smorgasbord of styles and varieties. I was lucky on Mary and Max because we had $8,000,000. My producer Melanie said go nuts and choose whatever pieces you want, so I did, but once we started to investigate how much it was going to cost, we were quite shocked. A lot of the cheesy music I'd chosen was actually quite expensive because it was used in advertising, for jingles. There was a lot of negotiation and begging, and it still went into the hundreds and thousands of dollars for licensing. We also had a composer and an orchestra, so that became quite expensive as well.

Peter Walker, the sound mixer, was great. He was fantastic because he was more of a perfectionist than I was, and always reminded me of how important the sound was. He spent a lot of time getting the sound right on *Harvie Krumpet* and I don't think he's been given enough credit for that over the years. Most of the music was from CDs, and we didn't have a composer, so he wasn't given a lot to play with, but we did put a lot of effort into Foley. It is a shame, because my films are narrated and the narration often wins, so the music and effects have to be pulled down. Just like a lot of shots and scenes end up on the cutting room floor, so does a lot of fantastic sound. On *Mary and Max* I also had a wonderful film editor, Bill Murphy—he was just as much of a perfectionist as Peter Walker was. The edits to all my films have taken weeks and weeks and weeks, and months for *Mary and Max* because of that very fact, the narration was always competing with all the other elements. So it was very manicured, extremely slow, and therefore expensive to get it all balanced.

Ernie Biscuit is more of an experimental short to test out new types of software and plasticine. We realized after *Mary and Max* that $8,000,000 was a luxury, so we had to work out ways of getting our budgets down, particularly as we want to keep making art house independent films. I certainly never want to make a high-end kids' film—not that there's anything wrong with that, but my films are for adults. So we realized that we had to come up with new ways of making films, in a cost-effective manner, and that was what *Ernie Biscuit* was primarily about. Surprisingly, it's doing quite well for a film that was extremely low budget. In regards to the sound, I did most of it myself. That's always dangerous, when you try and do everything yourself, particularly sound, because it's such a specialized component of making a film. You should never edit your own film, and I think I'll add to that, you should never do all your own sound. I had a wonderful sound mixer, but as I self-financed *Ernie Biscuit* I couldn't afford hundreds and thousands of dollars to employ a team of sound designers. I think more than ever I've realized the importance of a good soundscape. In an ideal world, I would continue to employ John Simpson, who does incredible Foley. We had him on *Mary and Max* and he's a genius. Having said that, I have done my own Foley, I've now downloaded Foley, so there are always ways. You have to think laterally; there's a lot of compromise,

Mary in *Mary and Max* (2009)

Max in *Mary and Max* (2009)

as with any low-budget film. I love Foley and will always go for something real and authentic over something that comes from a library, but they are a cheap and efficient way of gathering material. I think the danger for animation is, if you go for cartoony sound effects, unless that's what you're aiming to do, to make a cartoon animation, it's *doinks* and *dings*, and I hate all that.

For me it's about creating authenticity and believable characters. Ultimately I'm trying to convince the audience that these lumps of clay are real people, so when they die you are genuinely affected and moved. The last thing you want is your soundtrack to sound clinical or fake. You need to put as much effort into sound as into vision. There's a piece of music from *Eye Level*, a 1972 single by the Simon Park Orchestra, used in a Dutch detective series. I just had to have that piece of music. It's also the intro to the film and the credit film. It's a very cheesy, upbeat, '70s instrumental, and I quickly discovered that it was also expensive. I had to decide whether I was going to go with it and sacrifice a lot of the money that I had saved for the film. It cost thousands of dollars to license and I had to negotiate heavily for it, but without that music I think the film would suffer. I just had to have it. I also had Tchaikovsky's 1812 Overture, but luckily he's dead, so that's a lot cheaper. The luxury with *Harvie Krumpet* was we had $300,000 so could proportion a lot of that to sound. On *Ernie Biscuit* I had to do all that myself. I managed to do it, and it works for this film, but it certainly doesn't have the layered richness that *Mary and Max* and *Harvie Krumpet* had.

There's an assumption sound happens in post—it's an afterthought. It's very dangerous to just approach sound when you're sitting in the edit suite. Talk to a sound designer early on and start planning at the storyboard stage. We have the luxury of creating very dynamic

Ernie Biscuit (2015)

soundtracks if we chose, with time and money. Give your sound mixer lots to play with, just as you would give your editor lots to play with. Strive for authenticity and try to be a lateral thinker. If you can't afford a certain piece of music, don't be scared to negotiate or find something similar. Always get a good sound mixer; don't attempt to sound mix yourself. Budgeting is a tough one. It really comes down to what sort of story you've written. It also depends on the scene, but sound is just as important as the visuals. With any short film or independent feature film, there's always budget constraints. The mistake a lot of filmmakers make is that they don't put enough emphasis and money into the sound. They'll have very high-resolution images, but they think high production values are just visual. To me that's also the sound. I worry that a lot of emerging filmmakers are obsessed with the look of their films, and sound and story is secondary. For me the story is always paramount, and then of course I want my films to look and sound as beautiful as possible. (Elliot, 2016)

TIPS AND TRICKS

Having the right personnel, talent, facilities, and tools is important, as is preparation. Make sure your supervising sound editor or sound designer has read your script well before production begins to ensure all audio requirements are identified, so that they can be planned and budgeted for in advance.

In live action, the production focus is on the shoot, capturing quality dialogue, room tone, atmos, wild tracks, and other effects where appropriate. If the script involves any unique sounds, props, or specific vehicles, make sure they are also recorded (wild); they will probably be more authentic and of a higher quality than the material found in most sound libraries. If the script involves crowd scenes, utilize talent and extras and make sure these are also recorded separately. Large crowds can be difficult to emulate in postproduction.

In animation, by the end of production, the soundtrack should be relatively well conceptualized. When hearing sound with pictures, dramatic opportunities and dynamic moments are easier to realize. Being selective and story focused also helps streamline the postproduction process; the mix should be taken into account and planned for during preproduction and production.

6

Postproduction

Postproduction is considered the final stage of creating a film, encompassing many different processes: picture editing, VFX, grading, music composition, ADR, sound editing, design, mixing, and mastering. The majority of work undertaken in audio postproduction is sound editing and design, followed by premixing and the final mix. Soundtracks are mixed, mastered, and encoded relative to the project's distribution and release model: Web, broadcast, DVD, and cinema, Since the late 1990s, animated, CGI, and VFX-heavy films have dominated mainstream cinema, which has altered approaches to film production. Pre-visualization techniques have gained wider acceptance across the media and entertainment industries. Cameras that capture 3D volume information are also being designed to make it easier to integrate live action with CGI, and cinematic VR has become a reality. Animation, digital migration, and emerging technologies are essentially redefining conventional film production processes and blurring the lines between mediums and production stages. Some practitioners maintain that a film is created in post because of the impact editing has on a film, however the general trend is greater consideration of postproduction in preproduction.

Sound and Picture Editing

Postproduction supervisors are responsible for managing postproduction and maintaining good channels of communication between the producer, editor, supervising sound editor (or sound designer, audio director), external facilities, and the production accountant. The complexity varies according to the type of project and budget. On low-budget projects and shorts, the producer or director may take on the role. On animated films and feature films incorporating CGI, the postproduction supervisor is usually involved during preproduction and throughout production. In games production, the role of narrative designer is evolving, which incorporates assembling prototype story components such as storyboards and animatics; working with animators, artists, editors, designers, and programmers; and liaising with the sound department throughout the production phase. The increasing popularity of pre-visualization processes has introduced the role of "pre-vis editor," someone who edits animated QuickTime movies and is responsible for recording temporary dialogue and editing sound effects and music.

Traditional live-action film postproduction starts with the logging/ingestion of dailies or rushes, followed by the first assembly and a rough cut, a first cut, a fine cut, and a final cut. Edit changes make finalizing sound and music difficult, which results in delays and budget issues. Conversely, it's difficult to lock a picture edit without sound. There are various ways of handling picture changes across departments. The picture editor can supply a new OMF/AAF export or a new QuickTime with guide audio for smaller manual revisions. Applications such as EdiLoad allow editors to conform location .WAV files in a DAW such as Pro Tools, and re-conform after any picture edit revisions. Conforming (or assembly), is the process of enforcing the edits made by the picture editor using a guide audio track. There are a few different applications for both conforming and re-conforming, which work in much the same way. "VirtualKaty" was developed during the postproduction of *Lord of the*

Rings to handle numerous picture edit changes; it compares the differences between EDLs on completion of a new cut. The picture editor exports an EDL from Avid to the sound department, which VirtualKaty compares with the previous version and updates Pro Tools sessions to reflect any changes. These types of tools and processes are important for large-scale productions such as feature films and fast turnaround projects like television series.

In live-action films, there are usually several takes and angles to select from, whereas an animated film is largely "pre-edited"—the editor usually starts working with the director and/or story supervisor once the script and storyboards are finished. Story reels set up the timing of the film before animation begins. The editor times sequences, and in collaboration with the sound department, adds or replaces dialogue, temporary SFX, and music. The edit is updated and revised as shots progress, from rough animation to the final render, composite, and output. The differences between a story reel and the final edit of an animated film can be marginal, whereas in live action the film editor cuts the film based on available footage, which means a film can change quite dramatically during the editing stage. After test screenings are conducted, a cut is then finessed unless there is a need for additional shots or major changes. Once revised, a film is said to be "picture locked," which means no more edit changes are to be made. However, the ease of making changes in nonlinear editing systems has resulted in picture changes being made right up to the final mix stage.

Editing Theories

Picture editing, like sound, is another film craft that's often underappreciated, largely because the work involved goes unnoticed. Picture editors bring a fresh perspective to a project. Walter Murch defines the ideal picture edit as adhering to six priorities: It's true to the emotion of any given moment, it advances the story, and it works rhythmically. Secondary is the consideration of "eye trace," or where the audience is looking, 2D place, and 3D space, which concerns the coherency and cohesion in placement and movement of people in places and in relation to one another. Both sound design and mixing recognize similar guidelines: the selection and creation of sounds, the relationship between sounds, the perspective of sounds relative to and situated in a given plane, and the relationship between sound and image. The sound design needs to suit the narrative and become part of the film's aesthetic.

You have more freedom with sound than you do with picture. There are, consequently, fewer rules. But the big three things—which are emotion, story, and rhythm—apply to sound just as much as they apply to picture. You are always primarily looking for something that will underline or emphasize or counterpoint the emotion that you want to elicit from the audience. You can do that through sound just as well as through editing, if not more so. Rhythm is obviously important; sound is a temporal medium. And then story. You choose sounds that help people to feel the story of what you're doing. (Murch in Jarrett, n.d.)

Both picture editing and sound are concerned with timing, pacing, and rhythm. The pacing of an edit is determined by a combination of kinetic qualities: the length of shots, the rhythm of editing, the number of cuts, connections between edits, and the relationship between sound and the visuals. The way a film is edited influences soundtrack design and in turn, sound influences the picture edit. Sound can smooth or accentuate edits and slow down or accelerate the pacing of a scene. There are no hard and fast rules as to how a film is cut or how sound is designed or mixed, but there are some basic principles to keep in mind. Some sounds are difficult to understand without an initial visual reference for support, and audiences need a period of time to hear and register certain sounds. Too much sound, too quickly, makes it difficult for an audience to "focus," especially when there's also a lot of visual detail and/or fast cutting. Having an understanding of how shots are assembled and how an edit will affect sound and vice versa is invaluable when it comes to conceptualizing a film.

Typically, most commercial films and television or Web series are dialogue driven and cut in consideration of the dialogue, although different editors employ different ways of working. During the first assembly of a film, Walter Murch turns off the dialogue and any production sound to focus on the visuals. This makes him pay more attention to sound and the possibilities for sound design, which helps generate sound ideas. As an edit progresses, Murch adds sound and assesses the impact on visuals. By not focusing on dialogue and production sound, the film is acquiring shape while welcoming the influence of sound. Like many film editors, Murch also avoids too much focus on music until the picture edit feels complete. Music is treated with restraint and primarily used to underscore and support the emotion that's in the images. In the lead-up to any test screenings, he prepares the edit with sound so that the film feels as finished as possible. While he may not always formally take on the role of sound designer, he's affecting the design and mix direction through editing with sound.

My heart aches for people who work the other way because they have to start from a dead stop. They have to come up to speed not having really any idea of what is going to happen. And the bad thing that happens is everything gets put in and, as a result, you get a logjam of sound at the mix that frequently results in a kind of conceptual muddiness. . .and this I think is related to some general criticisms of films being too loud. Because it is so dense, the ear can't make any sense out of it, so the director asks to increase the level. The mixers make it louder, and you quickly arrive at the threshold at which you can endure it, hoping for some kind of clarity to emerge from the loudness. But it's the clarity of the mallet on the head, and what an audience hears is noise. Because it's conceptually muddy, they can't begin to separate out what they're supposed to hear. And when they don't know what they're supposed to hear, their threshold of where loudness begins is much lower. (Murch in Kenny, 2000)

Evolution of the Invisible Arts

The first films consisted of one shot, so there was no editing. Edwin S. Porter pioneered the use of dramatic editing in the early 1900s. Porter's *The Great Train Robbery* (1903) was groundbreaking at the time and considered the first narrative film to achieve continuity of action. D. W. Griffith was

Intolerance: Love's Struggle throughout the Ages (1916, dir. D. W. Griffith)

later credited as the inventor of modern editing and establishing the basic grammar of film editing. His 1916 film *Intolerance* is considered a landmark in cinematic history largely due to the film's nonlinear plot structure, which consists of four separate yet parallel stories spanning 2,500 years.

Intolerance also initiated an examination into the impact of film editing by Soviet filmmaker Lev Kuleshov. Kuleshov was among the first to experiment with the effect of juxtaposition, which evolved into what became known as the theory of montage or Soviet montage theory. Kuleshov cut a shot of an expressionless actor with shots of three different subjects, a girl in a coffin, a hot plate of soup, and a woman. Audiences perceived the actor's performance differently relative to the different shots. At first he looked sad, then hungry, then lustful. Kuleshov discovered that depending on how shots are assembled, audiences attach a specific meaning or emotion to the shot, and he concluded that the essence of cinema is in the way a film is edited.

Sergi Eisenstein adopted and expanded on montage theory, believing that multiple images edited together created a "tertium quid," which is Latin for "a third thing" and refers to an unidentified third element, which is greater than its individual parts. The phrase is associated with alchemy, a form of chemistry and philosophy practiced in the Middle Ages and Renaissance period. A general use of the word is to describe a process that transforms a common substance into a substance of greater value. Eisenstein's *Battleship Potempkin* (1925) is hailed as a classic example of experimentation with the montage. Images of marching soldiers are cut with fleeing citizens to incite a feeling of helplessness, and then oppression as soldiers are seen firing on the crowd. In his film *Strike* (1925), Eisenstein included a sequence that cuts between the slaughter of a bull and police attacking workers, drawing a metaphorical connection between an assault on workers and a slaughtered bull. Some film theorists further define the montage as "intellectual montage." A well-known example is *2001: A Space Odyssey* (Kubrick, 1968). An ape beats another ape using a bone as a weapon for the first time. He tosses the bone into the air, which cuts to a satellite in space, depicting years of human evolution in two shots. The cut draws a connection between the two objects, bone and satellite, primitive and advanced tools, quickly summarizing humanity's technological advancements.

After the introduction of sound, both Kuleshov and Eisenstein started to explore sound in a similar way to their experimentation with pictures. Sound or sound montages achieve the same effect as the visual montage, albeit more subconsciously. Sound can support and enhance the idea behind a visual arrangement or create an idea of its own in the mind of the viewer/listener. In his book *On Directing Film*, David Mamet describes how filmmakers take unrelated shots and juxtapose them to convey an idea. Mamet uses the example of cutting two shots that have nothing to do with each other, a bird snapping a twig and a fawn raising his head. The combining of the two images gives the viewer the idea of alertness and/or danger. Imagine these two shots as mute, without sound, and then imagine them with sound. The sound of a twig snapping would give the viewer/listener the idea of alertness. A distant gunshot would give the viewer/listener the idea of danger. The sound of a gunshot would also tell the audience how close or far away the potential danger is and give some clues as to what it is—a hunter, perhaps? The gunshot could also be replaced with any number of sounds, each of which would tell the audience something beyond what they're seeing and hearing. Audiences make connections between seemingly unrelated images and sounds, which gives filmmakers an extensive tool kit when it comes to creating meaning and emotion—a fourth dimension.

The advent of sound in the 1930s expanded and complicated the film editor's role. There were two mediums to be cut and then synchronized. Directors were rarely involved in the process, which was controlled by the studios and their supervising editors. Editors were called "cutters" and viewed as highly skilled mechanics. MGM's Margaret Booth mastered the transition to sound and became known as one of the first film editors. Booth is acknowledged for introducing the concept of cutting for emotion and initiating a shift in perceptions. Editing evolved from being seen as "mechanical" to being understood as a creative and editorial discipline. Until the 1950s, film editing was largely formulaic; scenes opened with establishing shots that cut to medium shots and close-ups. Dissolves and fades were frequently used to signal changes in time and place. Film editor Dede Allen rejected formula and introduced new techniques such as making sound precede picture (or pre-lapping), rapid cutting, using slow motion, cutting before the end of the scene, and altering time by changing the sequence of scenes. Allen was also the first film editor to receive a solo opening credit on *Bonnie and Clyde* (Penn, 1967). Thelma Schoonmaker is another widely regarded film editor and has worked on all of Martin Scorsese's films since *Raging Bull* (1980). She has received seven Academy Award nominations for Best Film Editing, winning an award for *Raging Bull* (1980), *The Aviator* (2004), and *The Departed* (2006). One of Schoonmaker's techniques is to cut alternative versions of a scene, one that she feels matches Scorsese's vision and variations if she thinks there are better or different ways of editing a scene. In the same way a scene can be shot or animated different ways, it can be edited, sound designed and mixed in a number of different ways. It's difficult to gauge the impact of different approaches without experimentation.

Montage and Continuity

All films are edited, but the most successful films use a variety of editing techniques to tell and enhance the storytelling. There are two main approaches to editing, montage and continuity. Continuity situates editing as the driving force of narrative films but adheres more to the script, whereas montage is more concerned with associations between shots and is more commonly employed as an emotive, dramatic, and aesthetic-narrative device. Montages in contemporary films also build upon the same principle developed in early film: a series of images that condense time and story. Continuity editing is about invisibility. A film feels seamless when the audience is focused on the story, not the production. The key considerations in continuity editing are screen direction, eye lines, and adhering to the 180-degree rule so that action unfolds with spatiotemporal consistency and smooth transitions of time and space. Disorienting an audience pulls them out of the story. Editors create sequences that flow, as if everything is happening continuously, unless for effect. In *The Lord of the Rings: The Two Towers* (Jackson, 2002), the rules are broken to make a "conversation" between Gollum and Sméagol feel like it's occurring between two different characters (the good and the bad).

The sequence starts with the camera panning the line so the audience becomes aware they're watching one character having a schizophrenic conversation. The scene is dialogue driven, with forest atmos constant across picture edits. Music underscores the taunting of the tortured Sméagol, which fades in after Gollum calls Sméagol a "murderer," increasing in intensity as Sméagol demands that Gollum leave, and then dropping out completely as Sméagol realizes he's been talking to his evil self.

The Lord of the Rings: The Two Towers (2002, dir. Peter Jackson)

Sound is often used to bridge cuts or transitions between shots and scenes, which is sometimes written into the script. Continuing sound across a shot transition can smooth an edit and reinforce a sense of narrative continuity, which helps sustain the illusion that events are taking place in a continuous space or time. Sound and picture cuts are often staggered and known as a "split edit." When the sound of the next shot or scene is introduced before the next shot, it can set up a sense of anticipation. On the other hand, cutting or fading a shot and sound simultaneously emphasizes the edit, which is common in location, time, and scene changes. In continuity editing, shots are commonly cut together on an action, but if the action isn't "matched," sound can exaggerate the cut. If someone is closing a door and the action is not seamless across the edit, the sound either doubles up (the door closes twice), or there is something unnatural about the sound/cut (because the door is closing, and then it's closed). In live-action films, issues like this are apparent. In animation, problematic edits can

sometimes be "cheated" with sound; a continuous sound can fool the eye into seeing continuous movement. At times it's preferable to allow moving objects to leave or enter the frame and cut after or before an action. This technique can also allow for greater use of sound and sound-image arrangements. For example, someone walking into a frame can be heard prior to being seen. We could hear the sound of heavy combat boots on gravel walking slowly, which would "subconsciously" tell the audience something about the location, character (soldier, military?), and possibly intent (uncertain, confident, measured?).

Creative Editing Techniques

Narrative films are complex; they involve internal states, psychological or emotional, which are not necessarily "seen" or expressed in dialogue. There are a number of relational concepts that underpin creative sound and picture editing used for narrative, aesthetic, and emotive effect.

Graphic-Sonic

Interest, emotional engagement, and meaning can be created by graphical information (shape, color, composition, and treatment) and/or aural information (shape/envelope, color/timbre, composition/frequency, and treatment), which is similar when cutting from one shot to another. In *The 39 Steps* (Hitchcock, 1935), a shot of a woman screaming cuts to a shot of a train sounding its whistle. In *Psycho* (Hitchcock, 1960), the shower scene ends with the camera tracking blood and water as they flow down the bathtub sinkhole, which dissolves into a match cut of Marion's eye. The sound of the shower still running overlaps the match cut, which tracks out, revealing Marion dead on the floor, before cutting to a shot of the showerhead. In *Apocalypse Now* (Coppola, 1979), the sound design and imagery connect the ceiling fan with helicopter blades and to war and Willard's emotional state.

Aural-Visual Rhythms

Movement within a shot can be used to set the tempo of an edit, which can also extend to sound associated with, or attached to, that movement. Camera movement, character performance, dialogue, sound design, and music all embody and define rhythm, and therefore can determine the tempo and pacing of an edit, either separately

Delicatessen (1991, dir. Marc Caro and Jean-Pierre Jeunet)

or as combinations. *Delicatessen* (Jeunet and Caro, 1991) is an example of using aural-visual rhythms and creative sound design to connect characters within an environment. The film is set in a run-down apartment building owned by a butcher. The building is in constant need of a handyman, because the butcher routinely butchers them to sell as food to the apartment's kooky occupants. Food is so scarce it's used as a form of currency. Louison, a former clown desperate for work, applies for the job of handyman and forms a relationship with the butcher's daughter, Julie. Julie and a team of underground vegetarian rebels save Louison from the meat cleaver. The film takes place in, on, around, and underneath the delicatessen and uses an old heating pipe running through the building to connect characters and the storyline. The opening sequence sets up the narrative and aesthetic of the film with the butcher sharpening his tools. The sound (and camera) travel through the pipe to a room upstairs, where a terrified tenant is wrapping himself in newspaper. He hides in a dustbin in an unsuccessful attempt to escape the butcher. Later the other tenants are introduced through connecting sound and image. An amorous butcher sets off the sequence with bedsprings squeaking rhythmically, while his daughter is practicing the cello, a woman slaps the dust from a rug, another tenant is pumping up a bicycle wheel, an elderly woman knits, a metronome ticks, two men make and test novelty sheep "baaing" toys, and the clown is painting the ceiling. The intercutting and sound get faster and faster until the sequence climaxes and concludes with the tire popping, a cello string breaking, and Louison falling off his ladder.

Temporal Manipulations

Film is the manipulation of time. Time is expanded (slowed down), for example in a slow-motion fight scene. More commonly time is compressed, and the story takes place over a longer time period than the duration of the film. Elliptical editing is the technique used in film editing to reduce the duration of an event. Flashbacks/forwards are also common manipulations of time and can be objective, from an "observer's" point of view, so the audience feels as if they are in the scene, but somewhat removed, or subjective, which gives an audience the illusion that they are the character in the scene. Flashbacks/forwards are often initiated by sound; sometimes a reoccurring design effect signifies a shift in time for the audience, or a sound effect acts a memory and triggers a flashback/forward. Most flashbacks/forwards include changes in visual and aural treatment, dissolves, and fades and are sometimes superimposed text with sound effects. Music can also be used to signify changes in time and period. Flashbacks/forwards are a narrative device that offers character insights and helps advance the story. In *The Sixth Sense* (Shyamalan, 1999), psychologist Dr. Malcolm Crowe (Bruce Willis) attempts

to uncover the truth about a young boy's (Cole) supernatural abilities. Through flashbacks, he re-experiences earlier conversations and realizes that he is dead. In *The Jacket* (Maybury, 2005), Jack Starks, a Gulf War veteran, is accused of murder and incarcerated in a mental institution. Starks is forced to undergo an unauthorized treatment with experimental drugs. Bound in a straitjacket and placed inside a morgue drawer as a form of sensory deprivation, he is somehow able to travel fifteen years into the future for short periods of time. The flash forwards are visually and aurally stylized, fragments and flashes of sound and image.

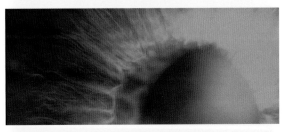

The Jacket (2005, dir. John Maybury)

Themes and Subtext

In thematic editing, images are cut together based on a central theme to communicate feelings or experiences. Montages are often thematic. Cross-cutting (or parallel editing) is another common method of editing in which the POV (point of view) switches alternately from events at one location to those of another. The action is usually simultaneous and creates dynamic tension, or the "third thing," which is often thematic. The baptism scene in *The Godfather* (Coppola, 1972) is a well-known example of parallel cutting. Michael Corleone and his nephew are seen getting baptized, while leaders of five rival families are being murdered. The juxtaposition of violence with baptism, birth, and death, emphasizes Michael's transition from the Marine who initially shunned the family business to a mobster and then Godfather. He orders the murders, which seals his transition, and re-establishes the Corleones as the nation's most powerful crime family. The scene starts in the church, with organ music and the sound of the baby crying. As the scene unfolds, the organ music bridges the action, creating a tension between the baptism and the murders. The organ music and dialogue from the priest performing the baptism drive the scene, while the baby crying is heard out of visual context. The reality and "grittiness" of the murders is set up through the use of Foley (guns, footsteps, cracking of glasses), sound effects (gunshots), and screams from the victims, juxtaposed with Michael calmly renouncing Satan as his enemies are eradicated.

Dreams and Nightmares

Dream and nightmare sequences in films are often used to give the audience insight into a character's mind-set, usually in reflection of a conflict or fear the character is facing, which advances the narrative. The use of symbolism and metaphors is common, as is the stylized treatment of both sound and image. In the case of horror films, dreams and nightmares are often central to the narrative. In *Nightmare on Elm Street* (Craven, 1984), college students experience nightmares involving a figure with razor-sharp "finger knives," and they realize they have to stay awake to keep alive. *Waking Life* (Linklater, 2001) explores a range of philosophical questions, including the nature of reality, dreams, consciousness, and the meaning of life,

through the central character, who wanders through a succession of dreamlike realities. The entire plot of *Inception* (Nolan, 2010) is based on dreams, as a thief, Dominic "Dom" Cobb, uses dream-sharing technology to steal corporate secrets. Dom and his team of "extractors" use experimental military technology to infiltrate the subconscious of their targets and extract information through a shared dream world. Dom is then contracted to do the reverse and plant an idea in the mind of a CEO. Most of the film takes place in these interconnected multilevel dream worlds, which sound reflects by combining literal, nonliteral, and sub-textural sound.

Sometimes when people are dreaming, external sound is incorporated into the dream. Walter Murch explored this in the opening scene

Inception (2010, dir. Christopher Nolan)

from *Apocalypse Now*. At first the helicopter is a more abstract electronic sound, but then it becomes the sound of a real helicopter as Willard wakes from his jungle dream into the reality of the hotel room. When he opens his eyes, he thinks the helicopter sound is coming from the ceiling fan until he realizes that the sound is a real helicopter flying over the hotel. The intention of the effect is to mimic the disorientation that happens when dreaming; a sound from the real world enters the dream and is incorporated into the dream reality. According to psychologists, 10 to 20 percent of people also experience "exploding head syndrome," which is hearing a sound that can't be explained. People are woken by an abrupt imaginary sound, ranging from explosions and fireworks to slammed doors, the sound of a gun firing, an enormous roar, shouting, thunder, or a crack of lightning. Doctors suspect it stems from problems with the brain shutting down; instead of shutting down properly, the brain cells responsible for sound fire at once, creating a blast of energy that the brain interprets as a loud sound. Dreams and nightmares are mysterious occurrences and so open the door for interesting approaches to both sound and visual design.

Jump Cuts

A jump cut occurs when two sequential shots of the same subject are taken from positions that vary only slightly. The effect can be jarring and generally perceived as a bad edit. French filmmaker Georges Méliès accidentally created the jump cut in 1896. He was filming a bus driving through a tunnel and his camera jammed. When the film began to roll again, the bus had already gone and another vehicle was in its place. Méliès later used the jump cut to create VFX. Jump cuts are often used for effect, be it tension, urgency, the passing of time, or as a means of dramatic punctuation. They need to serve the story, and if sound is not considered with pictures, sound can amplify what can be perceived as a bad edit. Sound can smooth a problem cut to some extent, but it can't "fix" a poorly conceived edit.

Flash Cuts

Flash cuts, or fast cutting, and sometimes called "hip-hop" montages, involve consecutive shots of a brief duration, sometimes interspersed with black frames for effect, are used to convey a lot of information quickly.

In Requiem for a Dream (Aronofsky, 2000), the technique is used to show the main character's entry into drug taking and the impact of addiction through the use of extreme close-ups and equally "magnified" sound effects. The approach to editing and sound design effectively highlights the short-lived euphoria of drug taking, the subsequent despair and destruction that addiction causes. The same technique has since been used in films like *Shaun of the Dead* and *Hot Fuzz* (Wright, 2004, 2007, respectively) for comedic effect.

Smash Cuts

A smash cut is when one shot abruptly cuts to another for aesthetic, narrative, or emotional purpose, usually at a crucial moment in a scene. Smash cuts are unexpected and therefore "jarring"; the intention is to startle the audience. Smash cuts are often used when a character wakes up from a nightmare to simulate the jarring nature of that experience. Typically, smash cuts rely on a big shift in both aural and visual information, such as a tranquil wide shot of a quiet, peaceful town, with a close-up of an axe splintering wood. Smash cuts are common in horror films, which rely on the shock factor. A sudden appearance of a boy in *Children of the Corn* (Kiersch, 1984) startles both the audience and the couple who hit him with their car. In horror, jump, flash, and smash cuts are usually coupled with sound effects, often visceral and "shocking" in nature. The many layers of a film's sound design are manipulated at specific points to scare. In Stanley Kubrick's *The Shining* (1980), treated dialogue, sound design, and music build tension, which helps the smash/flash cuts to deliver shock. We see Danny riding his tricycle down empty hotel corridors and we hear squeaky wheels; music and sound design preempt his vision of twin girls followed by a flash of seeing them murdered.

The Shining
(1980, dir. Stanley
Kubrick)

VFX, Lighting, and Grading

While the design and mix of a soundtrack should be discussed in preproduction and production, it's not usually until postproduction that all the separate soundtrack elements are heard together with complete and final pictures. VFX need to be locked before sound effects can be finalized, and any VFX revisions will affect sound. Most VFX work is planned in preproduction and completed during postproduction, but if the sound department is aware of the VFX being undertaken, then sound effects for the corresponding VFX can be prepared. Certain VFX can also be aided by sound effects, and sometimes sound effects are created first, before VFX, and then later revised alongside VFX. The way a shot or scene is lit also influences sound in different ways. High-key lighting makes a scene feel bright or soft, whereas low-key lighting is used to isolate a subject, convey drama, or set a dark and mysterious atmosphere. Color grading also alters the tone, mood, and feel of a scene or film. As these processes happen at the end of the postproduction stage, sound may not see the overall effect until quite late in the production cycle. This makes viewing concept art early on helpful for understanding how the final film will look and how that might influence sound design.

Audio Post

As previously discussed, the majority of audio work undertaken in postproduction is sound design/editing and mixing, but this is influenced by the move away from relegating sound design to postproduction in favor of greater collaboration between sound and image throughout pre and production.

Track Laying and Session Management

In soundtrack production, a project or job is typically called a "session" (a dialogue, Foley, SFX, edit, mix, or mastering session) and arranged in a way that makes it easy to manage the soundtrack, general workflow, and the transferring of sessions when working across studios. Feature film soundtracks are typically split across dialogue, effects, and music departments and therefore sessions are separated until brought together for the final mix. Small projects like a short film can be undertaken within one session and resaved and renamed as per the stage in the process (from edit to mix). Different studios have their individual methods or session templates, but they typically lead with dialogue tracks, followed by walla, atmos, room tone, SFX, Foley, sound design FX, and then music. This is because dialogue leads the mix, serving as a reference point, and other elements are "mixed against" the dialogue. Specific tracks are named according to the type of effects, for example, "foley1_ footsteps." The number of tracks in a session depends on the number of characters and how effects-driven the project is. A feature film, especially an action film, will involve hundreds of tracks, whereas shorts tend to have smaller track counts. In most DAWs, tracks can be moved around, so sessions can be easily rearranged, dependent on the type of project and the production stage.

Dialogue and ADR are laid up against either a guide dialogue track or conformed to an EDL. A track is set up and named for each character, and each line is placed in a "checkerboard" arrangement. Dialogue tracks are named as per the character for easy identification. Individual character lines are placed onto separate tracks so their dialogue can be treated independently. Perfect sync can be difficult to achieve, so dialogue or ADR editors use dedicated software such as VocAlign or Revoice Pro, which compares one line against the other and alters the duration of the rerecorded line to match the original sync line. This can also be done manually in most DAWs, but it is time-intensive and can involve stretching or reducing individual words separately.

Atmos and room tones are laid up against and balanced with dialogue. This fills the spaces between dialogue lines or across dialogue in animation and ADR to ensure what is seen and heard feels natural and consistent. Once dialogue is balanced, it becomes clear as to where other elements of the soundtrack should "sit" relative to the scene. A busy city street will be louder than an empty warehouse situated on the outskirts of a city. Atmos (or ambience) and room tone also play a grammatical role in a soundtrack; when atmos is constant before and after a picture cut, it indicates the scene has not changed, and we are in the same location even though the shot perspective has altered. Changes in atmos typically signify changes in location and time.

Foley sound effects enhance detail and create the illusion of "reality," or hyperreality when exaggerated. Like sound effects, atmos, and room tone, Foley can also be sweetened and in such a way that tells us something—a squeak added to a footstep, or a heavier sound like a "thump" to suggest weight. Despite the perception that "quiet sounds" don't have the dramatic power of big or loud sounds, subtlety and overall dynamics add realism and emotion. However, if a scene is dialogue or musically driven, the subtlety and nuance of Foley is often lost, and especially if certain frequencies are being masked. If Foley is made louder to compensate, then the realism Foley brings to a soundtrack is lost. What takes priority always has to be ascertained, and once dialogue has been balanced, it's best to pull down levels as opposed to increasing levels. There is only so much headroom to push into.

SFX and sound design effects play a large part in building tension and anticipation. Most sound designers and editors will create effects for everything on the screen, offscreen, and in the case of sound design effects, everything "in-between." "Sweetening" is an expression used to describe the adding, mixing, and finessing of additional sound(s) to an effect to "sweeten" it. A gunshot could be sweetened with a cannon blast, a low-end rumble, or a boom. A flame burst could be sweetened with an animal roar. Sweetening makes an event feel bigger or more dramatic and adds an emotive or psychological component. Integrating sound design elements adds another dimension to an organic physical place or space. In some films, especially the more abstract, or "otherworldly," environments, the space or place is not real but built from sound design effects and textures. Music is often one of the last elements added to a soundtrack and is also laid up on individual tracks so that different music tracks can be cross-faded if needed. One of the key questions to consider or reconsider when laying up music is, Where should music start and finish? This could be at the start and end of a new act, scene, or sequence. The other main issue is where music is sitting in terms of the overall mix. Is it competing with dialogue and effects?

Basic Pro Tools SFX session template and 5.1 mix template

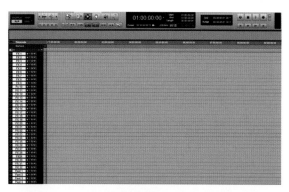

Groups, VCAs, and Auxiliaries

As soundtracks involve potentially hundreds of tracks or channels, most DAWs allow for controlling multiple channels as if they were one. Groups allow you to combine (group) and control a number of related tracks or "subgroups" together. In soundtrack production, this is generally dialogue, effects, and music, but on larger-scale projects effects are often broken down further. Groups allow you to mix or "sum" inputs in varying amounts to a single output bus. Auxiliary sends/returns are typically used to create individual mixes and/or route a number of signals to an EQ or compressor or effects plug-in such as reverb. For example, sending all ADR tracks to a room reverb. Voltage controlled amplifiers (VCAs) are similar to groups, because you assign a number of channels to a single VCA, but a VCA is only a level (or volume) control. Adjusting a VCA adjusts the faders for all channels assigned to it. For example, if all the Foley tracks were assigned to a VCA and the VCA was turned down 3 dB, each individual Foley channel fader is automatically turned down by 3 dB. The relative balance between channels stays the same, yet the overall level is reduced. Since no audio passes through a VCA, you can't insert any signal processing (compression, EQ) like you can with an auxiliary send.

Stereo or Surround

Most commercial project deliverables include both stereo and surround mixes. There are a number of different strategies for working with surround sound, which involves deciding what elements will go where and why. Surround sound must serve the story and should be discussed in preproduction. Audiences generally don't like surround sound if it distracts or detracts, and many directors aren't fond of the overuse of surround for the same reason. Some directors opt for creating a largely stereo mix and only using surrounds for atmos and certain sound effects, or alternatively creating effects specifically for the rear and LFE (Low-Frequency Effects) channels. Working in surround will also have an impact on budgets, schedules, and workflows between sound and picture editors. When working in surround both sound and picture editors need to be able to monitor in surround. On low-budget projects, filmmakers sometimes receive postproduction grants for a theatrical surround sound mix if their film has been selected for a "name" festival or has distribution interest. Most DAWs and picture editing systems support a variety of surround sound formats, 5.1 being the most common. This breaks down into the standard channels of left, center, right, left surround, right surround, and LFE. Most DAWs can also convert a stereo session to a surround session via altering the I/Os. There are a number of plug-ins for "up mixing," which is the term used to describe the process of taking a stereo mix and making a 5.1 or 7.1 surround mix from it.

As surround sound and home theatre systems evolve mixes can include extra channels for overhead speakers. A 7.1.4 system is the traditional 7.1 layout with the addition of four over-head speakers.

Spatial Audio

With the increase of 360 video and cinematic VR, spatial audio has also become a greater concern for content creators. In games, immersion is typically separated into three categories: narrative, tactical, and strategic. VR adds spatial immersion. Spatial audio immerses the user in a virtual space and "anchors" individual elements in that space to create a believable experience through headphones. The key difference between surround sound and 360 audio is playback; surround sound is played back through speakers, whereas 360 audio is played back through headphones. Ambisonics is the term used to describe full-sphere surround sound. Spatial audio is associated with the sense of "presence," which is defined as a psychological state or subjective perception that "overlooks" artificiality and the role of technology in creating the experience. Dedicated software and plug-ins are used for creating soundtracks for 360 video and VR films.

Re-Recording Mixing

From the 1930s on, re-recording technology was constantly advancing, and the soundtrack evolved from a mono track to several tracks. Re-recording, or "dubbing," as it was called in the early sound era, was understood in much the same way as postproduction image was. Early practitioners compared both sound design and re-recording to the practice of shooting against a blue cloth (blue/green screen) and adding in backgrounds. Dialogue was recorded in the foreground, and then any background sound could be added. Other parallels between sound-image practices included matching photographic treatments and techniques with the similar approaches to sound. The process of re-recording was likened to playing music, except the picture on the screen served as the sheet of music.

The Re-recording Mixer

Postproduction culture varies from project to project, city to city and country to country. On a large-scale feature film, re-recording mixing is undertaken by a team of mixers, usually three, separated into dialogue, effects, and music, whereas on lower-budget films and in many countries, the re-recording mixer is only one person. Sometimes individual editors/designers come together and mix their component as a team; for example, the dialogue editor would mix his or her dialogue tracks. The role of re-recording mixer is usually separate from that of sound designer, but sound designers typically attend the mixing session, and on smaller and independent films, the sound designer is often and increasingly the re-recording mixer. The main difference between the two roles is that sound designers are more concerned with content and re-recording mixers with context. It's the sound editor's, designer's, and composer's job to supply the re-recording mixer(s) with the *content*, and the re-recording mixer is responsible for shaping that content within the *context* of the film. Undertaking both roles requires creating and managing content in consideration of context. Key to a successful mix is objectivity

in terms of the overall soundtrack, which is dialogue, effects, and music.

There are four phases to the entire mixing process: temporary mixes, premixes, the final mix, and M&Es (music and effect mixes). Once an edit is locked, sound design and music can start finalizing work in preparation for the mixing stage. Some directors are heavily involved in the process of film mixing, particularly the final mix, while others leave it up to the sound team. Sometimes directors are already on another project or are still working on finalizing pictures. Most re-recording mixers prefer the director to remain "fresh" and objective, which can be difficult to arrange in terms of scheduling, but it's always a good idea to have a break between processes to retain objectivity.

Temporary Mixes

Temporary (temp) mixes for test screenings are useful for assessing if further experimentation is required and/or the degree of refinements to be made. Sometimes new and better ideas arise. A test screening is a preview screening conducted before its general release in order to gauge audience reaction. Preview audiences are selected from a cross-section of the population and are asked to provide feedback in some form. After audience previews, films are often recut, which means sound editorial changes and new mixes are needed. It's difficult to "lock down" a soundtrack before a final cut, so temporary mixes should be treated objectively. Test screenings are commonly conducted around the premix stage, which can be problematic for schedules, particularly if the soundtrack is still in development.

Most picture changes will also require sound changes, which is where costs and schedules can blow out, especially if a number of test screenings are conducted with corresponding revisions. The types of revisions that commonly occur are usually story oriented, which can result in the shortening or extending of shots and scenes and/or shot and scene changes. A close-up (CU) could become a wide shot (WS), or the scene order could change. Sound revisions can often take longer than picture edit changes, depending on the scale of revisions, which needs to be factored into revised schedules. Swapping a CU for a WS could result in the original sound design needing to be redesigned. Issues such as missing visual effects, and on animated films, inconsistencies such a prop design, can also arise.

Premixing

The next step in the film mixing process begins with the preparation of premixes, which involves the sub-mixing of many—up to hundreds—of tracks into a more manageable state. Dialogue, music, and effect premixes are mixed into what's called a stem. A stem is a completed premix and is usually in multitrack format, three to five 5.1 stems in the case of 5.1 surround sound. They are typically mastered through Dolby meters and bussed out as 5.1 stems of dialogue, music, and effects. Premixes can also be divided further if the mix contains a large number of sound effects, for example separate spot, Foley, or atmos premixes. Twenty tracks of atmos could be mixed down to one or two six-track stems. Retaining some separation allows for the manipulation of individual elements during the final mix if required.

During the premix, groups of tracks are combined and equalized in relation to each other. During premixing, the different elements are further assessed to "see" how sounds and different layers are working together before moving into the final mix stage. Sound editors/designers are often working in isolation, so it helps to have dialogue and music to work with during both design and premixing stages. The same applies to music composers; it helps to hear the dialogue and even temporary sound design. Each element of the soundtrack has volume, pitch, rhythm, and pacing, which need to vary to create interest and drama over time.

Sound editors/designers generally do as much in advance as possible and often premix as they design. Certain sound and design effects need to be premixed as part of the sound design. It can be difficult to know if something "feels right" without some preliminary mixing. Sound editors/designers will adjust levels and add fades and volume automation. Premixing helps set up the mix so that the mixer(s) can focus on finessing the overall balance, instead of making a lot of small adjustments. As the soundtrack builds, a rough mix of the individual elements is created from scene to scene; however, it's not until sound design is complete that an effective mix is possible.

The Final Mix

During the final mix stage, the soundtrack is further refined in consultation with the director. Some directors are not always actively involved in the mixing stage and may only attend review sessions. The final mix for a feature film can take between two and twelve weeks, and sometimes much longer depending on the film's scale, budget, and how much premixing has been undertaken. During the mix, all the soundtrack elements or stems are adjusted in volume and equalized relative to each other and the image. Reverbs are added and individual elements and effects are panned. The key decisions made during the final mix are which sounds should be emphasized, thinned, or dropped depending on the impact of the overall sound within the context of the pictures.

M&E Mixes

M&E stands for "music and effects," which is the entire soundtrack minus the dialogue, and is used as the basis for foreign-language dubbing. The dialogue is recorded and dubbed in the relevant language. It's easier and less expensive to prepare an M&E after the final mix as opposed to at a later stage. Creating an M&E is an additional cost, so some independent films opt for using subtitles instead, particularly for short and non-commercial films. For commercial films, M&Es are typically part of the deliverables required for distribution and include dialogue sheets, which are transcriptions of all spoken language (dialogue and voice-over or narration) and where in the film dialogue occurs. Dialogue sheets are then transcribed into different languages for either subtitles or foreign language dubbing.

Mixing Tools and Techniques

Since the late 1970s, films have become increasingly more complex, which means the process of mixing film soundtracks is more complicated. The mixing process "refocuses" attention to what's important at a given time, and even a small adjustment in level or frequency can have a dramatic effect. Sound is perceived both emotionally and intellectually. Constant choices are made as to what elements need to be heard and to what extent. Film is an illusion, so it works by suspending disbelief, and different genres demand different approaches and sensibilities. A good mix feels seamless and doesn't distract or make the audience conscious of the soundtrack and the film itself. The main aim or purpose of the soundtrack is to support the emotion and story, and generally the better the mix, the less the audience is aware of it.

Dialogue Mixing

After the coming of sound in the late 1920s, the use of dialogue became more prevalent in both animated and live-action films. Dialogue is often considered "king" and the most important element of the soundtrack mix. Dialogue is mixed first and all other soundtrack elements are then mixed against the dialogue. Films are mixed with the dialogue set to a specific level, and all other audio elements are "subordinate" to the dialogue. When at home watching TV or a film, most people will adjust the volume to comfortably hear the dialogue.

The easiest way to balance dialogue is by locating and leveling the loudest line so that all other lines can be adjusted in reference to the loudest line. Perspective is important. For example, if the audience sees a WS and the dialogue sounds too loud or "present" or "close," it will feel as though something isn't right. Audience members will be unlikely to isolate the problem, but they will notice and be critical of it. As a rough guide, dialogue levels will generally sit within an *average* range of around -24 dB to -18 dB relative to the visual perspective. A CU shot of a character

yelling may *peak* at around -10 dB. Aside from elements like crowd walla, offscreen and muffled conversations through walls, or effected elements such as radio "chatter" and telephone conversations, important dialogue needs to be audible and understood. In live-action film, matching location sound and ADR is challenging because of the variations in microphone placement, reverb, and locations. The same problem can occur in animation if dialogue has been recorded with different microphones in different studios. A common solution is to paste and cross-fade atmos, room tone, and/or use software to match room tone, atmos, and ambiences. Depending on the quality of the recording, unwanted noise is removed, either edited out/around or through the use of EQs and dedicated noise reduction plug-ins. The dialogue mixer focuses on getting all the dialogue levels right, EQ, adding reverb, and other effects to ensure what we are seeing and hearing feels "real" and is consistent.

Effects Mixing

The original thinking behind the concept of sound design was to establish a person who took on the responsibility of "auralizing" the sound for a film, like a director of photography or art director, but for sound. Sound effects mixing is often compared to cinematography and compositing. Cinematographers focus the lens on a specific area of a shot, which draws the audience's attention. Other elements are still visible but are soft or out of focus. This applies equally to sound design and mixing; raising or lowering the volume or equalizing a sound effect, or stem influences the audience's focus. Compositing is the combining of visual elements from separate sources into a single image, sound design is effectively combining a number of separate sounds into what feels like a single sound effect. A mix combines many elements into a soundtrack. Sounds are chosen and mixed to make each moment realistic and/or emotionally targeted. Different films have different mix aesthetics, particularly when it comes to effects. Some mixes involve grouping layers of sounds within a frequency spectrum. Another approach is to focus on one or two principal foreground sound effects at any given moment, which makes the audience think they are hearing more than they are. The more pared down a soundtrack becomes, the more freedom there is for events and moments to feel bigger than they are. Films perceived as "quiet" take the "less is more" approach to a greater extreme. *No Country for Old Men* (Coen Brothers, 2007) is well documented for being a "quiet" and tense thriller. There is minimal dialogue and music, but as Ethan Coen described it, it's "maximal" in terms of sound effects and how they were handled. Sound can be emotionally effective even when reduced to near inaudibility, and the sudden absence of sound can have a dramatic impact.

Music Mixing

One of the biggest conflicts that happens in the mix is competition between dialogue, sound effects, and music. When a mix is "muddy" or lacks "definition," it's usually because it contains too much energy in the lower mids and/or bottom end. A certain type of sound with a certain type of music can muddy a mix. Ideally, sound designers and composers are collaborating to avoid this, but because of budgets and schedules, it doesn't always happen. More often than not, either sound effects or music are removed, thinned, or reduced in level. Music doesn't have to be there all the time, but sound effects do to some extent. Music can come and go, start and end, whereas effects in the wider sense are always present, often synced and/or "attached" to the visuals and story world. Early discussions between the sound designer and composer can isolate pitch/frequency "double-ups" to inform instrumentation and sound design to set up clarity in the mix. This is what Murray Spivak and Max Steiner were exploring on *King Kong*, and what Skip Leivsay and Carter Burwell do on Coen Brothers films.

Panning

Dialogue comes from the center speaker irrespective of the placement and movement of characters. Panning dialogue is distracting and sounds unnatural to audience members who aren't sitting in the center of the cinema. Spot sound effects are positioned carefully and generally not too far left or right. A door might appear on the left edge of the screen visually, but if panned hard left, it may appear too far away from audience members

sitting on the right. Atmos, music, and reverb can generally be panned anywhere in the stereo and surround spectrum because they're not visually "anchored"—not something that you see, so not something that will make an audience member turn away from the screen. Certain sound effects and elements like helicopters are panned relative to visual suggestion; they can fly over the audience, or from front left to rear right. Creating soundtracks for VR film is different to working in traditional film; sound is 360, often used to direct the audience/user, and there is no screen.

EQ

One of the most common EQ techniques in film sound mixing is "notching," which is essentially pulling down the volume of a specific frequency or frequency band, particularly when faced with masking issues. For example, if dialogue and music are competing, "notching" frequencies common to dialogue, from the music will make the dialogue "pop" through. Dialogue can start to sound unnatural when certain frequencies are pushed or pulled too much, so a good rule of thumb is to look at EQ'ing effects and music, not dialogue, when dealing with masking issues. When in doubt, using frequency analysis plug-ins helps to ascertain frequency issues. Another common technique in effects mixing is "rolling off the bottom end", which involves EQ/ing or using a HPF (high pass filter) to reduce lower frequencies. This can add "clarity" to mixes that are going to be played back through consumer headphones and speakers, which are not designed to reproduce much in the way of lower frequencies.

7-Band EQ: notching filtering

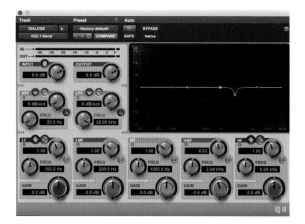

iZotope, Inc.'s mastering tool Ozone 7 (www. izotope.com)

Compressors and Limiters

Compressors are used extensively in audio post, especially for broadcast applications. Compression is the process of lessening the dynamic range between the loudest and quietest parts of a stem or entire soundtrack. Compressors boost the quieter signals and attenuate the louder signals. Theatrical mixes can have a huge dynamic range because they are played back in a quiet, controlled listening environment (a theater). Broadcast, video, and online mixes have lesser dynamic range because of the final listening environment. However, over-compressing can destroy a mix, making it feel "squashed" and lacking in detail and dynamics. Limiters are commonly used in broadcast mixes to ensure that they do not peak over a set threshold in adherence to delivery specifications. A compressor smoothly reduces gain above a threshold, while a limiter prevents any additional gain above a threshold.

Reverb

In the early days of film, it was difficult to get realistic-sounding reverbs, reverb units were unnatural and metallic sounding. The way around the problem was to rerecord material in a similar acoustic environment to the film. This involved playing back the original material on one machine, usually a Nagra, recording that in a space with another machine, and then blending the two together. Today, there are a number of reverb plug-ins used to recreate reverb and therefore spatial realism. Mixers adjust perspective, determined mainly by the ratio of direct to indirect or reflected sound, which creates a sense of depth and space. Surround reverb plug-ins are typically used for overheads or surround

Waves compressor

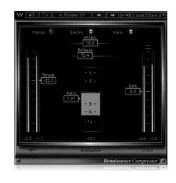

Altiverb convolution reverb

objects to create a sense of depth and space. Interior spaces such as different rooms are relatively easy to re-create with reverb plug-ins, but exteriors are more difficult to get sounding natural. Sound in a forest or sound reflecting off a building is a more complex event. As previously mentioned, convolution reverb allows an impulse response or "snapshot" of the acoustic characteristics of real locations to be recorded and converted into set parameters. In postproduction these are used to create more realistic and accurate reverbs.

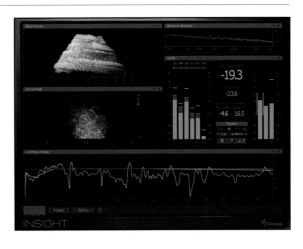

iZotope Insight
Loudness Meter
(Surround)

Monitoring the Mix

Professional mixing studios are acoustically treated and calibrated for accurate monitoring of mixes relative to the type of mix. Large mix facilities at 85 dB, and smaller facilities at 79 dB. Monitoring too loud in small mixing studios causes inaccuracies because the ear hears frequency response differently at different levels.

Monitoring a mix involves looking, listening, and metering. The mix should feel balanced, and sound and image should present as a unified whole. In mixing sound for film or television, there are specific standards that have been established and passed into law. Loudness meters provide precise loudness measurements and are compliant with all international specifications and broadcast deliverables. They measure audio like the way we perceive sound, taking into account duration as well as frequency.

In addition to loudness, content is also assessed on dialogue, or "dialnorm" (dialogue normalization) to ensure consumer dialogue levels are consistent from program to program and channel to channel. There are variations in how we judge loudness, but we're fairly consistent when assessing dialogue, and most people react negatively to dialogue that is too loud.

Monitoring a mix involves looking, listening, and metering. The mix should feel balanced, and sound and image should present as a unified whole. Audiences will always notice and complain about badly recorded, synced, and mixed dialogue. Atmos creates the story world and affects the illusion that what we are experiencing is "real." In mixing sound for film or television, there are also very specific standards that have been established and passed

into law. There are different audio metering scales, which have been developed by different industries in different countries, for different applications. Loudness meters provide more precise loudness measurements and are compliant with all international specifications. They measure audio similarly to the way humans perceive sound, taking into account duration as well as frequency, which is more consistent with the way we hear. They are used to evaluate everything from trailers and commercials to feature film soundtracks, for comparison purposes, to alert mixers to the potential for audience complaints about loudness, and to adhere to broadcast industry standards.

Mastering, Encoding, and Delivery

Film soundtracks don't get mastered in quite the same way as music is mastered. Music mastering engineers fine-tune levels and equalization of music so that it's balanced and the levels are constant with other CDs or tracks on the market. The process involves optimizing average and peak volume levels; signal processing (compression and EQ); removing unwanted noise like clicks, pops, and hisses; arranging tracks in sequence; and inserting codes for replication. Most of this work, applicable to film, is conducted during editing, premixing, and the final mix of a film soundtrack.

The way a soundtrack is mixed, mastered, and encoded depends on the project and the distribution model. As previously discussed, delivery requirements need to be ascertained, planned, and budgeted for in preproduction. Most audio postproduction facilities take care of deliverables for broadcast, Web, mobile, over-the-top and streaming, games, DVD and DCPs (Digital Cinema Packages). Commercial feature films are mixed on a calibrated mix or dubbing stage with dedicated personnel to particular specifications, and then mastered and encoded relative to distribution and replication requirements. A consultant ensures the mix theater is aligned and calibrated correctly, evaluates the mix so it translates to cinema, helps in the creation of other deliverables (Blu-ray etc), and checks the first copy of the DCP or 35 mm print so it meets standards. The certification of theatrical mix theaters is dependent on room acoustics, audio and visual monitoring standards, equipment selection, installation standards, synchronization accuracy, mixing competence, and technical experience.

Common Mix Issues

On large projects like feature films, the sound department is often working individually, which can result in the preparation of too much material. Despite advancements in audio technology, there is only so much information that can actually "fit" into a soundtrack. Dialogue, sound effects, and music regularly "compete" for space. As an example, a dialogue-driven scene will not benefit from overly loud music that employs common audio frequencies to the human voice. A poor-quality dialogue recording will add to the problem. If music is not lowered in the mix, the music will "mask" the dialogue and make it even more unintelligible. If the scene also requires a number of sound or sound design effects, the problem is magnified. If the scene lacks emotion and the music is expected to bring emotion to the scene, a director will not want it lowered in the mix.

"Auditory masking" (or frequency/spectral masking) is the term used to describe what happens when one sound is affected by the presence of another sound. When too many sounds with the same frequencies are layered together, the louder sounds mask the quieter sounds, diminishing them. Certain sounds (with a broad frequency spectrum) like running water, traffic, and air-conditioning tend to mask higher-frequency and softer sounds. The brain is able to single out simple frequency ranges but has trouble when too many frequencies are heard at once. The knee-jerk reaction is to make the quieter sounds louder, which in turn masks and therefore diminishes other sounds. When music and effects contain the same frequency range as dialogue, depending on the level, they will mask the dialogue and the dialogue becomes inaudible. The same problem occurs if music and effects are both punctuating the same screen action and in the same frequency range. EQs and filters are used extensively to create greater separation between dialogue, effects, and music. When composers and sound designers collaborate, they can create "space" by avoiding hitting a specific sync point at the same time, or by avoiding creating material in the same frequency range.

TIPS AND TRICKS

Ensure all production sound, not just a production mix, is ingested for editing, so that all tracks are available to ascertain the quality of recordings. Both dialogue editing and dialogue mixing can be labor-intensive, so the sooner any issues are isolated and addressed, the better. It's also important to be aware of the picture editing environment. If editing suites are not acoustically treated or calibrated, it can be difficult to fully assess the quality of production recordings. It's more advantageous to assess the quality of production sound in a sound studio.

Try to avoid using temp music if possible, and consider editing scenes that are going to be musically driven sooner rather than later. Ideally, the composer has plenty of time and is not "hindered" by a cut that has been locked to temp music. When working with sound designers and composers, think about what will or could help the visual edit. Dialogue aside, it is advantageous for picture editors to have key spot sound effects, sound design material, and music to inspire the edit and help with pacing, rhythm, and timing. The ideal workflow is fluid, but keep in mind that both sound designers and composers need to see the film as a whole. The picture edit and any VFX should be locked before the mixing phase begins.

Most of the problems that occur in postproduction stem from a lack of planning and collaboration between sound, music, and image during preproduction and production. Rango (Verbinski 2011) is a good example of a collaborative production model. The creation and development process maximized on the potential for creative sound design, picture editing techniques and resulted in a seamless final mix.

The mixes for Rango were the easiest mixes I've ever done. We weren't concentrating on solving any problems; all we were doing is concentrating on getting a great mix, because we'd solved all the problems. We were building this great sonic environment for the whole film and because of our entire creative process we knew we had it, so the mix was about taking it up another level. Every discussion we had was about how to get it sounding better. There was no, this doesn't work; we need to fix this, no discussions like that at all, no arguments or disagreements because everybody knew what we were trying to do because it was all there in the edit. All of the hard decisions were made as we were building the soundtrack. If you deal with all those decisions during the creative process of building the film, which you should do, when you get to the mix you do the job that the mix is there for, which is to get all your sounds sitting nicely, not to fix problems. On most films you get to the mix and there's a heap of crap you have to fix; dialogue problems, and noise, and you just don't want to know about it. This scene doesn't work, I don't like those sound effects, have you got something that sounds better here. We didn't have any of those issues when we got to the mix.

In the old days there was a distinct line between production and postproduction. You had preproduction, which was all about getting the shoot done. You'd shoot on film, and then you'd have your dailies, wrap your sets and commence postproduction. That doesn't exist anymore. The whole film is now postproduction more or less, because even when you shoot, unless there's some imperative for shooting at a certain time, like because an actor is moving on to another project, you can keep on shooting. Animation is a really prime example, you start shooting your Claymation or whatever it is, start cutting, and if you need another shot of him looking back over his shoulder, no problem, shoot it again and add that in. Production and postproduction are overlapping, so you really shouldn't think about your sound as being postproduction. A sound person should be in your mind from the beginning, which will prevent problems and result in a better film. Hire a sound person when you start your film and problems will be solved as they come up. That's how you do it. (Miller, 2016)

SPOTLIGHT ON: Shane Acker, Filmmaker

Shane Acker wrote, directed, and co-animated the award-winning animated short film 9 while a student at UCLA (University of California, Los Angeles). He has since worked on a number of different projects, currently developing an animated series with French comic company Humanoids and working as a professor in the Animation Department at Loyola Marymount University in Los Angeles. 9 tells the story of 9, a "sentient rag doll," or stitchpunk, living in a postapocalyptic world where humans no longer exist. The only "living things" are other rag dolls and the machines that hunt them. The short led to a feature-length adaptation, also titled 9 (2009) produced by Tim Burton and directed by Acker. The feature version is based on the short, maintaining the overarching narrative and steampunk-esque aesthetic. The characters and environments are visually and therefore sonically detailed and textured, bringing them to life and giving both films a tactility.

Stills from the short film 9 (2005, dir. Shane Acker)

I think the short feels like a window into a much larger world, like one moment in a larger narrative, yet it still stands as a complete story. I think that made it satisfying as its own thing, but also got people excited to see more, which is something you always want to do as a film-maker. I spent a lot of time on the short—over four years—and I put a lot of craft into making it as good as it could be. My hope was that it would stand as a director's piece and it would lead to more work as a director. The production wasn't constant; there were gaps in the process where I would go work professionally to support myself. I think this allowed for some critical distance from the work, so when I came back to it I would have fresh eyes again, and I could see problems more clearly. I was also becoming stronger as an animator and a storyteller. It meant that I had to repress the urge to redo everything that I had done before, but there was so much left to do, I just had to push on. I hoped the whole would be greater than the sum of its parts.

I got a lot of exposure at Sundance, but in truth, the feature was already in development when I went to Sundance. I had already signed up with ICM and they had been sending me out on rounds meeting producers in Hollywood. I had a general meeting with Bonnie Curtis and that's where I met Jim Lemley. They were making a film together; Red Eye, I believe. Jim and I started developing a treatment for a feature version of 9 after that, which I later pitched to Tim Burton, sometime after Sundance.

Tim was very gracious and complimentary, and wanted to help me make a feature. After he came onboard, things moved quickly. The short opened doors, but I think timing and luck played a huge part in getting it set up.

I think the best advice I could give is don't rush into production before you have a solid storyboard. It's easier to shape your story with pencil and paper (stylus and Cintiq) than through CG animation, and it's far less painful to throw away a sequence of storyboards than a sequence of animation, or a drawing rather than a CG asset you modelled and textured. Story really is the most important thing, so take your time with it, and show your animatic to as many people as possible to get feedback. Remember, you are making your film for an audience, not yourself, and when you are in the middle of making, it's really hard to separate yourself and take a critical step back. Having other people watch your film allows you to see it from a fresh perspective.

As far as working with other artists and sound designers, I think the best approach is to try to be as clear as possible about your intentions and to explain what you are trying to say or convey at different moments in the film, rather than being too specific and saying "I want this" and "I want that." This allows the space for people to creatively solve the problem and to participate in the making. Guaranteed they will give you something you are not expecting, and most times it will go beyond what you imagined. After all, they are the experts of their field. If they go too far off target, then you can bring them back or describe something more specific, but I find that if you empower them, they will come up with something cool more often than not. That's the magic of collaboration.

We did a spotting session with Danny Elfman where we walked through the movie and talked about where we wanted music and the dramatic peaks in the story. We had already created a temp score, but Danny didn't want to hear it, he didn't want to be influenced, so we just watched the movie without sound and talked. He would play a little on the keyboard, sketching out some themes. I was scared shitless—I knew I was in over my head with no experience directing an amazing composer, but I just went with my gut. He was very accommodating, and it was an amazing experience. A few weeks later we went back and he played the themes he had developed for the characters and a few sketches for some of the larger scenes. I got goosebumps hearing his music with my film. He worked for another week or so and then handed it over to the amazingly talented composer, Deborah Lurie. She was great, really creative, and we explored more of the soundtrack together for another three weeks. Then we flew to London to score it at AIR studios, which is located in a historic church. It was unbelievable. It sounded so good. Tim Burton would come down every day and hang out. That was an amazing time on the production, because the bulk of my work was done and I was just enjoying watching other artists contribute to the film.

Story is king. If you have a great story, the audience will forgive marginal animation, but great animation will never save a bad story. And story is character. Films aren't about plot, but about what characters do when placed in situations of conflict. So I often try to think of everything through the lens of the story, a story which is being told in a visual medium. The goal is to try to tell the story purely through the visuals, so that an audience could turn off the sound and still understand what's going on and how the characters feel. So all visuals should be contributing to the telling of the story. Everything from design, composition, color, staging, lighting, all the way down to the poses and the motion of the characters, because that's how characters really communicate, through their actions, not through their words. As an animation director, you are always trying to find the truth behind the words, because people rarely say what they mean. If you can show that truth in the acting, even if the words are betraying the truth, then you are getting to the essence of the story, and the audience will pick up on it.

Once the performance is complete, you keep applying this approach that everything supports the story, and this informs your sound choices. Sound is a great medium to impart emotion, depth, and a sense of presence, or "being there." Visuals will always be two dimensional; even in 3D movies you are cognizant of the frame from which you are looking in on the world. This keeps you at arm's length, but sound immerses you. Good sound design can pull you into an artificially created world and add an audible tactility that lends to the believability and the experience. When correctly married to music, this can lead the emotion and support the dramatic moments within the film. It really is another layer of storytelling, and one not to be overlooked. (Acker, 2017)

Stills from the feature film *9* (2009, dir. Shane Acker

Looking Ahead

In summary, having an understanding of sound and picture postproduction concepts enables a much greater insight into how creative sound and image techniques can be explored earlier. The success of a project is dependent on a good story, and the ability to exploit sound and image to their full capacity. The traditional film production model is an outdated convention. Collaborative workflows are the way to achieve this. In animation, the edit and the soundtrack are effectively being developed through story reels, and increasingly live action is following suit. As VR film evolves, sound will need to be considered earlier and alongside image, particularly if the intention is to creative immersive cinematic experiences.

I think this collision of gaming and live action and animation is changing the way films are made. Often, before I have a screenplay for a movie, I'll have story room, or locations photos and bits of character design, and pin it all up. The idea of narrative being informed by visuals and storyboards and text is exciting, and there are a lot of thumbprints on the sculpture by the time you're done with it. Everything's progressing, especially in terms of post. Looking ahead, I'd love to have more of an open format and the conventions of how we manage post done away with. As much as I enjoy sitting in a room alone with my editor for 10 weeks, I also can imagine a Star Trek Enterprise bridge version of the edit room, where you look over to Uhura and they're your sound design person. We seem to edit and then do sound, or finish things and then do visual effects, and I feel more and more that it should be far more fluid—I've got a new idea, let's try it and loop a line of dialogue, do a quick character sketch, change what we're not happy with, and maybe that will lead to a re-shoot or a pick-up or a new visual effects shot, but we're going to try stuff. So the sound designer informs how you're going to cut things, and maybe the composer comes on earlier. Instead of traditional post where it all stacks up at the end of the schedule, I'd love to open it up in the editing process, with everyone in there together. (Verbinski, 2011)

Picture Credits

Chapter 1

pg. 1   DBS Publications, Inc. / Drama Book Specialists, New York, New York (1930)

pg. 2   George Routledge and Sons, New York (1900)

pg. 3   University of Houston Clearlake http://coursesite.uhcl.edu/HSH/Whitec/terms/S/slapstick.htm

pg. 3   Scanned from *Winsor McCay: His Life and Art*, John Canemaker, 2005

pg. 4   *The Boys Playbook of Science* (p. 306) London; George Routledge and Sons, Pepper, John Henry 1866

pg. 5   Le praxinoscope à projection d'Émile Reynaud pour La Nature, revue des sciences - 1882, n° 492, page 357.

pg. 6   The British Museum

pg. 7   Jules Jamin, Edmond Bouty, *Cours de physique de l'École Polytechnique*, ed. 2, vol. 2, p. 629 (fig. 515)

pg. 8   Courtesy of George Eastman House

pg. 9   New York Herald, April 17, 1910

pg. 10   Lyman Howe's *Ride on a Runaway Train* (1921) / Educational Films Corporation of America

pg. 11   p. 24 Tower Radio, January 1935

pg. 12   *Back of the Mike* (1938) / Jam Handy Organization (JHO)

pg. 13   Scan of black-and-white promotional photograph released without copyright notice by Culver Pictures, Inc.

pg. 14   Taken from http://www.victorian-cinema.net/

pg. 15   Keystone-France / Getty Images

pg. 15   U.S. National Archives and Records Administration

pg. 16   ERPI/Warner Vitaphone

pg. 17   *Finding His Voice* (1929, dir. Max Fleischer and F. Lyle Goldman) / Western Electric Sound System, Inkwell Studios

pg. 18   Imagno / Contributor / Getty Images

pg. 19   *M* (1931, dir. Fritz Lang) / Nero-Film AG

pg. 19   *The Triplets of Belleville* (2003, dir. Sylvain Chomet) / Les Armateurs, Production Champion, Vivi Film

pg. 21   *Dizzy Dishes* (1930, dir. Dave Fleischer) / Fleischer Studios

pg. 23   *Sinkin' in the Bathtub* (1930, dir. Hugh Harman and Rudolf Ising) / Leon Schlesinger Studios

pg. 24   *Fiddlesticks* (1930, Ub Iwerks) / Celebrity Productions

pg. 27   *Porky's Hare Hunt* (1938, dir. Ben Hardaway and Cal Dalton) / Leon Schlesinger Studios

pg. 28   *Fast and Furry-ous* (1949, Chuck Jones) / Warner Bros.

pg. 29   *King Kong* (1933, dir. Merian C. Cooper and Ernest B. Schoedsack) / RKO Radio Pictures

pg. 31   CBS Television

pg. 32   *Crusader Rabbit* (1949-57, dir. Alexander Anderson and Jay Ward) / Creston Studios, Jay Ward Productions, TV Spots

pg. 32   *Space Barton* (1950) / Telecomics

pg. 33   Colonel Bleep (1956-57, dir. Robert D. Buchanan and Jack Schleh) / Soundac

pg. 34   *Gerald McBoing-Boing* (1950, dir. Robert Cannon) / United Productions of America [UPA])

Chapter 2

pg. 37   *Ornament Sound Experiments* (1932, dir. Oscar Fischinger)

pg. 38   *Synchromy* (1971, dir. Norman McLaren) / National Film Board of Canada

pg. 39   *The Tell-Tale Heart* (1953, dir. Ted Parmelee) / United Productions of America (UPA)

pg. 41   *The Tell-Tale Heart* (1953, dir. Ted Parmelee) / United Productions of America (UPA)

pg. 42   *Now Hear This* (1962, dir. Chuck Jones and Maurice Noble) / DePatie-Freleng Enterprises (DFE), Warner Bros.

pg. 43   *The Last Trick of Mr. Schwarcewallde and Mr. Edgar* (1964, dir. Jan Švankmajer) / Josef Soukup

pg. 43   *A Game with Stones* (1967, dir. Jan Švankmajer) / Studio A See

pg. 44   *Meat Love* (1989, dir. Jan Švankmajer) / Koninck Studios, MTV Productions, Nomad

pg. 45   *The Grandmother* (1970, dir. David Lynch) / American Film Institute (AFI)

pg. 46   *Eraserhead* (1977, dir. David Lynch) / American Film Institute (AFI), Libra Films

pg. 48   INA / Contributor / Getty Images

pg. 49   © Luigi Russolo

pg. 51   Hulton Archive / Stringer / Getty Images

pg. 51   INA / Contributor / Getty Images

pg. 52   Frans Schellekens / Contributor / Getty Images

pg. 53   *Enthusiasm: Symphony of the Donbass* (1931, dir. Dziga Vertov) / Ukrainfilm

pg. 54   *Forbidden Planet* (1956, dir. Fred M. Wilcox) / Metro-Goldwyn-Mayer (MGM)

pg. 55   Walter Daran / Contributor / Getty Images

pg. 55   *Forbidden Planet* (1956, dir. Fred M. Wilcox) / Metro-Goldwyn-Mayer (MGM)

pg. 56   Forbidden Planet (1956, dir. Fred M. Wilcox) / Metro-Goldwyn-Mayer (MGM)

pg. 57   *La Jetée* (1962, dir. Chris Marker) / Argos Films, Radio-Télévision Française (RTF)

pg. 58   *La Planète Sauvage* (1973, dir. René Laloux) / Argos Films, Les Films Armorial, Institut National de l'Audiovisuel (INA)

pg. 59   *THX 1138* (1971, dir. George Lucas) / American Zoetrope, Warner Bros.

pg. 60   *THX 1138* (1971, dir. George Lucas) / American Zoetrope, Warner Bros.

pg. 60   *THX 1138* (1971, dir. George Lucas) / American Zoetrope, Warner Bros.

pg. 61   *Apocalypse Now* (1979, dir. Francis Ford Coppola) / Zoetrope Studios, Zoetrope Studios

Chapter 3

pg. 74   *Gravity* (2013, dir. Alfonso Cuarón) / Warner Bros., Esperanto Filmoj, Heyday Films

pg. 75   *Raging Bull* (1980, dir. Martin Scorsese) / United Artists / REX / Shutterstock

pg. 70   Waves' PAZ analyzer, Courtesy of Waves

pg. 79   iZotope, Inc.'s metering suite, Insight (www.izotope.com)

pg. 80   Paragraphic EQ (Waves Q10), Courtesy of Waves

pg. 80   Pitch and time shifters (Waves' Graphic SoundShifter / x-form), Courtesy of Waves/ Avid Technology

pg. 81   iZotope's sample-based synthesizer Iris (www.izotope.com)

pg. 85   Waves' TrueVerb and Audio Ease's Altiverb Convolution Reverb, Courtesy of Waves/ Audio Ease

pg. 83   Waves' Meta Flanger, Courtesy of Waves

pg. 92   © AKG Acoustics, Vienna

pg. 93   Courtesy of Schoeps Mikrofone

pg. 94   Courtesy of RØDE Microphones

pg. 96   Photo Courtesy of Sound Devices, LLC

pg. 97   Photo Courtesy of Sound Devices, LLC

Chapter 4

pg. 100   *Sin City* (2005, dir. Frank Miller, Robert Rodriguez, Quentin Tarantino) / Elizabeth Avellan, Frank Miller, Robert Rodriguez

pg. 103   *Barton Fink* (1991, dir. Joel Coen, Ethan Coen) / Circle Films / Working Title Films

pg. 104   *Panic Room* (2002, dir. David Fincher) / Columbia Pictures Corporation / Hofflund/ Polone / Indelible Pictures

pg. 112   *Coraline* (2009, dir. Henry Selick) / Focus Features / Laika Entertainment / Pandemonium

pg. 114   *The Ring* (2002, dir. Gore Verbinski) / DreamWorks / Parkes+MacDonald Image Nation / BenderSpink

pg. 115   *In the Cut* (2003, dir. Jane Campion) / Pathe Productions / Pathé Pictures International / Red Turtle

pg. 116   *Rango* (2011, dir. Gore Verbinski) / Paramount Pictures / Nickelodeon Movies / Blind Wink Productions

pg. 123   *The Conversation* (1974, dir. Francis Ford Coppola) / Directors Company, The / The Coppola Company / American Zoetrope

pg. 123   *Chico & Rita* (2010, dir. Tono Errando, Javier Mariscal, Fernando Trueba) / Isle of Man Film / CinemaNX / Estudio Mariscal

Chapter 5

pg. 131   *Fantastic Mr. Fox* (2009, dir. Wes Anderson) / Twentieth Century Fox Film Corporation / Indian Paintbrush / Regency Enterprises

pg. 135   © 2017 Avid Technology, Inc.

pg. 139   Courtesy of Waves

pg. 140   Courtesy of Kiwa Digital Ltd (www.voiceq.com)

pg. 143   Courtesy of Native Instruments

pg. 145   Courtesy of Native Instruments

pg. 146   Anzel Greyling in T Is for Talk / AFK: The Webseries, JF2: Primal Fury

pg. 146   Aoterroroa, series launch / Keira Christina in A Christmas Wish (H2Ow Ltd)

pg. 148   Adam Elliot Clayographies and Melodrama Pictures

pg. 148   Adam Elliot Clayographies and Melodrama Pictures

pg. 149   Adam Elliot Clayographies and Melodrama Pictures

pg. 149   Adam Elliot Clayographies and Melodrama Pictures

pg. 150   Adam Elliot Clayographies and Melodrama Pictures

pg. 151   Adam Elliot Clayographies and Melodrama Pictures

pg. 151   Adam Elliot Clayographies and Melodrama Pictures

pg. 152   Adam Elliot Clayographies and Melodrama Pictures

Chapter 6

pg. 157   *Intolerance: Love's Struggle throughout the Ages* (1916, dir. D. W. Griffith) / Triangle Film Corporation, Wark Producing

pg. 159   *The Lord of the Rings: The Two Towers* (2002, dir. Peter Jackson) / New Line Cinema, WingNut Films

pg. 160   *Delicatessen* (1991, dir. Marc Caro, Jean-Pierre Jeunet) / Constellation, Union Générale Cinématographique (UGC), Hachette Première

pg. 161   *The Jacket* (2005, dir. John Maybury) / Mandalay Pictures, Warner Independent Pictures (WIP), 2929 Productions

pg. 162   *Inception* (2010, dir. Christopher Nolan) / Warner Bros., Legendary Entertainment, Syncopy

pg. 164   *The Shining* (1980, dir. Stanley Kubrick) / Warner Bros., Hawk Films, Peregrine

pg. 166   © 2017 Avid Technology, Inc.

pg. 172   © 2017 Avid Technology, Inc.

pg. 172   iZotope, Inc.'s mastering tool Ozone 7 (www.izotope.com)

pg. 176   *9* (2005, dir. Shane Acker) / UCLA Animation Workshop

pg. 178   *9* (2009, dir. Shane Acker) / Focus Features, Relativity Media, Arc Productions

Index

9 (film), 176–78
2001: A Space Odyssey (film), 74, 157

A
Acker, Shane, 176–78
Acoustic ecology, 53
ADR (automated dialogue replacement), 65–67, 69
  dialogue editing, 139–40
  distortion, 138
  performance and direction, 139
  phase issues, 138
  plosives, 138
  production, 138–40
  sibilance, 138–39
AFK: The Web Series (film), 145–46
A.I. (film), 145
Alexandrov, G. V., 18, 108
Allefex, 8
Allen, Dede, 158
Amplitude, 81
Analogue-to-digital conversion (ADC), 88, 136
Anderson, Wes, 130, 131
Animation
  development of, 147
  early films, 4–5
  finding its voice, 20–23
  limited, 31–32
  production, 98
  recording, 121–22
  recording dialogue for films, 130–31
  stylized, 32–34
Animation director, Adam Elliot, 147–53
Aoterroroa (film series), 146
Apocalypse Now (film), 58, 61–62, 113, 144, 159, 163
Artists, unsigned, 124
The Art of Noises (Russolo), 49–50
Atmosphere, soundtrack, 67
Audio post
  groups, VCAs, and auxiliaries, 166
  session management, 165–66
  spatial audio, 167
  stereo or surround, 166–67
  track laying, 165–66
Audiovisual development
  concept art, 109–14
  project planning, 119–24
Audiovisual synergy, 75–76
Audio waveforms, 38
Auditory masking, 174
Avraamov, Arseny, 37

B
Barker, Robert, 5
Baron, Auguste, 14

Barron, Bebe, 54–56
Barron, Louis, 54–56
Barton Fink (film), 103, 124
Battleship Potempkin (film), 157
Becker, Franz, 18
Belar, Herbert, 58
Bell Telephone Laboratories, 14
Belson, Jordan, 37
Black Diamond Express (film), 8
Blackmail (film), 18
Blanc, Mel, 27
Bolt (film), 113
Boom operator, 127
Booth, Margaret, 158
Bosustow, Stephen, 34
Boyd, Jack, 32
Brother (film), 147–48, 150
Brown, Tregoweth, 27, 41
Browne, Van Dyke, 2
Bureau, Fréderic, 14
Burton, Tim, 176–77
Burtt, Ben, 62–63, 69, 75–76
Burwell, Carter, 103, 171
Buster Keaton Show (television series), 32

C
Cables and connectors, 96–97
Cage, John, 52, 54–55
Cannon, Johnny, 22
Cannon, Robert, 34
Cartoon Network, 23
Case, Theodore, 16
Caul, Harry, 123
Chaplin, Charlie, 3, 32
Chico & Rita (film), 123
Chladni, Ernst, 5
Chomet, Sylvain, 19
Chronophone, 14, 15
Cinema Novo, Brazil, 57
Cinematography, 75, 88, 99, 103, 170
Cinephone, 22
Citizen Kane (film), 13
Clark, Les, 22
Claymation, 147–53
Clayton, Jack, 51
Clipping, 90
Coen Brothers (Joel and Ethan), 103, 124, 171
Coffin, Pierre, 66
Colonel Bleep (television series), 32–33
Comb filtering, 82–83
Composers, 123
Concept art, 109–14
  design direction, 112–14
  pre-auralvis, 110–11
  research and referencing, 112
  scratch tracks, 111
  shot lists, 110
  storyboards, 109–10
  story reels, 110
  temp music, 111–12
Concrete music, 47–49
Consumerism, 59–60

Continuity editing, 158–59
The Conversation (film), 58, 123
Coppola, Francis Ford, 57–59, 61, 123, 159, 162
Copyright, 122–24
Coraline (film), 112–13, 149
Cousin (film), 147–48, 150
Craft, Edward, 15
Crusader Rabbit (cartoon series), 31–32
Cubism, 49, 60

D
Dahl, Roald, 130
D'Alesi, Hugo, 5
Da Vinci, Leonardo, 50
De Forest, Lee, 16, 17, 20, 22
De Vries, Marius, 123
Delicatessen (film), 160, 161
DeMille, Cecil B., 27
Dennis, John, 1
Derbyshire, Delia, 52
Design duality, 75–76
Development stage, 99–102
  genre and style, 99–100
  outlines and treatment, 100–102
  story and/or theme, 100
  story development, 100
Dickson, William, 10
Dickson Experimental Sound Film (film), 10
Digital audio fundamentals, 88–89
Digital audio workstations (DAWs), 135–36
Digital-to-analogue converter (DAC), 88, 136
Diorama, 5–6
Disney, Roy O., 21
Disney, Walt, 20–23
Dizzy Dishes (film), 20, 21
Don Juan (film), 15
Doppler, Christian, 49
Drury Lane Theatre, 1
Duchamp, Marcel, 52
Dugan, Dan, 1
Dynamic range, 90
Dynamism of a Car (Russolo), 49

E
Eastman, Phil, 34
Edison, Thomas, 7, 8
Editing techniques, 159–63
  aural-visual rhythms, 159–60
  dreams and nightmares, 162–63
  flash cuts, 163
  graphic-sonic, 159
  jump cuts, 163
  smash cuts, 163
  temporal manipulations, 161
  themes and subtext, 161–62
Eidophusikon, 6

Eisenstein, Sergi, 18, 108, 157–58
Electronics, film and, 54–56
Elliot, Adam, 147–53
Emotive and psychological sound, 73
Eng, Ron, 112
Engl, Josef, 16
Enthusiasm: Symphony of the Donbass (film), 52, 53
Equalization (EQ), 79, 80, 171
Eraserhead (film), 44–46
Erlenborn, Ray, 32
Ernie Biscuit (film), 149–52

F
Fantasound, 22
Fantastic Mr. Fox (film), 130–31
Fast and Furry-ous (film), 28
Fiddlesticks (film), 24
Figurative/metaphorical sound, 73
Film, electronics and, 54–56
Film soundtracks, live, 7–8
Finding His Voice (film), 17
Fischinger, Oscar, 37, 52
Flanging, 82–83
Flash cuts, 163
Fleischer, Dave, 20, 21
Fleischer, Lou, 20
Fleischer, Max, 17, 20
Foley, Jack, 67
Foley effects, 2, 13, 20, 40, 42, 65, 67, 69, 70, 84, 95, 104, 109, 127, 128, 132, 141
Forbidden Planet (film), 54–56, 58
Foster, Don, 30
Foster, John, 21
Free Cinema Movement, 57
Freemantle, Glenn, 110
French New Wave, 34, 36, 56–57
Frequency, 78–79, 92–93

G
Gaiman, Neil, 112
A Game with Stones (film), 42–43
Gaumont, Léon, 14
General Electric, 16–17
Gerald McBoing-Boing (film), 34, 39
Gertie the Dinosaur (film), 3
Gizicki, Steven, 123
The Godfather (film), 58, 162
Goraguer, Alain, 57
Grainer, Ron, 52
The Grandmother (film), 44, 45
Gravity (film), 74, 110
Grieg, Edvard, 18
Griffith, D. W., 156, 157
Gunshot, 30–31
Gunsmoke (television series), 31

H

Han Dynasty, 3
Hanley, Tom, 31
Hanna-Barbera, 32–34
Harline, Leigh, 26
Harmon, Hugh, 23
Harvie Krumpet (film), 147–52
Haynes, Peter, 145
Headphones, 94, 136–37
Hendrix, Jimi, 52
Henry, Pierre, 51, 54
Hilberman, David, 34
Hitchcock, Alfred, 18, 55, 110, 159
Howe, Lyman, 8, 10
Hoxie, Charles, 16–17
Hubley, John, 34
Humphriss, Eric, 37
Hyperreal and surreal sound, 73

I

Inception (film), 162
Intensity, 81
Interaural level difference (ILD), 86
Interaural time difference (ITD), 86
In the Cut (film), 115–16
Intolerance (film), 157
Inverse square law, 81, 82
Ising, Rudolf, 23
Italian Commedia dell'arte, 3
Iwerks, Ub, 21–22, 24

J

Jack Benny Show (radio show), 32
The Jacket (film), 161
Jackson, Wilfred, 22
Jacob, Abe, 1
Jarre, Jean-Michel, 49
Jazz Singer (film), 15, 21
Jones, Chuck, 27, 28, 31, 41, 42
Julian, Paul, 39
Jump cuts, 163

K

Kabuki theater, 1
Katz, Stephen, 63
Keaton, Buster, 3
Kemper, Ray, 31
Kinetophone, 10, 14
Kinetoscope, 14
King, Jack, 31
King Kong (film), 28–29, 64, 66, 142, 171
Kremenliev, Boris, 40
Kubrick, Stanley, 19, 74, 157, 163, 164
Kuleshov, Lev, 157, 158
Kunz, Jacob, 16
Kurtz, Gary, 62

L

Laemmle, Carl, 21
La Jetée (film), 57, 100
Laloux, René, 57, 58
Lang, Fritz, 18, 19
The Last Trick of Mr. Schwarcewallde and Mr. Edgar (film), 42–43
Lauste, Eugene, 16
Leivsay, Skip, 103, 171

Library music, 124
Literal and real sound, 72–73
Live film soundtracks, 7–8
Looney Tunes, 23, 27–28, 41
Lord of the Rings (film), 114, 158–59
Loudness, 81
Loutherbourg, Philip James de, 6, 25
Lucas, George, 57, 59–63, 74–75
Lye, Len, 37
Lynch, David, 44–46

M

M (film), 18, 19
McAlpin, Fred, 33–34
Macbcth (play), 1
McCay, Winsor, 3
MacDonald, Jimmy, 24–26
Macdonnel, Norm, 31
McDonnell, George, 11
Mackenzie, Louis, 47
McLaren, Norman, 37–39
Mad Max: Fury Road (film), 110, 112–13, 142
Magic lantern shows, 4
Mamet, David, 158
Mangini, Mark, 112
Manifesto of Futurism (Marinetti), 49–50
Manne, Maurice (Morris), 21
Manne, Max H., 21
The March of Time (radio show), 13
Marinetti, Filippo, 49–50
Marker, Chris, 57
Martinville, Édouard-Léon Scott de, 7
Mary and Max (film), 149–52
Mason, James, 39
Massole, Joseph, 16
Master and Commander (film), 112
Méliès, Georges, 54, 163
Meat Love (film), 43, 44
Mental imagery, 11–13
Merrie Melodies, 27
Metaphorical/figurative sound, 73
Metering, sound, 89–90
Metro Goldwyn Mayer (MGM), 23, 32–34, 55, 158
Mickey Mouse, 20, 22, 24–25
Microphones
accessories, 94
digital, 94
frequency response, 92–93
polar patterns, 92
recording chain, 91–97
shotgun, 129
stereo, 93
surround, 94
Miller, Frank, 99, 100
Miller, George, 110
Miller, Harry, 18
Miller, Peter, 114–18
Mintz, Charles, 22
Mixing tools and techniques
common issues, 174
compressors and limiters, 172
dialogue mixing, 170
effects mixing, 170–71
EQ, 171

mastering, encoding, and delivery, 173–74
monitoring the mix, 173
music mixing, 171
panning, 171
reverb, 172–73
Montages, 158–59
Moog, Robert Arthur, 58
Moog synthesizer, 55, 58
Moores, Dick, 32
Moorhouse, A. H., 8
Morgan, Kenneth, 19
Morphophone, 49
Motion Picture Editors Guild, 119
Mott, Robert, 12
Murch, Walter, 58–60, 61, 85, 87, 155–56, 162
Murphy, Bill, 151
Music
mixing, 171
soundtrack, 68
Musique concrète, 47–49
Muybridge, Eadweard, 7

N

Narration, 39–41
New German Cinema, 57
New Waves, 56–57
Nicholas, Ora, 11
Nichols, Arthur, 11
Nightmare on Elm Street (film), 162
Noble, Maurice, 41
Now Hear This (cartoon), 41–42
Nyquist theorem, 88

O

The Old Mill (film), 24, 26
Olson, Harry, 58
On Directing Film (Mamet), 158
Ono, Yoko, 52
Oram, Daphne, 51–52
Orloff, Lee, 131
Ow, Hweiling, 145–46

P

Pallophotophone, 16–17
Panic Room (film), 103, 104
Panning, 171
Pepper, Henry, 4
Pfenninger, Rudolph, 37
Pfleumer, Fritz, 47
Phantasmagoria, 4
Phase, 82–83
Phonautograph, 7
Phonograph, 7
Picture editing
creative techniques, 159–63
evolution of invisible arts, 156–58
montage and continuity, 158–59
theories, 155–56
VFX, lighting, and grading, 164
Picturesque of sound, 4–6
Pitch, 78–79
Pitch shifting, 79–80
Place
distance localization, 87
perception of space, 85–86

reception of direction, 86–87
sound as a, 84–87
Poe, Edgar Allan, 39
Porky's Hare Hunt (film), 27, 28
Portable field mixers, 96
Portable field recorders, 94–96
Porter, Edwin S., 156
Postproduction, 98, 154, 175
audio post, 165–67
mixing tools and techniques, 170–74
re-recording mixing, 168–69
sound and picture editing, 155–64
Poulsen, Valdemar, 47
Powers, Patrick, 22
Praxinoscope, 4
Preproduction, 98
concept art, 109–14
development stage, 99–102
project planning, 119–24
sound in script, 103–8
Production, 98, 126
ADR (automated dialogue replacement), 138–40
development, 147
Foley and sound effects, 132, 141
on location, 128–31
sound, 127
sound design effects, 143–44
sound effect libraries, 134
sound mixer, 127
studio recording, 135–37
Project planning, 119–24
ancillary and marketing materials, 121
budgets and scheduling, 119–20
copyright, 122–24
recording, 121–22
tech, format, length, and deliverables, 120
voice casting, 121
Provas, Alex, 114
Psycho (film), 18, 159
Psychological and emotive sound, 73
Pudomn, V. I., 18, 108
Pulse-code modulation (PCM), 88–89
Puppetry, 2–3
Pyne, William Henry, 6
Pythagoras, 48

R

Radio, television killing, 30–34
Raging Bull (film), 75, 158
Rango (film), 114, 116–18, 122, 131, 175
RCA's Photophone, 16–17, 37
Real and literal sound, 72–73
Realism, television, 30–31
Recording chain, 91–97
cables and connectors, 96–97
digital microphones, 94
frequency response, 92–93
headphones, 94
microphone accessories, 94
microphones, 91–97

Recording chain (*continued*)
 polar patterns, 92
 portable field mixers, 96
 portable field recorders,
  94–96
 stereo microphones, 93
 surround microphones, 94
Re-recording mixer, 70
Re-recording mixing, 168–69
 final mix, 169
 music and effects (M&E)
  mixes, 169
 premixing, 169
 temporary mixes, 168–69
Reverb, 84–85, 172–73
Reynaud, Charles Émile, 4, 5
Rickard, Dick, 26
Ride on a Runaway Train
  (film), 10
The Ring (film), 114–15
Robert, Etienne-Gaspard, 4
Roberts, David, 5
Rodriguez, Robert, 99, 100
Rogan, Jim, 12
Room tone, soundtrack, 67
Russolo, Luigi, 49–50, 53
Rydstrom, Gary, 72, 75, 109,
  113, 145

S
Sabbatini, Nicola, 1
Schaeffer, Pierre, 47–49, 51,
  53, 54, 81
Schafer, R. Murray, 53
Schary, Dore, 55
Schoonmaker, Thelma, 158
Schwartz, Zachary, 34
Science fiction
 ambiguous twilight zone,
  58–60
 architects of sound,
  61–63
 film and electronics,
  54–56
 New Waves, 56–57
 sonic-psychedelia, 57–58
Scorsese, Martin, 57, 61, 75,
  110, 158
Scott, Bill, 34
Scott, Ridley, 110
Scratch tracks, 111
Script
 breakdowns, 108
 sound in, 103–8
*Secrets of Scene Painting
  and Stage Effects*
  (Browne), 2
Seibert, Fred, 34
Selick, Henry, 112–13, 149
Selznick, David O., 29
SFX (sound effects), 26, 107–8,
  132, 165–66
Sholpo, Evgeny, 37
Short films
 aural junk, 44–46
 rated X, 39–41
 sound cards, 37–39
Shotgun microphone, 129
Signal-to-noise ratios, 90

Silence, soundtrack, 67
Simpson, John, 142, 151
Sin City (film), 99, 100
Sinkin' in the Bathtub (film), 23
The Sixth Sense (film), 161
Slapstick, 2–3
Smash cuts, 163
Smith, Harry, 37
Snow White (film), 25–27
Sonic sculpturing, 47–53
Sound
 animation incorporating,
  20–21
 audiovisual events and
  installations, 5–6
 behind the scenes, 2
 fallacy of silence, 7–10
 picturesque of, 4–6
 puppetry, slapstick, and
  vaudeville, 2–3
 radio with pictures, 11–13
 sculptors of, 51–53
 sonic sculpturing, 47–53
 sound-on-disc, 14–15, 51
 sound-on-film, 16–17
 staging of, 1–3
 stop-motion film, 28–29
 story and workflow, 24–27
 thunder, 1
 transitioning to, 14–19
Sound cards, 37–39
Sound department
 re-recording mixer, 70
 sound designer, 69–70
 sound editor, 69
 supervising sound editor, 69
Sound design
 effects in production,
  143–44
 effects mixing, 170–71
 frequency modulation
  synthesis, 143
 granular synthesis, 144
 hyperreal and surreal
  sound, 73
 metaphorical/figurative
  sound, 73
 modes of thinking, 71–76
 phase distortion
  synthesis, 144
 physical modeling
  synthesis, 143
 psychological and emotive
  sound, 73
 real and literal sound,
  72–73
 samplers and sample-
  based synthesis, 144
 as score, 124
 subtractive and additive
  synthesis, 143
 symbolic and subliminal
  sound, 73–75
 synthesizer and
  samplers, 143
 wavetable and vector
  synthesis, 143–44
Sound design effects,
  soundtrack, 66

Sound designer, 69, 114–18
Sound designer's tool kit
 capturing sound, 88–90
 recording chain, 91–97
 sound as a place, 84–87
 sound as medium,
  77–83
Sound editor, 69
Sound effects
 artistry, 11–13
 libraries, 134
 machines, 8–9
 production, 132, 141
 soundtrack, 66
Sound in script, 103–8
 marking up and SFX lists,
  107–8
 script breakdowns, 108
Sound installations, 53
Sound ornaments, 37
Sound propagation, 77
Soundscape, 53
Soundtrack
 atmosphere, 67
 dialogue, 65–66
 Foley effects, 67
 live film, 7–8
 mastering, encoding, and
  delivery, 173–74
 music, 68
 room tone, 67
 silence, 67
 sound design effects, 66
 sound effects, 66
 walla, 67
Space, perception of, 85–86
Space Barton (film), 32
Spivack, Murray, 28–29, 171
Splet, Alan, 44, 113
Spotting sessions, 147
Stalling, Carl, 25, 27
Stanfield, Clarkson, 5
Star Wars (film), 63, 74–76
Star Wars: Episode IV (film), 62
Steamboat Willie (film), 20, 22,
  23, 29, 107
Steiner, Max, 29, 171
Stop-motion film, 28–29
Studio recording, 135–37
 audio interfaces, 136
 control surfaces, 136
 digital audio workstations
  (DAWs), 135–36
 hard drives, 137
 headphones, 136–37
 monitors, 136
 plug-ins, 136
 transfer formats, 137
 video, 137
Subliminal and symbolic
  sound, 73–75
Supervising sound editor, 69
Surreal and hyperreal
  sound, 73
Suzuki, Koji, 114
Švankmajer, Jan, 42–44
Symbolic and subliminal
  sound, 73–75
Synchromy (film), 38

T
Talbot, Frederick A., 9
Tarantino, Quentin, 68, 99, 100
Television, killing radio, 30–34
The Tell Tale Heart (film), 39,
  41, 66
Temp music, 111–12
Terry, Paul, 21
Thom, Randy, 62
Thunder, sound effect
  machine, 8
Thunder sound, 1, 6
THX-1138 (film), 59–60, 62, 99
Tigerstedt, Eric, 16
Timbre, sound as, 80–81
T Is for Talk (film), 145, 146
Topor, Roland, 57
Trap drummers, 9–10
The Triplets of Belleville
  (film), 19
Trombley, Gene, 32
Tsekhanovsky, Mikhail, 37
Turner, Edward, 24
Tushar, Steve, 112
Tykocinski-Tykociner,
  Joseph, 16

U
Uncle (film), 147–48, 150
Utilities person, 127

V
Valdés, Bebo, 123
Vaudeville, 2–3
Verbinski, Gore, 114, 116–17,
  122, 131, 175, 179
Vertov, Dziga, 52
VFX (visual effects), 26,
  108, 164
Vitaphone, 15, 16, 51
Vogt, Hans, 16
Voice casting, 121

W
Walker, Peter, 151
Walla, soundtrack, 67
WALL-E (film), 66, 69, 76,
  104–5
Warner, Frank, 75
Warner Bros., 15, 23, 27, 39
The War of the Worlds
  (Wells), 13
Waveform, 16, 37–38, 82,
  88–91, 93, 96, 139–40,
  143–44
Waves, sound as, 77–78
Welles, Orson, 13
Wells, H. G., 13
Wiener, Norbert, 55
Wireless telephony, 11
Wood, Craig, 114
Wul, Stefan, 57

Z
Zimmer, Hans, 114
Zoetrope, 4, 58
Zuro, Josiah, 28